DATE DUE

AP 03 '09			
3 -23			
MAR 2 3 '10			

Demco, Inc. 38-293

Profession
Vide

Professional Techniques for Video Game Writing

edited by

Wendy Despain

A K Peters, Ltd.
Wellesley, Massachusetts

Editorial, Sales, and Customer Service Office

A K Peters, Ltd.
888 Worcester Street, Suite 230
Wellesley, MA 02482
www.akpeters.com

Library of Congress Cataloging-in-Publication Data

Professional techniques for video game writing / edited by Wendy Despain.
     p. cm.
  Includes index.
  ISBN 13: 978-1-56881-416-2 (alk. paper)
 1. Video games–Authorship–Vocational guidance. I. Despain, Wendy.
  GV1469.34.A97P76 2008
  794.8–dc22

                  2008007163

Printed in the United States of America
12 11 10 09 08   10 9 8 7 6 5 4 3 2 1

To Chris and Rich for encouraging my crazy ideas, and
Kevin for keeping me sane throughout the process.

And special thanks for the editing help from:
Ahmad Saad
James Swallow
Beth Dillon
Richard Dansky

Contents

Preface

Game writer is a job title many people kind of squint and tilt their head at. Even people who work in the video game industry sometimes wonder what it is a game writer does. When I meet new people, I always have to explain that when I say "game writer," I mean writing dialog and documents, not code or systems design. Even then, I usually have to break it down further. "You know when you shoot someone in a game and the guy says some clever quip as he dies? Someone has to write that so the voice actor knows what to say." A few people outside the industry have a vague idea that they want to be a game writer, but they don't know how that works out day to day.

And those of us who actually have this rare job title often wonder if the methods we've come up with for doing the work are the best way of getting things done. There are more than 12,000 members of the International Game Developers Association (IGDA) and only 350 members of the IGDA's Game Writing Special Interest Group. Only about a third of those are working game writers, either freelance, full-time staff, or part-time staff. Granted, not every writer in the game industry is a member of our special interest group, but many are and the ratio is pretty accurate. In the grand scheme of things, there just aren't that many of us. The techniques we use today have evolved from a varied background of writing and code-building traditions, and every one of us has had to make up big parts of it as we go. That's why we wrote this book: to share our experience and learn from each other. Ultimately, if we share our knowledge, we'll all get better at what we do and raise the state of the art.

Why We Wrote This Book

Once I get done explaining what it is I do as a game writer, the next question I'm almost always asked is, "How does that work? Do you get to play video games all day?" The short answer is "Some days, yes. But it isn't as much fun as it sounds." I play other people's games with a critical eye, learning from them. And I clunk through playable builds of my own games to look for typos, mistakes, and continuity errors.

But days when I'm heavy-duty gaming are not the norm. Most days I'm wrangling spreadsheets and team dynamics. I'm updating game documentation and trying to find the umpteenth way of saying "ouch." Sometimes I wonder if my methods are really the best way to approach the down-and-dirty doing of the job of game writer, but there aren't very many methods available for comparison.

That's where this book comes in. The IGDA Game Writing SIG had already written one book about the dirty details of game writing, but one book can only scratch the surface of a new narrative media as it's being created. *Game Writing: Narrative Skills for Videogames* is full of excellent information on the basics of the craft, but there's so much more beyond the basics.

So I went out and convinced experts who are in the trenches doing this work day in and day out to take some time and download their brains onto paper. We've broken the job into its component parts and examined each one individually. I won't say yet that these are best practices. In order to formulate those, we have to find out what the baseline practices are. So this book is a meeting of the minds and a sharing of experiences. It's an examination of the techniques working game writers are using right now.

How to Use This Book

This book doesn't replace the first book by the IGDA Game Writers SIG, *Game Writing: Narrative Skills for Videogames*. Instead, *Professional Techniques for Video Game Writing* builds on and goes deeper into specific points raised there. You can understand the material here without having read the first one, but we assume you have a working knowledge of the basics. Some chapters refer back to it in a few places where we don't have space to cover the material it includes. This book uses the *Narrative Skills* book as its foundation and looks in-depth at the methods and techniques we use to get our jobs done.

Each chapter is an essay by an individual writer or team of writers. They may build on each other in some places, but in general, each one stands independently. So, you can skip ahead to the area you're dealing with today, or read straight through and get a broader view of how these techniques impact each other. Even if you've never had to write for a game manual or develop a new IP, you'll gain a fresh perspective on your own work by looking through these windows and seeing how other people tackle their problems.

These writers have shared their processes and techniques at a very detailed level. Working game writers will be able to compare their own methods, see where there are differences, and incorporate new ideas into their systems. Ultimately, we'll learn what the best practices are from our own experience, and we can share that knowledge as well. Soon we'll get started on an upward spiral of constant improvement as we all learn from each other.

Those who are hoping to break in to the game industry can use this book to learn the more advanced aspects of the craft. They'll be able to see how it's similar to writing for other media and how it's different.

Also, this book is a hands-on guide and includes writing prompts and exercises at the end of each chapter. They'll get your brain and your pen moving in the right direction to apply the tips and techniques described in the chapter.

What You Need to Know to Make the Most of It

Writers working on interactive narratives are still writers at the core. Spelling, punctuation, and grammar are still vitally important, but we're not going to cover those principles here. Techniques from other books on writing should be applied to game writing as well. What this book offers is a look at those circumstances unique to writing for an interactive medium.

This can be a solitary job. Even if you're a staff writer who goes into the office every day, you're surrounded by programmers and systems designers who don't really get how writers work. But we still need to share techniques and work together to improve our own skills and the medium as a whole. You're not really alone. Other writers have encountered similar problems and lived to tell the tale.

Wendy Despain

1

How to Break In and Stay In

Beth A. Dillon

Breaking in to the game industry isn't easy. It's an entertainment industry and has the same problems as movies and television and novels. Everyone wants to be a star. Inevitably, there are far more applicants than there are positions to fill, and when it comes to writing for video games, the imbalance is even more extreme. While every developer knows they need several programmers and at least one designer, they're still not entirely convinced they need a dedicated writer. Some companies have caught the vision and employ entire writing staffs. Others are beginning to see the benefits of hiring freelance writers. It's a situation in flux and it could explode one of these days, but don't hold your breath.

This isn't to say there's no room for new blood. It's entirely possible to break through and get those game-writing jobs. In fact, for someone with the know-how, it's just a matter of making the right contacts and being patient until the right opportunity comes along. The know-how isn't just about writing, though. Some excellent writers from other media have floundered in the video game space. Writing for games requires additional skills beyond generating good narrative and dialog. There are technical aspects that can't be ignored. This book and our first book, *Game Writing: Narrative Skills for Video Games*, provide a look at exactly what those skills are.

Once you have the tools in hand, getting a job in the industry is mostly a matter of social networks, availability, and luck. But there are a few things you can do to stack your hand. I've broken them down into five elements: education, experience, portfolio, networking, and applying.

1.1 Education

Having an education doesn't necessarily mean getting a degree in creative writing or game design. Your writing skills and ability to work within a team in a quirky company culture will speak louder than any diploma. Focus your college education on any degree that gives you a chance to develop your writing, your interpersonal skills working with other students, and a broad grounding in a variety of topics. You never know when that class in early Bronze-Age military strategy will come in handy. Michael Fiegel from Ninja Burger and aethereal FORGE says, "I have a Bachelor of Arts in English Honors and I know for a fact that it was my college years that really honed my writing skills. In particular because I was encouraged to take a wide variety of writing courses and got excellent feedback on what I was doing wrong and what I was getting right."

College also gives you an opportunity to learn about other aspects of game development. Matt Forbeck, who has worked full-time on games and fiction since 1989 with many top companies, including Atari, Ubisoft, Wizards of the Coast, and Games Workshop, advises, "Having a computer programming course or two under your belt will help you know how to talk with the rest of the game development team." Ben Serviss, Associate Producer/Designer at Saber Interactive, comments, "If you want to write for historical real-time strategy games, concentrate on world history and geography."

Some writers even go past the bachelor's degree. Andy Walsh, who has worked on more than 25 games for companies such as EA, Sony, SEGA, and Eidos, completed a master's in television and radio scriptwriting. Through it, he learned narrative theory (the three-act structure), format, process, and industry principles.

Internships through your school are one way to get a toe in the door. These part-time positions with companies usually earn you course credit and will provide both real-world experience and networking opportunities that may transition you directly from school into that company if you work well for them and they have need for a writer when you graduate.

Whatever route you take to getting an education, finding mentors and getting real-world experience are invaluable. If you only want to write for your own satisfaction, nobody else's opinion will ever matter. But if you want to share your words with the world, it's crucial to get constructive feedback from experienced writers—if they work in video games or not.

1.2 Experience

Get writing! And write anything. If you're interested in creative writing, forge ahead with media like film, television, radio, novels, short stories, and comic books. The important thing is to learn how words go together and develop your voice. You'll also learn your strengths and weaknesses, learn how to give and take feedback, and generate new ideas on demand.

If you're more interested in technical writing, you can still stick within the area of games while you develop your skills. Write game reviews and journalistic news. This will give you fundamentals to fall back on when you write game documentation and manuals. Writing for pen-and-paper games is also highly relevant if you want to transfer your experience over to role-playing games.

At its utmost, every job or project you take on should concern either games or writing. Even jobs you may not see as relating to game writing can lead to more creative positions. Tracy Seamster, Sony Online Entertainment, whose entry came from a customer-service job in a text-based game company, points out: "If you can demonstrate the ability to respond to customers in a quick, concise, and clear manner, your writing skills will be evident."

There are, of course, ways to build experience strictly in video game writing. "One frequently overlooked avenue into the gaming industry is the modding community. Getting to work with a serious mod development team can give you invaluable experience that translates directly into the professional world," recommends Jay Posey from Red Storm. The same goes for working on game development projects with other students as course assignments and landing internships during your education.

1.3 Portfolio

Some writers opt to keep permanent portfolios, while others don't, but rather make portfolios for each job they're applying for. If you're a freelancer just starting out, you'll need an online presence, possibly with a blog or another way of providing consistent updates to show possible employers that you're active in your interests.

So what should you include? All of that experience you've been building up. "The wider range of samples you can provide, the better. Detailed character biographies, dialogue samples, short prose, gameworld descriptions or history, cutscenes in screenplay format; all would be valuable examples of your particular talent," says Posey. Keep samples brief, and if you don't have any material you can show from published games, use an idea of your own and write a script or some character descriptions.

If the work you've contributed to a project is protected by a non-disclosure agreement or can't be shown separately from the final work, you should still reference the project and your role in it. "Your portfolio should contain your greatest hits, including pieces that demonstrate a variety of techniques. I refer people to a game's website in which all the text is mine, pointing out that I wrote both the long, serious stories as well as the humorous blurbs. That way, my ability to switch styles/voices is evident," recommends Seamster.

Posey points out, "If you're interested in or applying for a specific kind of writing job (say, writing quests for an massively multiplayer online game), you should include similar samples." Be clear and concise about what you're capable of and interested in contributing to a company.

1.4 Networking

When you set out to network, always have in mind that everyone is a resource. Whether it's another student, a fellow writer, the CEO of a company, or even an audio director, anyone involved in the game industry will be able to share their opinion about you—for good or ill. So even if you're talking to someone who doesn't work for a company you want to work for, or do the job you want to do, put your best foot forward. They may change companies or jobs in the future and be asked by a hiring manager if they've met you and what they think of your interpersonal skills. You don't want them remembering you as the pompous jerk they ran into at that one bar that one time.

Some events are designed for networking, include the Game Developers Conference and the Game Writing Conference section of the Austin Game Developers Conference. This is where being a game journalist specializing in event coverage can be a real boon. You can attend with a press pass, write about sessions, and interview industry professionals to learn about the game industry.

Also keep an eye out for local events and especially International Game Developers Association (IGDA) chapter meetings. Connecting with IGDA will inform you about the companies in your area. Although not many companies explicitly put out requests for game writers, you may be able to suggest your services as a freelancer with a solid portfolio.

Serviss comments, "The funny thing about networking is that you never know who will be able to help you down the line. Someone in a senior position miles above you may come to you in a few years looking for opportunities. The way events unravel, you'll never be able to predict who will or won't be able to give you a push. So while keeping this in mind, keep yourself open to helping others who don't appear to need your assistance. Plus, if you help someone out in even a small way, they'll remember what you did for them."

Forbeck echoes that sentiment. "The secret to networking is to enjoy it for what it really is: meeting people. You never know who's going to be in a position to hire you in the future, so be kind to everyone you meet and work with. I get jobs all the time because of people I first worked with 15 or more years ago. We started out in the tabletop industry, but lots of refugees from that industry turn up in computer games, mostly chasing larger audiences and better pay."

So how can you be remembered? First, think mostly about other people. If you can help other people get hired by making connections, you'll be remembered for your helpfulness. Second, get yourself a nice professional business card with your name, title, location, email, phone number, and Web address. This of course means you need to have a website, which ties back to your portfolio. Having some kind of online presence with a simple bio and your professional interests will make it easier for people to keep you in mind for work they may run across. Also, just be yourself. Don't try to be someone you're not or you'll find yourself in a company you may not be happy with. Look for the company culture that works for you, and you'll have better quality of life in the long term.

And finally, a word about alcohol. A lot of socializing and networking at industry events take place in a bar, and game industry veterans will drink you under the table, so don't even consider making it a competition. Remember that you're trying to make a good impression, not a sloppy drunk impression. If you're not a fan of bars, consider eating meals with people you meet at conferences. It's almost as good—and better if you can pick up the check on occasion.

1.5 Applying

First, don't cold call a company. It won't do you any good. If there's a particular company you know you'd like to work for, try to get to know people who work there through mailing lists, message boards, and conferences. The IGDA can be invaluable for making these connections. The people you get to know will think of you the next time there's an opening in their company, and you'll learn volumes about the company culture long before your first day on the job. Sometimes companies make games you admire but don't have a corporate culture you could stomach. Better to know ahead of time, and networking will answer a lot of questions for you.

Ads for game-writing positions are pretty uncommon, so don't wait for them to show up even on game industry specific job boards. Most game-writing jobs get filled through word of mouth.

If you do see one of the rare ads for a writer, or someone tells you about an opening at their company, there are a few things to keep in mind when putting together your application. First, write it specifically for the company you're applying to. Don't just use the same materials for every opportunity. Second, be aware of exactly what they need in an application. Some companies, such as BioWare, require that you make a game mod with their game engine with an emphasis on the writing.

If you don't get a reply, don't badger them. Move on to the next opportunity. It won't do any good to send in a new application over and over again. Spend careful time on your first application so that it grabs their attention. Your cover letter should show how you fit with their company but also what you can bring to them, in a humble and direct manner. The best strategy is to reference your experience and portfolio.

Once you get past the application process, you're up for an interview. Here's the time to prove yourself. As Serviss recommends, "Know the company you're interviewing with. Be familiar with their games, the critical and commercial receptions they've received, and think about elements you would improve upon if you had the opportunity. Have a basic game plan of how to present your background and interests, but don't try to memorize anything and stress yourself out. Have a few questions for the person you're interviewing with at the end that show you're serious."

Forbeck adds, "Be polite and prepared. Dress well, but in most cases you can forgo the suit or business dress. To call the dress code in some studios 'business casual' would be generous. If you're not sure and you have questions, call the company and ask human resources for advice. That could be your first friend on the inside."

Overall, if you're polite and prepared, you should be relaxed when getting interviewed. If you're a writer who hasn't yet worked with the game industry, as Posey suggests, "showing an understanding of games, and story execution in them, can give you a leg up on others."

1.6   Staying In

Once you break in with your first job, that's not the end of your personal skill development and keeping an eye out for future positions. If you're having problems with building up more material for your portfolio, Seamster and Posey both recommend volunteering to help showcase your writing skills.

If you're full-time but looking to move to a different company or get more attention, Serviss notes, "Noticeably reaching out and doing twice the work in your current job as well as handling writing duties will get you noticed. Once you've made your ability to write known, smart studios will realize the asset they have and will work to keep you happy doing what you can do best."

If you're freelancing, you certainly have to look ahead. "Keep offering your skill up. Talk openly about your ambitions as a writer and ask advice from others in the company about how you can crack that nut," advises Forbeck. "Publish your work. Start a blog or LiveJournal. Link to other writers and get them to link back to you," adds Fiegel.

Above all, just keep writing.

1.7   Breaking-In Stories

Ben Serviss, Saber Interactive

When I first decided to break in to the game industry, I started small, leveraging the skills I already had as a writer for a small-time game site. I wrote features, previews and reviews for months, getting paid little to nothing—but the real experience came in covering events. Through this job I was able to cover GDC, E3, and countless small-scale game nights and press gigs. All this exposure to the professional side of the industry was great experience and gave me plenty of opportunities to start networking and making contacts. Shortly afterwards I joined the New Jersey chapter of the IGDA, where again I offered my skills to help out with events, writing meeting reports, and generally making myself useful. This gave me even more industry connections to like-minded people, and I soon found myself as the lead writer at a small indie startup. I stayed busy, continuing to write articles for various game news outlets and even doing some consulting work on a 'serious' military game. Eventually, I was approached by an established game studio and signed on as an Associate Producer/Designer. While the duties of the job are highly varied, my skills as a writer consistently come in handy.

Matt Forbeck, Freelancer

I started out in tabletop games, which is still what I'm best known for, and I write novels, too. I've won a lot of awards for it and even served as president of a fairly popular publisher (Pinnacle Entertainment Group) for four years. That gave me a huge in when Human Head Studios went looking for a director for its tabletop games division. I worked for them for about two years before going back to freelancing, which I'm still doing today.

Michael Fiegel, Freelancer

I emailed a friend of mine to tell her I was getting married, and she emailed me back her congratulations, and informed me that she had a writing position open at her company, in her department. I sent in some samples and arranged an interview for the day before my wedding. Six days later I got married, and five days after that was my first day at my new job. The whole thing seemed somewhat serendipitous.

Tracy Seamster, Sony Online Entertainment

My start was on GEnie playing *GemStone III*, particularly its test version because it was free (whereas the "real" game was subject to hourly GEnie subscription rates). Fascinated by the idea of interacting with people from all over, I applied to work as a volunteer board moderator with Simutronics. Not long after they selected me for that role, they began hiring Assistant GameMasters (a combination role entailing both customer service and design) and picked me up for that as well.

When I spoke at GDC 2007, I said half-jokingly that my start in games began with a job at McDonald's, and in many ways that's true. That job taught me the basics of customer service, which I used later on to obtain experience in other customer-related fields. Working as a GM with Simutronics bridged my customer-service background with game (some might call it level) design. Breaking in to full-time game design came about because of the contacts I'd made while working with Simutronics, as well as the design skills I learned. My current job is a blend of "who I know" and "what I know."

Jay Posey, Red Storm

"Breaking in" for me was a several-stage process. My first job out of college was in tech support at a game company. I left the industry for a few years, but when I wanted to get back in, I was able to get a great reference from one of my tech-support buddies who had become a designer at Red Storm Entertainment. He helped me get in as a Scripter at Red Storm (where I was responsible for implementing gameplay elements, not writing). Though it wasn't my primary job, I had opportunities to provide writing help on a couple of projects and eventually was promoted to Narrative Designer.

Haris Orkin, Freelancer

I worked in advertising for a number of years before I broke in to screenwriting, selling scripts to Disney, Fox, Sony, and Paramount. I was a gamer all along and became something of a hardcore gamer after my son turned 10. When he was 15, he was kicking my butt pretty bad at *Counter-Strike*, so I'd stay up late, after he went to bed, and practice. At one point we started playing this other online shooter, *Soldier of Fortune II*, and I became pretty good at it.

So good, I was recruited by a top clan that competed in matches. Eventually, I ended up meeting one of the producers of the game. He was also the writer of the single-player version of *SOF2*. I asked him how he got the job of writing the game, and he quizzed me on how I broke in to screenwriting. We exchanged information and contacts, and through him I met quite a few other developers and producers.

I called them, e-mailed them, and took the ones in Southern California out to lunch. I picked their brains and pitched my services. A former Blizzard producer who went to work for Atari in L.A. finally offered me a project. The developer was Liquid Entertainment, and the game would be a *Dungeons & Dragons* RTS. I submitted some writing samples to the developers, met with them a few times, and was eventually hired. That was my start, and my subsequent jobs have come to me much the same way. If you want to be a freelance game writer, you need to do a lot of schmoozing and networking. It's not something I'm completely comfortable with, but I've gotten better at it and now, occasionally, I even enjoy it.

Wendy Despain, International Hobo

My path to breaking in is winding and weird. I got a degree in magazine journalism with an emphasis on science writing back when the World Wide Web was being invented. Since it was an interesting tech story, I learned the basics and got sucked into the world of Web development. My journalism contacts got me a job making Web features for Tribune Company—the owner of the *Chicago Tribune*, *LA Times*, and other newspapers and TV stations. My contacts and experience there got me work producing websites for television shows, and in the course of working on some Gene Roddenberry projects, I designed and wrote for two alternate reality games.

I had always enjoyed playing video games, and in college that led me to MUDs, the very first massively multiplayer online (text) games. That's where I developed a love for interactive narrative that I put into practice with the alternate reality games. When those completed their runs, I realized video games were more invested in interactive narrative than television was at the time, so I decided to transition into the game industry and started networking. I also went from working full-time as a Web producer to freelancing as a writer for magazines, novels, and television. I got involved in an interactive fiction project and joined the IGDA.

The IGDA Game Writing SIG gave me an opportunity to showcase my writing and organizational skills to a group of industry insiders, and after being very active in that organization for a while, I got into a conversation with one of the working game writers who was also active there. He mentioned in passing that he was slammed with work, and I reminded him that I was a freelancer. He asked for samples, and within a few weeks I had a freelance job writing for a video game.

The moral of the story is to never underestimate the value of networking and practicing your craft. That's how I've gone from one job to the next to the next, and now I'm even the chair of the IGDA Game Writing SIG.

Andy Walsh, Freelancer

Some days it feels like I still am breaking in; I'm not sure the process ever stops, though it does get a bit easier. I started writing at university while I was doing a law degree and wanting to become an actor... so I took a few turns on my way to writing for games! The great thing about starting this way was that I'd written and produced seven original plays, adapted another, and had a half-hour comedy shot and broadcast for cable TV by the time I left university. This experience meant I'd not only got a healthy resume, but I'd also had a chance to see how a theater audience reacted to my material, what they liked, as well as what they didn't respond to, and what my writing style and technique was. By the time I'd done all this, I'd caught the writing bug and decided that writing and directing was what I wanted to do as a job.

Luckily, as I left university without a clue as to how to manage this massive life decision, my mum found an MA course in television and radio scriptwriting at a local university. I knew practically nothing about TV or radio writing, but I recognized that theater didn't pay much, so TV and radio might be a way to earn a living. During this time I got my first paid job. A local theater had heard of me... er... through my mum again!! The interview took place in a pub, and the fact that I'd already written so many plays in my spare time gave me a good resume and a range of samples to show the producer. When we negotiated fees and rights, I must admit that I'd arrived with the thought that I didn't care if I got paid nothing, but I didn't say this—*never say that!* By the end of the interview I'd not only negotiated a reasonable fee, but I'd kept all the rights to my work. This is a good model to remember... never go in shooting too low. If you shoot too low thinking this is the only way to break in then you will end up with nothing. While you need to be realistic, don't be too fast to give away rights or to ask for too little money. If you're not sure what to ask for, talk to other writers, look on the Internet, or contact groups that represent writers such as IGDA or your national writers' guild.

A little time after this I landed my first TV job through a professional tutor I met on my MA course. I'd gone the extra mile on my assignments and worked well with him, so when he got a job story producing a new soap opera, he made it a contractual point that he brought me with him as a storyliner. Walking up to the TV station the first day was incredible... I was on a pretty nice salary, I was breaking in to TV, and I felt I was off! The job was a short-term one to do development work, and after a six-week whirlwind I left the station, having learned a lot and convinced this was it!! I'd worked for a major TV company, I'd written the play that had opened the Ben Kingsley Theatre—what was to stop me?! Surely now I could pick and choose from jobs... er... no. As it worked out I didn't get paid to write again for another seven months.

I wasn't idle during this time. I wrote and toured another two plays with my own theater company, started work on a play for a local school, and worked on completing my MA. All the time I was applying for jobs and sending off writing samples until I got my next writing job. From that point on, I've not stopped.

Okay, so this is all theater and television...so what has it to do with the games industry? Well, most of my work in the games industry has followed the same pattern. The standard ways of getting a job are simple—hard work, persistence, and meeting as many contacts as possible. On top of this you have to have skill, you have to learn your craft, and you have to listen to those with experience...this will get your writing into shape for when you meet the right person. Keep writing even in fallow periods; the better your resume and sample list, the better your chances of getting a job and, hopefully, the more honed you are as a writer.

Once you have these things in place, it's all about perspiration and convincing people you're serious. I know a lot of people who say that they're writers...but they have yet to complete a project...they spend very little time writing. You need to be passionate about what you do, or why would someone employ you? You also need to be someone people can work with. While you need conviction, being confrontational is a big turn off. People want someone who can work in a team, and if you make yourself a pain to work with by arguing over everything and failing to listen, then chances are you either won't get the job or you'll get a bad reputation that will close doors to you in the future.

1.8   Resources

Groups

- International Game Developers Association: http://www.igda.org/

- Game Writing Special Interest Group: http://www.igda.org/writing/

- Online game scripts and documentation library: http://www.igda.org/writing/library/

Magazines and Sites

- *Game Developer*: http://www.gdmag.com/

- Gamasutra.com: http://www.gamasutra.com/

- Game Career Guide: http://www.gamecareerguide.com/

- Gamedev.net: http://www.gamedev.net/

Books

- IGDA Game Writing SIG's *Game Writing: Narrative Skills for Videogames*, edited by Chris Bateman

- Lee Sheldon's *Character Development and Storytelling for Games*

- Steve Ince's *Writing for Video Games*

- Robert McKee's *Story: Substance, Structure, Style, and the Principles of Screenwriting*

- Christopher Vogler's *The Writer's Journey: Mythic Structure for Writers*

2

Interactive Script Formatting

Wendy Despain

If you look at a book editor's desk, every manuscript sitting there in piles has the same format—1-inch margins, double-spaced, 12-point type, specific information in page headers. If you look at a stack of screenplays on a showrunner's desk, you'll see they all have their own format, too—dialog centered, certain words in all-caps, spaces between paragraphs, 12-point type.

But as a freelance gamewriter, no two of my jobs have been in the same document format. I've worked in three different Excel spreadsheet layouts and two kinds of modified screenplay format. Some of my big-picture interactive narrative assignments are turned in with a modified memo style along with an intricate, hand-drawn, Photoshop-edited flow chart. Conformity is not common in this industry. I've seen this realization put writers from other disciplines into prolonged panic attacks.

Writing has a long history of appreciating structure—just ask the fans of haiku and limerick. Writers are accustomed to being given a structure set in stone and the freedom to fill in that structure and decorate it any way they like. Game writing doesn't work that way. In fact, sometimes it's exactly the opposite. You get an assignment where you're told they don't care what format it's in, but your narrative needs to have a princess, a plumber, and a bunch of mushrooms.

2.1 There Is No One True Interactive Script Format

I don't want to shatter anyone's world view, but there just is no one true interactive script format. There are a few very good reasons for this and a few less good reasons. Let's start with the less good reasons. They're partly cultural, partly habitual, and partly arbitrary.

For one thing, the video game industry has a long history of independence. The first computer games were written by lone artists on borrowed machines in their basements. Although huge teams are brought together by big corporations to make games today, the organizations still have a maverick, rebellious culture. Everyone thinks they can do this better than the other guys, so they start from scratch and reinvent as many wheels as possible. Every developer has a different workflow and a different set of development tools and a different philosophy about narrative. They all have their own way of dealing with dialog and narrative planning.

Secondly, the added position of "writer" on these big development teams is fairly new. Up until about 2002, game designers and programmers did what we today call narrative design and dialog writing. Many of them didn't have the background in traditional forms of writing but were very inventive, so they created a system that worked for them on the particular game they were building at the time. As writers were hired onto teams and as contractors, they mostly worked in isolation—again, coming up with their own formats.

Historical and cultural reasons aside, there are two very good reasons for not having one consistent script format across all games. For one thing, games are still a young medium. New ways of playing games, new ways of building games, and new genres of games are still being invented all the time. If we get too hung up on back-end procedures too soon, we may tie our hands for future innovation. Games are not novels, they're not screenplays, and they need to develop their own format. It's going to take us more than a few years to develop best practices.

And possibly the most important reason for not having one consistent format is that games don't have one consistent format. Consider writing quest dialog for a role-playing game versus commentary for a sports game. They have different requirements, different delivery methods, and different purposes. They can't effectively share a common format.

Within the game-development process there are even needs for presenting the same information in different formats. The programmers need to put dialog text into games, the animators need to lip-sync the words to the images, and the voiceover actors need to put feeling and tone into an audio file. All these people need different things when they're looking at your words, and format can go a long way to bringing out the best performance and presentation for the game.

2.2   How Format Works in the Real Development World

It's a cliche because it's true. You've got to use the right tool for the job. It's possible to pound a nail in with a screwdriver, but it's much better to use a hammer—or even better a pneumatic nailer. The same goes for script formatting. Game developers today use different formats for doing different jobs.

If you're writing a cutscene or cinematic or scripted event—anything that ends up being presented to the player in a noninteractive, movie-like fashion is best communicated using a movie-like format. This is either the "traditional screenplay" or "modified screenplay" format. Examples of these formats from real games are included in Appendix A.

More interactive portions of the game are usually presented in a spreadsheet format. Often, writers aren't familiar with Excel, but when the end product needs to be put into a database and triggered by code or randomized, that's the best format to put it in.

And when it comes to planning nonlinear narrative, nothing beats pictures. A lot of times, the first draft is done in pen on the back of a napkin, but this isn't very effective when presenting to a development team. The format here is really up in the air. I've seen whiteboards with color-coded markers, bulletin boards with note cards and magazine photos, sticky notes on a blank wall, and modified PowerPoint and Visio org charts.

And these three formats are just scratching the surface. Individual developers often create proprietary development tools to help streamline the production process. To get some idea of how these work, take a look at the level-customizing features some PC games provide. The most famous one is the *Neverwinter Nights* mod kit.

2.3 What You Need to Know about Screenplay Formats

Many other books have been written on the subject of screenplay format and will do a more thorough job of explaining it. Personally, I think the best way to learn the format is to get a screenplay from a movie or television series you admire and take your cues from that. Even if you think you'll never write a film, every game writer should learn how to write their ideas as a screenplay. Most games today include dialog voice talent, and actors are used to seeing their material in the traditional screenplay format. Your original material may be in some other format, but you should do everything you can to provide the actors with a script that looks familiar. They've got enough to worry about without having to squint at 9-point Arial type in a grid.

The modified screenplay format is essentially the same but with everything aligned to the left instead of centered. As far as I know, the only reason for this change is that game developers are in a hurry and most of them don't have Final Draft or another program that does the centering with no fuss. They use Microsoft Word or a bare-bones text editor and just go straight down the page.

The screenplay formats are best used for cinematic sequences and linear game narratives. If there aren't very many branches in the plot, the screenplay format can just chug along with occasional notes for interactive elements such as boss battles and the like. Don't try to describe the player's fight scenes blow by blow. A simple note introducing the big bad guy and listing some randomized fight barks is sufficient.

One thing to keep in mind while working in this format is that all your dialog will eventually be put into a database, and you may or may not be the one to do the data entry. So group like things together and include many, many notes to clarify what you were thinking when you wrote this.

And never think you've got this script-format thing licked. There are writers in other media who have dealt with many of the same problems we face in game writing. For instance, writers who have penned animated series and movies know a lot about writing for characters who aren't entirely human. Take every opportunity to learn the methods writers use in other media and take whatever you can use.

2.4   Learning to Love Excel

Microsoft Excel and other spreadsheet programs aren't as antithetical to narrative as you might think. Most writers know how to work with an outline, and that's just a spreadsheet without the dividing lines. It's also not confined to the 8.5 × 11 blank white page writers tend to think in. Your outline can go down one column, the next column can hold fleshed-out dialog, the next column can hold delivery notes for the actors, and so on off to the right and down forever.

I learned how to use Excel back in college during my short stint as a physics major, but there are easier ways to learn its quirks. Online classes and tutorials can demystify things like how to automatically wrap cells and change how they're displayed. Don't let the accountant-style layout intimidate you. This is just another program to learn. Jump in and take charge of your knowledge acquisition. You'll be far more valuable to an employer.

There are a few things I really love about Excel when working on game projects. For one thing, the tiny little cells encourage brevity. Players don't want to listen to long monologues—they want their information delivered in a punchy, pithy sound bite. If you only see a small space to write in, you're going to think in terms of short sentences.

Spreadsheets are also really good at managing huge volumes of data. When you're facing 100,000 lines of dialog, it can be incredibly helpful to sort these by character or quest or whatever. Having the lines automatically numbered can also be very helpful for planning purposes, and if you learn how to use some of the more advanced controls, you can have the program automatically generate numerical filenames and fill in a series of cells containing identical content.

Nobody needs page numbers in the video game world anyway, so why use a word-processing program designed to break things up by the page? What programmers and level designers need are line numbers. They need to be able to instantly find the dialog they're looking for. Audio engineers find Excel very helpful for organizing the voiceover sessions from the back end. The actors may not need all the columns and cells, but audio engineers can automate the gargantuan task of attaching multiple takes of each line to the spreadsheet script.

When I sit down to start a new project I know needs to be in a spreadsheet, I start out by building the skeleton. I put headings on all the columns and set the program to keep those headings at the top of the window at all times. I also set it up to sort those columns without messing up the relationship to data in the rows. This way I can tell it to just show Grandma's lines, and it won't reorder just the data in that one column, lining up the name Grandma with dialog for Ninja #3.

Once I have my skeleton in place, I start filling it in. See the sample of the skeleton with a little meat on its bones in Appendix A. I usually work scene-by-scene or quest-by-quest, making sure to name or number the scenes and beats so they can be grouped together this way later on. Those columns can be filled in automatically. Then I type the character name in the appropriate column, the line in the cell next to it, the trigger for that dialog, and notes for the voice talent. Then I move on to the next line of dialog. I find it much easier to write all of these notes at the same time I write the dialog, rather than powering through the conversation and then going back and adding actors' notes and triggers.

I also like to start my dialog-writing time by editing something I wrote two or three days before. The work I did yesterday is usually too fresh and still looks fine. Material from a few days ago has had enough time to age, and I have enough distance to be able to tell if it's starting to stink or not.

Sadly, Excel is not the most ideal program of all time. The spell checker can be spotty, formatting can be tricky, and files can grow to astronomical sizes some computers will choke on.

If you make yourself learn the tools available to you, you'll get a feel for which will work best for the job ahead of you. And if you're not sure which is most appropriate, just pick one and get started. If it's not right, you'll feel it soon and can make the switch.

2.5   Representing Branching and Nonlinear Narrative

In both spreadsheet and modified screenplay format, plot branches can only be represented in a linear way. For instance, making a note where the branching possibility happens and going through dialog for one possible path, then writing through the dialog for the next possible path, and so on. The *Bratz* script in Appendix A is an example of the linear "if choice B" strategy.

Because this is kind of clunky, most writers resort to visual representations of their nonlinear narrative. These methods truly have no standard. It comes down to using whatever works. Some people list one event per note card and pin them up on a big bulletin board, then use string to show paths between events. Others draw it out on a big whiteboard or sketch it on paper and then scan it into a computer for digital editing. I've seen trees, webs, matrices, and spirals.

Some writers say they can keep the narrative and all its branches straight just in their own head, but in game development you have to be able to communicate your vision to others, and sometimes there's nothing like a flow chart or diagram to get the point across. In these cases, a cleaner presentation can be critical, so consider using a program like PowerPoint, Visio, or Dia to pretty up the scribbles.

2.6   Specialized Tools

Many writers look at the current state of patchwork solutions and think there has to be a better way. Tools programmers do, too, and I know of at least three possible solutions in the works. The tech guys see programs like Final Draft and Movie Magic

Screenwriter and think there must be a way to make a tool for speeding up the process of formatting and writing interactive narrative. So far, I'm unconvinced it's possible to have a perfect tool for all games, but some of the proprietary tools created for internal use at some of the larger developers may prove me wrong.

BioWare publishes something similar to their interactive narrative tool in the *Neverwinter Nights* mod toolset. Cheyenne Mountain Entertainment has contract writers use Movie Magic Screenwriter, then use a tool to automate the transition into the database. Another developer showed me their internal writing tool based on flow charts and stick figures.

You probably won't get to use these proprietary tools unless you're hired on staff at a company where they've built a writer's tool to interface with their unique workflow. However, you can get a feel for working this way by playing around with the mod tools distributed with some PC games.

Another way to learn how to work with specialized tools is to delve into the realm of interactive fiction. This community of independent text-based game developers have created some very interesting and intuitive tools for interactive narrative.

These specialized tools can mitigate some of the more tedious aspects of game writing that closely resemble data entry, but sometimes they just change the interface rather than cut down on real time spent. They do tie all the various formats together into one program and can integrate the writer more closely with the development team. No doubt about it, those specialized tools work wonders on the games they were created for.

The nature of the beast, though, requires that the writer's tool gets tangled up with the other proprietary tools a developer uses. So if your next game-writing job is with another developer, or if the developer you work with changes the game engine they're building on for the next game, you'll have to learn all new software. You may also have to wait while the new tools are being built–and the writers' tools are notorious for being last on the list of things the busy tools department has to conjure up. So you may have to submit scripts before your tool is finished. Don't let this stop you. Excel and Movie Magic will always be there on the shelf at the store, and they can be made to work with proprietary toolsets, too.

They're not likely to be joined there on the shelf by a box with a program specifically for game writing any time soon. If such a program were made flexible enough to work with every game genre in existence, it would look pretty much like Excel.

2.7   Free Your Mind

Writers can sometimes get hung up on format. Let's face it—we'll play around with fonts, margins, italics, and underlines till we're up against the deadline. Personally, I use it as a way to make that blank page not so scary and blank. Somehow having a title and a few headings makes the whole project look a little more possible.

But interactive narrative is young and still trying to find its way. Don't consider anything in this chapter as a standard or requirement. They're suggestions to help get your ideas out of your head and into a presentable state. If you think of a better way to do any of these things, give it a shot and see how it works. If it's better than what we're already using, please get together with other interactive narrative writers and share your methods. I still think there has got to be a better way.

2.8   Exercises

1. Convert one of the script samples from Appendix A into one of the other formats discussed in this chapter.

2. Choose a story-heavy game you enjoy and draw its narrative structure in the format you think best fits the design. Be sure you don't skip any side quests or alternative branches.

3. Create the skeleton of an Excel script format in Excel and fill in ten lines of dialog plus notes.

3

Writing Pitch Docs and Exec Docs

Erin Hoffman

3.1   I've Got This Great Idea for a Video Game

With rare exception, commercial video games get their start in the form of a *pitch document*, a very brief (usually under ten pages) description of the game that a studio proposes to create. This can also be called a *concept doc* or a *vision doc*, though those terms are usually applied to internal documents. A polished (and usually reduced) form of a vision doc will go to the prospective publisher and contain budgeting, team, and corporate information that a pitch doc doesn't need. But the two are closely related, and a pitch doc can serve as a core vision point to which the team returns for focus mid to late in the project phase when development can evolve away from its original concept. The vision or pitch doc also serves to communicate to the team early on what the project's core goals are. The larger the project, the longer its pitch or vision document will be, but the focus is on conciseness.

Understanding the techniques and standard formatting of a pitch document can help you present your project in its most crucial nascent phase as a professional product worthy of respect and consideration. With the growing roles of writers in game production, Pitch Writer has become a standardized job title, and particularly as games extend into other fields such as medicine and social services (a.k.a. "serious games"), wherein non–"game people" will be reviewing a project, a good pitch can mean the difference between landing a competitive gig and missing out.

Pitch documents are frequently collaborative, depending on a studio's structure, and can follow a brainstorming session including writers, designers, programmers, and artists. They frequently contain design mockups or art concepts, but in this chapter we'll focus on the communication-focused text produced by a pitch writer.

3.2   Parts of a Pitch Document

Most pitch documents follow a standard format. Individual studios may have their own style templates, but the basic components remain the same:

- Executive Summary

- Audience Analysis

- Story

- Competition Analysis

- Market Analysis

- Gameplay

- Budget & Schedule

Tips

- **Use bulleted or numbered lists wherever possible.** A pitch doc is not the place for your deathless prose—that goes into backstory documentation that in all likelihood no one will ever read.

- **Skim your document.** This is how your audience will likely review it. Does it communicate when read quickly?

- **Break up the text.** Keep your paragraphs short and, if you have a long section of text, such as in your gameplay or story sections, place concept art or design diagrams inside the block of text to break it up. A pitch doc is highly visual.

- **Don't use a paragraph where a table will work.** This is particularly true for any analytical section of the doc, e.g., competition analysis. Use language-free comparison charts where possible, but be careful of how this can expand your page count.

- **Read your executive summary aloud.** Does it sound exciting and new? Does it sound like the description of an existing game? If the answers are "yes" and "no" respectively, you're ready to go.

Executive Summary

The executive summary (ES), or alternatively overview (though the two are sometimes separated, with an overview being up to a page long for larger projects), leads a pitch doc. This is a two- to three-sentence description of the proposed title, and some consider this to be the most important part of the pitch as it may be all that certain portions of your audience, i.e., publishing executives, hear about the project.

The ES generally starts with the name of the title followed by a description of the genre and audience, as in "*GoPets: Vacation Island* is a social networking–focused pet simulator for the Nintendo DS targeted at boys and girls ages 6 to 14." This gives a concise description of the game and lets a publisher know where to "slot" it. Game publishers, like book publishers, frequently have genre slots that they are seeking to fill—"We need an action-RPG," or, "We need a platformer for kids." Many pitch documents are written specifically toward a slot, when a publisher has a license ("Cabbage Patch Kids® Game Boy Advance title for pre-teens") and is seeking a studio to develop it.

An ES may also contain or come in the form of a *high concept*, a term developed by Hollywood to streamline production of feature films. One method of high concept juxtaposes two existing properties in an immediately evocative way using the word "meets." For example, Stephen King's *Dark Tower* series can be described as "*Lord of the Rings* meets *The Good, the Bad, and the Ugly*." This form of high concept is particularly useful in early brainstorming but can sometimes backfire in a pitch document, depending on the audience (the high concept principle is seen by some as part of the high-speed downfall of cinema), and should be used with caution. But a high concept–style succinct description encompassing universal themes and familiar archetypes is especially useful in an executive summary.

The executive summary should, as concisely as possible (usually not exceeding 50 words), capture the *geist* of a game—that is, what it will feel like to play it. In creating pitch documents, I try to keep in mind Ursula K. Le Guin's description of an effective short story: she says in her highly wonderful *Language of the Night* that a truly effective short story should exist to convey *one* precise emotion. In a large game, you might be dealing with an array of emotions driven by a complex story, but in the end, the player should be left with a feeling of completion and theme. Find that theme, that one driving emotion, and you have the center of your pitch and vision.

Audience Analysis

The audience analysis follows the executive summary and makes a case for the game's role in the marketplace. It targets a particular audience as precisely as possible, e.g., "girls ages 8–14," "boys ages 6–12," "men 18–32." The audience analysis may come straight from the license of an existing product or, in the case of an original IP, serves to frame the potential player. This serves to define future marketing efforts and also conveys the studio's forethought in considering their design vector. Even a game intended as "fun for all ages" has a core audience, and defining your audience analysis as "all ages and genders" is risky as it does not help a publisher mentally fill a "slot" and can convey uncertainty or lack of research on the part of the developer. Even the hit title *Brain Age* for the Nintendo DS, which wound up being appealing to all ages, has a core audience and was initially intended for men and women over age 55.

The more precise your audience analysis—try to define one gender and an age range of no more than eight years—the clearer your document will be.

Story

All games, even simple puzzles like *Tetris*, have a story. This may not incorporate text in the final game version (as is the case in games for kids at pre-reading age), but it provides a mood for your project and a coherence of emotional content. Naturally, the story section for an epic RPG is going to be a lot more specific, and for a title like that, this section of the pitch can be both larger and more critical to the overall document. In a heavily story-driven game, the story section of your pitch will take the form of a plot synopsis similar to the one-page synopsis sent by novelists to prospective agents or publishers. For games of any type, all named major characters should appear in this section of the document, with their names **in bold** in the text.

Competition Analysis

In the competition analysis, you display your knowledge of current market forces and visually chart the necessary, amazing, so-crucial-it's-*obvious* niche that your game will fill.

Although your game will have a vast panoply of essential and unique features, for the purposes of this section you'll reduce those to a differentiating five to seven, depending on the size of the game. These core features—such as one-on-one Internet multiplayer functionality, sandbox-style freeform play, platformer action, or AI minions—give a quick picture of your game as compared to others with which it will compete for shelf space and audience attention.

The competition analysis chart for *GoPets: Vacation Island,* a sandbox-style social networking pet game for the Nintendo DS, looked like this:

Game	WiFi / Internet	Mobile	Items	3D Enviro.	Pet AI	Community
GoPets DS	X	X	X		X	X
NintenDogs		X	X	X	X	
NeoPets	X		X			X
Black & White Creatures		X		X	X	
Animal Crossing (DS)	X	X	X	X		X

The competition analysis will concisely tell your prospective client what your game offers that other games don't and what your game *doesn't* offer (but hopefully doesn't need). It also emphasizes your core feature set, which will be critical in maintaining focus as the development process continues. This chart may be followed by further analysis of other competing titles, but the chart should only focus on a top three to six, and the entire section should not be longer than about three-quarters of a page.

Market Analysis

A pitch document may or may not contain a market analysis, depending upon the pitch strategy of your studio. Larger projects almost always include a market analysis. Building on the image depicted by your competition analysis, the market analysis makes a case for why this game will be successful *right now*, citing the success of similar titles and the absence in the market of a game fulfilling a particular player desire.

Gameplay

Finally, in the gameplay section of your document, you'll get to talk about what the player will actually *do* in your game. This section is sometimes called "Game Mechanics" and, again depending on the size of the project, can be a brief summary of game functionality or a bullet-point rundown of a series of activities the player will engage in while playing. This section expands upon the core feature set outlined in your executive summary and competition analysis to give concise details on what the player will experience. In the full game design document, this section will take up a majority of your page count, documenting the fine details of the game experience.

Although your game will evolve through the pitch process and in development, this section should give a fast rundown of *every game feature* in single-line format.

For ease of communication, in a pitch document it's a good idea to lead with a summary paragraph followed by a bullet-point list, with "feature phrases" in bold that specify each game mechanic. For example, a partial gameplay summary for *Tetris* might look like:

- players manipulate **six puzzle block types** composed of four units;

- players can **rotate** puzzle blocks in 90-degree increments, and **speed up** descent;

- a **preview window** displays the next puzzle block to be dropped;

- forming a **contiguous horizontal line** of block pieces causes that line to disappear and score points to accrue;

- bonus points are given for strategically solving **four lines simultaneously**, called "**tetris**";

- etc.

Note that a great deal of specificity is conveyed through the gameplay section without using thick paragraphs or a lot of words. Your gameplay section should provide a complete picture of major game activities.

Budget & Schedule

In the last section of your pitch document, you'll seal the deal by outlining the staff size and development period for the project. In all likelihood, you, the writer, will not be completing this section, but you may polish the basics for presentation in the total pitch.

Depending on the phase of your project, the "budget" discussed here may not be a real budget. That will be hashed out in in-person or phone negotiations specific to the executives involved. But your budget and schedule breakdown should indicate the number of team members (broken down by role and "unit," where one developer equals one unit) and the length of time they will spend on the project. In an ideal world, this gives a natural budget as the hours devoted to the project result in direct quantifiable costs to the studio. This section will form the framework for a future production plan.

Additional Sections

Depending on the nature of your game, you may have select additional sections, such as a technical summary detailing specific technology your company will use to complete the project. If the game utilizes highly innovative graphics technology, a separate section on graphics can be warranted. Pitch documents are flexible and will differ by project and by studio; what you've just read are the basics for a core pitch template.

3.3   Executive Documents

Executive documents are documents frequently requested by the publisher or licensor after a project has been landed and/or is in development. These documents detail or clarify the design approach and are not always written by the game writer. As the project progresses toward attaining funding, the documents will get longer. Before a contract is signed, a publisher will want to see a detailed game design document (GDD) with milestones laid out and agreed to with delivery stipulations and dates, as well as a technical design document (TDD) laying out how, exactly, the team plans to achieve the objectives set out in the pitch. These documents represent the next step in the pre-production process.

During production, if any changes are made to the game's design, these documents can be revised, or new summaries issued. While the GDD and TDD are in the purview of the specific departments that use them, later-phase executive documents can be more language-oriented than technical documents and more geared toward communicating the creative intent of the project. Conciseness always counts, but solid, evocative executive documents can improve publisher-developer and licensor-developer relations substantially by conveying the competency of the studio and team. This side of game writing, similar to pitch writing, benefits most substantially from studying the art of succinct nonfiction. William Zinsser's *On Writing Well* is a superb resource for this.

3.4   Exercises

1. Take three of your favorite video games, from separate genres and audiences
   if possible, and write an executive summary for each. Focus on the game's
   core concepts; "sell" the product and do not exceed 50 words in your opening
   (short) summary. Test your short summary on a game-familiar audience and
   see if they can name the game from your concise description (leave out any
   specific character names, e.g., "Samus Aran").

2. Draft an original game concept and write a pitch document for it. If you're
   feeling frisky, create concept art or design diagrams and embed them in relevant sections of the document. Frame your competition analysis as a compar-
   ative table using at least three games created in the last five years.

4

Game Documentation Guide

John Feil

4.1 It Lives!

Game documentation is fundamental to the process of actually making games. This is the document that puts the plan into action, that gives the developers focus, that outlines what the game is and how the developers are going to bring it about.

The sad thing about game documentation, however, is that once everybody agrees that it represents the game everybody ought to be building, it becomes obsolete almost immediately.

Game development is a chaotic process and, like water, tends to seek out the earth that is easiest to carve. Sometimes, the earth sends the water in unforeseen directions. In game development, sometimes ideas that seemed so simple are suddenly revealed to be enormously complex. The amount of art you wanted in the game, once looked at closely, is projected to take months of extra time and millions of dollars more in extra cost. Characters are revealed to be cliché, game mechanics shown to be less than fun.

The great German strategist Moltke the Elder once said, "No battle plan survives contact with the enemy." The same goes for game documentation. Once the rubber hits the road, everything changes.

Thus, if you want your game documentation to survive, it must live! It has to be agile, to be able to change when it needs to change. It needs to be strong, so it can convince people to think twice before throwing it aside for the idea of the moment. It has to be charismatic, so it can sway people to believe in its vision. Otherwise, it will start gathering dust the minute the dev team writes its first line of code.

Currently, there are a few ways to make sure your game document lives. Everything depends on someone being responsible for it: someone needs to keep the document updated and current so that the developers on the team can refer to it with the confidence that it is accurate.

This person is usually the Lead Game Designer. As the core visionary of the team, the Lead Designer is the one responsible for navigating the development of the game through the shark-infested waters of entropy, rescoping, and lack of focus. Other personnel responsible for the upkeep of the game design document could be a producer, a writer, or it could even be a community affair, where responsible parties take the time to help maintain the document as changes occur in their own specialized bailiwick.

Keeping a live document is difficult. One problem is that it is a full-time job. Someone needs to be on top of all the changes that occur on almost a daily basis. The next problem is that you'll want to save your old work in case the original plan comes back into favor. For instance, the planners for the game might find that you can add back in a few enemy types to the design.

The next difficulty is that the latest document should be available to everyone who needs to refer to it, from the president of the company to the quality assurance team. If even one person is holding onto an old document, things can easily go wrong.

In modern game studios, game documents that live find themselves in one of two places: in the source control program, such as Perforce or SourceSafe, where old versions of the doc are easily accessible and everyone always has the most up-to-date version every time they sync to the depot, or in a wiki on the intranet of the company, where a quick launch of a browser of their choice gets people to the information they need.

Source Control

Leaving your game document on a source control program has benefits and risks. The benefits are that everyone always has the latest version of the documentation. You can lock out everyone but a few select employees from being able to change the document, so you limit the chance that somebody will edit the document in a way that proves disastrous. You also have the ability to recall your old versions in case you want to refer to or recover old design ideas from the past.

There are few risks to using source control to store your game documentation. However, in my experience, keeping your doc in a file structure can sometimes make it easier to ignore. If people have to go searching through their files to find the right doc, they may not check it at all. Instead, they'll just ask somebody what the game doc says. This increases the chance they may misunderstand the design and either do work that isn't necessary or waste time trying to figure out how to accomplish something that seems so out of place in the original design. Later in this chapter, we'll cover how to format your game design doc to limit this problem.

Wiki

Wikis have many advantages over the old "huge Word doc" method. Wikis are easy to edit, easy to place pictures in, easy to create hyperlinks between related pieces of information, easy to find information in, and generally kind of fun to explore.

However, wikis take a lot more work to keep updated. They encourage redundant information if people don't have perfect knowledge of the entire contents of the wiki. Multiple authors can cause much chaos. There is a certain technological barrier, where people have to learn the wiki's markup language in order to present their information in a nicely formatted manner. Finally, it's hard to make backups of the wiki, so older info may get lost after a certain number of iterations.

Whichever way you decide to take to keep your documentation alive, it must be done, or you'll find yourself constantly fighting fires that a quick reference to an updated document could have prevented in the first place.

4.2   The Evolution of the Game Design Doc

The game design doc and the other docs that accompany it are generally subject to a series of growth periods predicated by the doc being accepted and agreed upon by the stakeholders involved in the project. What this means is that the documentation starts small and high-level, and when everybody involved in making the game—from the development team, to the people supplying the money, to the console makers who allow the game to be published on their consoles—gives their thumbs up, the document goes back to become bigger, more focused, and granular. The document usually goes through several of these rounds until it reaches a final, comprehensive form. Even then, the doc may grow as changes are required, game features are cut or added, and even more granular details about the game are exposed and (hopefully) written down.

Below, I've outlined the evolution of game documentation, what is required in each form, and what types of things can be found in each stage of its life.

4.3   The Game Pitch

The game pitch is the seed from which all documentation will grow. The game pitch can contain the following information.

- The title of the game.

- The genre of the game: shooter, RTS, MMO, adventure, etc.

- The platforms the game will be made for: Xbox 360, PC, PS3, Wii, etc.

- The audience you intend to market the game to: boys, men, girls, frogs, etc.

- The ESRB rating you are aiming at: C, E, T, M, AO.

- The core concept of the game: what the game is all about.

- A summary of what happens in the game.

- The unique selling points that make this game distinct from other games.

- Possibly some concept art to fire the imagination of the reader.

The game pitch establishes the big, high-level ideas that define the game and attempts to get everyone excited about how cool this game could be. It is more marketing material than actual development information, and it concerns itself with emotional punch over technical feasibility or details. Basically, the reaction you want when someone sees your game pitch is a request for more information. You want the reader to think, "This could be cool! Tell me more!"

Once your targets have been wowed by your stellar pitch, the gate is unlocked, and you are allowed to go back to your computer to create a game treatment.

4.4   The Game Treatment

The game treatment is a larger version of the game pitch. It takes the ideas presented by the pitch and fills them in with more information. It begins to take into account more technical details, fleshes out the story being told in the game, and explores the look and feel of the game's art and playability in further depth.

Expanding the Game Pitch

Expanding the game pitch into a treatment is a fairly easy thing. Normally, it takes a lot of effort to take your game idea and put it into pitch format. You want to put in the entire story, along with the ingenious new control map scheme and the spiffy game mechanics. The pitch, however, is a teensy document meant to just whet the appetite of the reader. Now that you are writing the treatment, you can let all those ideas flow.

However, you still need to limit yourself. The game treatment needs to hover around 20 pages or less. While the pitch document looked like a vacation pamphlet, the treatment is more like an "information packet." It remains a fairly high-level document, with its main focus on making your game idea seem both attractive (which you did in the game pitch) and, perhaps more importantly at this stage, doable given your resources. The game treatment should convince your readers that your team can create this game in a reasonable amount of time given a reasonable budget.

Following are some things you generally find in a game treatment.

Full Story Overview

In the game pitch, you covered the game's core concept. The treatment covers the story in more depth. What was once, "A boy has adventures in his home-made flying machine in a modern take on Gulliver's Travels," now becomes, "Joshua, a boy genius, has built a home-made aircraft to help him find his missing mother, who disappeared when he was young. As he follows the clues into a strange land that isn't on any map, he encounters sights and peoples both strange and wonderful until he discovers the insidious plot of the malevolent Copernican League and their tyrannical leader, Dr. Indigo."

The game treatment should still be high-level, so while you won't need to (and shouldn't) write about every single moment of the player's experience in the game, you will need to cover the major characters of the game, especially the villains that comprise the main challenge to the player throughout the game.

Focusing on the Trailer Moments

"Trailer moments" are those moments in a movie that really sell the movie to its audience. They show some of the best parts of the movie while still leaving the audience hankering for more.

In writing the story treatment for your game, try to include the "trailer moments" that you see happening to the player as he plays. Not only will you be showing how exciting the game will be to the reader, but you will also be giving some idea of the scope of the game. If your game has a daring fight on the edge of a volcano, that gives the reader the information that you'll be building said volcano, that you'll probably have to build some sort of lava technology into the game, that there is combat in the game, and a host of other details. Writing these trailer moments should also ground you a little, too. Your team (who should read what they are getting into) might have an issue with your volcano and bring up the example of the failed "fight on the edge of the mammoth water geyser" scene that you had to strip out of the last game because of technical difficulties.

Gameplay and Specific Player Abilities

The treatment digs deeper into the technical specifications of the game. First and foremost it reveals the gameplay of the game. What fun things can the player do in the game? How is this accomplished using the standard controller that comes with the game console you're aiming at?

Include descriptions of what the player can do to affect the game world. Describe how he can attack, defend, use things and move. Describe the special game mechanics that are unique to your game. Remember, the game treatment is only a follow-up document, and that it still needs to convince the reader that the game is worth devoting time and money into making. These mechanics need to sound exciting and dynamic. They should be presented in a way that continues to sell the game as something the reader would want to play.

Also in this section, include some of the things that enemies can do to the player. This doesn't need to be an exhaustive list: you don't need to describe every single ability of every boss monster, but if the game world or enemies have abilities that are listed in your Unique Selling Points portion of your pitch document, you'll need to describe those things in greater depth.

Mockups, Maps, and Areas

Another thing that the game treatment document should include is a good amount of accompanying pictures. These can be hand-drawn concepts or fully rendered 3D models. There should be maps of significant areas, sketches of environments, anything that can help bring your game concept to life.

However, don't throw the kitchen sink in the treatment. Only include the best art you can. Stay away from including anything that looks like it was hand-drawn on notebook paper by a non-artist and scanned into the computer. Once again, the treatment is still trying to convince people to make your game. It should look as professional and as polished as possible.

Other things you should include in the treatment are control maps: pictures of the controllers for the targeted consoles shown with identifiers showing what each button does. This gives the reader a visual idea of how the game will be controlled and shows that you are already thinking ahead to how the mechanics of the game really work.

4.5   The Full Game Document

Once the treatment of the game has been given the thumbs up, you can now move on to the full game document. Usually, these are several documents that are made to guide each section of the team in their duties to create the game. Following are some examples of the types of documents the team will need to create for this purpose.

- The game design document, which includes the story of the game, along with game mechanics and systems, a list of assets that need to be built, such as player characters, nonplayer characters, levels, objects, units, weapons, etc., the user interface (UI) and heads-up display (HUD), and the game dialog script.

- The art bible, which is the style guide showing the artists concept art and reference they should be using to guide the creation of objects within the game.

- The technical design document, which lays out how the game will be programmed and lays down rules on how programmers should comment their work, which libraries they should use, what language the game will be written in, etc.

- Other assorted documents, such as the scheduling doc, which the producers create to illustrate schedules and show milestones, a testing plan that Quality Assurance follows to thoroughly test the game, and others.

The Game Design Document

The game design document (GDD) is the central document all stakeholders refer to so they know what the game is all about. It talks about the story, all the characters, and all the areas and levels. It goes in depth about gameplay and mechanics. In short, the GDD is the master document that all other documents derive themselves from. Following are the things that can be found in a game design document.

Full description of game mechanics and system design. This section of the game design document drives deep into the mechanics and systems the player finds in the game. In here, you will find the following.

- The controls the player will use to operate the game.

- The things the player can do in the game, such as

    - go into combat with enemy AI, both close up and from range;
    - jump over things;
    - climb up walls;
    - shimmy along ledges;
    - slide down ropes;
    - hit and destroy objects;
    - pick up or move objects;
    - use objects in some way, such as pulling switches or reading books;
    - talk with nonplayer characters;
    - upgrade the character by picking up weapons or growing in skills;
    - how different skills affect gameplay;
    - how the player loses or dies in the game;
    - multiplayer mechanics, such as
        * how the player interacts with other live players;
        * what is different between the regular game and the multiplayer version;
        * types of multiplayer options: multiple players on a single machine, players meeting through a network, etc.;
        * cheating countermeasures.

- AI behaviors.

    - How enemy or friendly AI should act in the game. This should have several examples listed to show how the designer wants the game to feel when the player encounters an AI.

- Boss design.

    - Much like AI behaviors, this lists the major bosses of the game and gives the reader an idea of what kinds of abilities they bring to bear to challenge the player.

Under-the-hood mechanics. Besides the mechanics the player can actually see, there are a host of other mechanics that he can't.

- How hit points work with combat.

- Weapon damage.

- Ranking systems and how to keep track of rewards.

- Accuracy in combat.

- Reputation systems.

- How traversal works, for instance, how a player dismounts from a climbing surface to the ledge above.

- How the player moves from one discrete area to another (is it streamed? Loaded during a cutscene?).

- And much, much more!

The interface and heads-up display. Also included are mockups of the interface, the menu screens, and the heads-up display (HUD) that the player encounters while playing the game. In complex games, the menus are normally presented in a flow chart that allows the players to see where they're going when they choose a certain option. Menus include the following.

- Front screen menu.

- Character creation menu/choose character menu.

- Multiplayer menu.

- Play mode menu (story mode, campaign mode, 1v1 mode, etc.).

- Save/load menu.

- Extra features menu.

- Options menu for controlling technical specifications.

- Credits screen.

The interface mock-up shows the placement of different meters, graphs, and maps that the player sees when playing the game. It also shows where text is placed on the screen (if text is shown) and possibly examples of interface-based systems such as conversation trees and on-screen help text.

Worlds, levels, missions, and quests. The game design doc also includes full details on the gameworld, the areas that the world is broken up into, and story-based gameplay such as missions or quests. In this section you might want to include the following.

- A backstory of the world: how the world got to the place where it is when the player meets it. This backstory may never be told to the player, but it is helpful to designers who must generate story from the higher-level narrative presented by the treatment doc. This is only for story-based games.

- Maps of all the areas of the game, showing where the player starts and ends, plus descriptions in text.

- A full rundown of the game's story, divided up in such a way that it follows the player's progress through the game. This will either be fairly high-level if the game is nonlinear (like Bethesda's *Oblivion*, where there are a host of ways to get from the beginning to the end) to very granular for linear games such as *Tomb Raider* or *Metal Gear Solid*.

  - This rundown may also include a ramp-up section that shows what skills or abilities or items the player has acquired progressing through the story. For instance, in level 3, the player should be power level 6 and should be capable of dealing 100 damage per second. He should have acquired the Gauntlet of Might and know that his chief enemy is the Scarlet Snake.

- A full listing of quests and missions, including

  - where the quest is found;
  - where the quest is turned in, if anywhere;
  - who gives the quests;
  - where the quest sends the player;
  - what the quest's reward is;
  - the story accompanying the quest;
  - any ramifications from fulfilling the quest (for instance, the player becomes an enemy of the God of Law).

The Script: Cutscenes and Dialog

Also included in the game design document, or if it's very lengthy, as a document in itself, is the game script. This document shows every line of spoken or written dialog in the game, from what goes on in in-game movies (cutscenes) to quest dialog to player shout-outs to sports commentary. Anything that the player reads or hears in the game should be written here.

In my experience, this document is usually broken up into separate lines and placed into a spreadsheet document such as an Excel document. Each line gets a separate identification name, such as Batman_001, so that developers can easily reference them and name each voiceline similarly.

Further, each line, if it is to be recorded by a voice actor or actress, should have a small note of direction in its row, giving the voice talent some clue as to how the line should be delivered and to whom they are talking. This makes things a lot easier when recording time comes along.

The Art Bible

The art bible is a document filled with concept drawings and reference images that the game's artists refer to when trying to build objects in the overall style of the game. Normally, it is created before production begins to serve as a guideline. This document will also include written instructions on how to implement the style of the game (e.g., "gritty, dark" or "cool blues") and possibly technical instructions on how the art pipeline will work. For example, artists may make objects in Maya, draw their textures from a central, shared folder on the network, export their objects into a specific folder associated with the area they are helping to create, and other pipeline info.

The Technical Design Document

The technical design document is the document the programmers will refer to when determining how the game will be programmed, what types of systems will go in the game, and other details. It's usually written by a game designer with a certain degree of technical expertise. The following should be included in the TDD.

- The system requirements that the programmers should be programming towards, including performance targets, and specific requirements that the game's engine has to have to implement the game's design.

- Architectural design of the engine, which includes the game engine's capabilities, including how it works with animation, lighting, shading, graphical effects, sound, and its abilities to interact with third-party solutions.

- A detailed design of the engine's components and modules. This should cover specifics for programmers to refer to in terms of how the engine's parts work and how they interact with one another. Included may be such things as how threading works, streaming, how the engine renders objects and scenes, how the engine works with multiple processors and other hardware, data structures, and so on. It should also deal with how artificial intelligence works within the game.

- A detailed design of how the engine will take advantage of the native tools the platform has available.

- A chapter on standardized development practices for programmers, including the environment they will be programming in, how to build the game, and how to treat each version.

- A chapter on how other nonprogramming roles will interface with the technology of the engine, such as how the artists export art into the game, the toolset the designers will use for scripting and placement, how sound engineers get sound into the game, how all members of the team will be able to test and play the game, as well as establishing size conventions for how much memory can be used at a single time, and other technical questions.

- A chapter on localizing the game content: how the game can easily be migrated into different languages and how to handle that migration.

Asset Lists

Other documents that should be created are asset lists. These are lists showing the available art assets that developers can place within the game. These are extremely helpful and can be exported into task lists by producers.

Schedules and Milestones

Producers and the people in charge of maintaining the schedules that the game developers must follow generally create scheduling charts detailing the entire team's tasks from the beginning of the game to the end. There are a variety of software solutions for these documents, led by Microsoft Project. These documents are continually monitored and updated, as their creation at the beginning of the project takes a lot of guesswork and conjecture to figure out how much time should be allotted for a specific task.

4.6   Conclusion

Game documentation can sometimes be the best part of the process of making a game. The initial potential of creating a game based on a single sheet of paper is intoxicating. However, as time goes by, maintaining those documents, especially the game design document, can be the last thing you want to do. However, you must remember that these documents are sometimes your sole means of communication with a diverse and spread-out team. They may be your only way of defending a feature that may be cut otherwise if you can show that the stakeholders already agreed to put that feature in at an earlier date. Game documentation is the truest source of the vision of the game, and if the documentation becomes stale or obsolete, you have to wonder what that does to your game.

4.7   Exercises

Take a game pitch and expand it into a treatment. Include maps of the world, pictures of the mapping of your controls, and details of how the mechanics of your game work.

5

Manuals, In-Game Text, and Credits

John Feil

5.1   Quick! Write this Manual!

In writing for games, there is no more harrowing task than writing the game manual. You're sitting there one day, writing dialog or prepping for a totally different game and then WHAM! You're stuck writing a piece of instructional prose with an extremely short deadline and a crippling word count. Further, you realize that the information you are going to use to build this document is changing on a daily basis and will do so until past the point when the manual is due to be finished.

If you are reading this chapter, it is entirely likely that you have just been assigned one of these things and are in a panicked frenzy. Relax for a moment. Take a deep breath. No one reads the manual, anyway. Well, except your boss, and all the people who are looking for their credit inside the covers, and the marketing department. Oh, and the legal department, so keep it clean. But those players out there? They only want to know some very specific things, like "What does the 'X' button do?" and "How do I chain combo attacks so I can get maximum damage on the boss enemy in level 8?"

Some of these questions you can answer; some are out of your realm. That is the essence of writing a good manual: knowing what the player has to know and what you send him to the strategy guide for.

5.2   The Short Manual

This section will go over the basics of what you need to put into a short manual. Short manuals are just that: short. They fit into a DVD case and are often about 14 pages long or less. Frequently, this won't be enough room for what you want to put in, so the overriding goal of the short manual is: keep it brief and don't put in anything the player can't use.

Where to Get Your Information

Before you start writing, you need to gather information. Sure, it would be easier to make stuff up, but you probably want to remain healthy and employed, so it's best to get it right.

The first thing you should do is go and collect a few manuals from competing games and study them for format and the kind of information they felt it was necessary to give to the player. These manuals should be fairly easy to find: the team working on the game you are writing your manual for probably has a few lying around. Check with the Producer or Project Manager of the game to see who might have one of these games gathering dust on a shelf in the corner somewhere.

Once you've collected some comparison material, read through them and see how they are formatted: what information goes where and how much of it is there. Also, take note of how much room the end-user license agreement (EULA) takes in the back, as well as the game credits. Make a mental note that you will probably have to save that many pages at the end of your manual, as well.

Next, you need to find the proper information to put into the manual. This is going to be a little harder than the previous task. First, go back to that Producer or Project Manager and get their opinion on what they want to see in the manual. Sometimes, this might be kind of a useless task, as they haven't thought of it. They might refer you to another person on the development team, most likely the Lead Game Designer. At this time, it is good to remember that you are writing your manual during the busiest time of game development, as the team is rushing towards the end at breakneck speed. Hardly anyone will have time to talk with you. It is also a good idea to remember that everyone will have a different idea of what should go in the manual. Congratulations: you have just become a diplomat.

The first place everyone will point you to is the game design document (GDD). Supposedly, this document contains all the necessary information about the controls and game features you will need to explain to the new user. The truth of the matter is that this document is frequently outdated and useless. During the last six months of an average 18-month development cycle, the game design document stops being updated because no one has the time anymore, nor the patience, to keep it up to date. However, it is a good starting point, and you can cut and paste sections verbatim from it to help you form the basis of your manual. Remember, however, that the design document was not designed for brevity, and it needs to be rewritten so that the necessary information can fit into the tiny, tiny manual.

Once you've talked to the Producer and the Designer, and have been shown the GDD, where do you go next? Usually, the answer is the Lead Tester. This person sees the game every day, is aware of the frequent control and feature changes that happen at a breakneck pace during this time of the development, and can usually spare a few minutes to help you get the information you need. The Lead Tester remains a good contact thereafter to inform you of sudden changes in control schemes and such so you don't kick out a manual that is completely useless.

Game Intro

Once you have collected your information, it's time to start writing! The first part of many manuals is the game intro. This is a short blurb encapsulating the game's main character and story. Once again, the essence of this section is brevity: it has to be done in one or two small paragraphs.

This intro will take much more work than you would expect. Many of the people who have a stake in your manual will want it to mention certain aspects of the game that you might not find important. Make sure you listen to them all and are polite to them. Remember that manual writers must be diplomats. If they aren't, then they find themselves in endless meetings about whether to use the word "obliterate" or "decimate" in a sentence.

The intro should also sound a bit like advertisement copy. The intro reaffirms to players that they made the right decision when they bought this game. Also, this section may be stolen at a later point to be the source for the back-cover blurb on the DVD case itself, so make this as engaging as possible.

The ingredients of the intro are as follows.

- Introduce the hero. If the game lets the player make his own character, like a multiplayer title, introduce the base concept of the character, like a WWII soldier or a star-spanning superhero.

- Introduce the world. Introduce the setting of the game, whether it is a fantasy village or an entirely new universe.

- Introduce the initial plot twist that gets the game going: the war that just broke out, the battle that must be fought, the princess that has just been kidnapped, etc.

- Introduce any secondary players, including named enemies that impact the plot in the first few minutes of the game. These introductions can be very general or fairly specific, depending on the amount of mystery you want to shroud the characters in.

"You are Mark Durable, a down-on-his-luck asteroid miner looking for his next job. While looking for a job in Star City 12, you find yourself launched on a quest to find the ancient relic of Exomar before the nefarious Squid-Lords of Volumina 7 can possess its awesome power!"

Contents List

The table of contents may or may not come before the intro. The table of contents is necessary for the player to find the information he wants without having to page through info he isn't interested in. The page numbers will change as the manual is edited, re-edited, formatted, reformatted, spindled, mutilated, and redone, so keep your eye on it and work with your editor (if you have one) to keep it as accurate as you can as the manual develops.

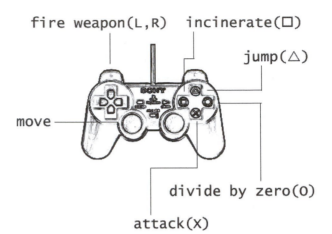

Figure 5.1. Sample schematic for the controller.

Controller

The first picture inside the manual that the player should see is a picture of the controller for the particular platform this game is for. Remember that you may be writing a different manual for as many as eight different platforms (Xbox 360, PS3, Wii, PS2, PC, PSP, GBA, DS) or more, so be extra careful that you have the right information for the right version of the game.

You may or may not be responsible for the final art of this graphic. Normally, bigger developers and publishers have graphic artists who are responsible for these duties. However, you will probably have to submit an initial schematic for the graphic artist to work off of (see Figure 5.1).

When identifying what each controller button does, make sure the graphic includes the button name along with its function (e.g., "attack (X)").

Guiding the Player Through Start-Up

The next section tends to be a quick run-through of starting up a game. Identify what the player sees on the initial menu screen and describe the fastest path to get the player in the game.

The Heads-Up Display

The heads-up display (HUD) is all the stuff the player sees that gives him vital game information like how wounded the character is, what unit the player has selected, what direction the next objective is, the minimap, etc. Once again, using screenshots of the actual game, point out what each individual element of the HUD refers to. Then include text descriptions underneath.

Menus and Options

After you've covered the HUD, start revealing the different menus and options the player will come across playing the game, such as the save menu, the load menu, and the options menu. Screenshots of these screens are optional, depending on space. Ideally, the player should be able to page to the information he needs quickly and read a short paragraph describing the function of each option.

Important Game Mechanics

In your game, there might be mechanics that are so obtuse that they need explanation in the manual. For instance, perhaps there is a mechanic where the player collects certain widgets that can be combined with one another to form some sort of other, more helpful widget. For example, armor parts to make armor, reagents to cast spells, or power boosts that can be combined to make more powerful or even different boosts.

When such a mechanic rears its ugly head and it's pretty apparent that the game itself doesn't teach the player how to use it, then you might consider putting an explanation and some examples of how this mechanic works in the manual. Make sure that graphical representations of the widgets appear here, so the reader can easily scan through the list to find the strange widget he's just collected.

Finally, just to state the obvious, if the widgets come in different power levels, like Power Boost (Level 1), Power Boost (Level 14), etc., just create a Power Boost category, and not a category for every level of the power boost, unless those powers actually have drastically different effects, such as one makes the player character pink and the other one allows him to smite like unto a god. (If you find that this is true, you may want to go back to the Game Designer and tell him this is confusing... the names may be placeholders, or someone may have forgotten to name things in their rush to, you know, get the game to actually work.)

Console- or PC-specific Guides

Sometimes, you'll want to put in console-specific information, like how to turn on the PS3, or how to install the game on a PC. If you have room for this information, it should precede most in-game information but be after the controller picture.

Got Free Space?

Sometimes, something miraculous happens and you find that you have a little bit of extra space to include something not so necessary. Here are some suggestions as to what you might put in there.

Hints and tips. It used to be that people could find helpful information on how to play the game in the manual. Lists of available combos are nice, as is a short tutorial on how to beat beginning monsters, where to look for collectibles and trinkets, or even a list of select cheat codes.

Fluff. If you have the extra space, you might want to put in extra fiction. Maybe a longer introduction, a description of the setting the player finds himself in, a short history of the cultures in the game and their relationship, character descriptions of NPCs, or lists of available weapon and armor types.

Awards. You may be directed to use the extra space to list different awards, good press quotes, and review scores the game has been gathering. For instance, if you are rewriting the manual for the Platinum version of the game, the game team might want to mention that the game was awarded the "Best Game of the Year" award from *Official Xbox Magazine*.

Advertisements. This probably won't be up to you. The marketing guys may slip an advertisement into this manual for upcoming games or already-released games made by the same developer or sold by the same publisher.

Credits

Who gets credit for what is a highly sensitive subject for most game studios. Normally, as the manual writer, you won't have to actually generate this list. However, if you do find yourself in the position of having to collect the credits, I've included some tips about this process in Section 5.5.

Legal Stuff

The end-user license agreement usually takes up a couple pages of the manual in a desperate attempt to absolve the game company of responsibility in case the game causes someone harm or discomfort, as well as scare the living heck out of wannabe pirates who might want to copy the game for their own profit (yar, matey!). You won't have to write this part: the legal team for the publisher will probably give you the text to include, if you touch the thing at all. Usually, it just magically appears in the manual, like little lawyer elves snuck in at the printers at night and filled up two pages with undecipherable legalese.

5.3   The Long Manual—Adding Content to the Basics

There are some types of games that demand a longer manual. Flight simulators, real-time strategy games, and massively multiplayer role-playing games come to mind. These games are so full of hidden commands, hard-to-understand mechanics, and distinct units and items that their manuals swell to near biblical proportions. A long manual takes a good chunk of time to write, so make sure you start early. You'll also need to find out just how much information the team wants to include about each separate item, unit, or spell.

Long manuals need to have the same information as short manuals: descriptions of the interface, how to control units or characters, what the game is about, and so on. Further, just because the manual is longer doesn't mean that the reader has any more patience. Keep your writing concise and easy to find.

Following are some of the things you'll want to include in your long manual.

Tutorials

Long manuals can sometimes do what manuals were originally intended to do: be a long tutorial on how to operate the software. This is especially true for manuals for games that are intended for serious simulations and other products of a "serious" nature. In these products, less emphasis is given to teaching the player as he plays the game, and thus it is up to you, the manual writer, to provide that education.

When creating a tutorial-style manual like this, you'll rarely want to keep any information hidden. The player is not expecting challenge in how to run the game, where he may need to learn new controls or functions as his avatar increases in powers or abilities. The controlling of the game is a known quantity; it's the difficulty in controlling that is the hard part.

There are entire books dedicated to writing technical manuals, so I won't delve into this too deeply. Once again, readers will want to skim through the tutorial to get to the parts that concern them, so make sure everything is well structured and labeled so they can flip to it quickly. As much as we'd like for players to sit down and read the manual before touching the software, it is much more likely that they'll want to learn while they are in the midst of playing, with one hand on the controller and one hand trying to find the appropriate page in the manual.

Try to include a quick-start section, so users can get in the game as fast as possible and get a sense of what the software is all about. This quick-start section should ignore extraneous menu information and unnecessary details and just concentrate on the vital information the player needs to get in and survive the first ten minutes of the game. For many users, this will be all they'll need, and they'll attempt to learn the rest of the game through trial and error.

After the quick start, start over and do the tutorial right. Start with basic descriptions of all the controls and menus, using lots of graphics to show what the different screens look like. If appropriate, insert short examples of play in narrative to reinforce the dry information of the lists and pictures. I would suggest that you keep things light and funny, but that isn't always appropriate given the nature of some games. Use your best judgement to relate the information to the reader in a way they'll find both appropriate and entertaining.

Story

Long manuals have a lot more room for story. You might find that you want to include narrative about what has brought the setting to this dire state. Describe the main antagonist (or at least the main apparent antagonist if there is a puppet master working behind the scenes) and what they are doing to make them the bad guys. Talk about the benevolent allies of the player: the wise council leader, the crusty general, the understanding significant other, etc. The story is here to give those players who crave backstory something to read while their game is installing. Well, and to give clues about where the game might take them. Remember that you're not writing a novel: keep the story to a couple of pages so those who may feel fear at the sight of words don't see too many and bolt for the nearest FPS.

Maps

It is likely that there will be maps included in your long manual. These will help the player navigate around important beginning areas in the game, like the character's home city or the first dungeon that he might encounter in the game. Make sure these maps are well notated, with important landmarks marked and named. You may also want to include some backstory on the location, but since the player will be able to see the place in the game, you can probably keep descriptions to a minimum.

Color

Color is nonessential stuff that nevertheless helps immerse the player in the game-world. Descriptions of important NPCs in the game, short histories detailing events that affect the story of the game in some way, essays and articles supposedly written by some of the NPCs that exist in the game world, all might be placed in the manual. You might also want to write the manual itself as if it were being written by an in-game character or some other colorful format.

Charts, Tables, and Lists

Charts, tables, and lists are core to the long manual. They detail all the "stuff" the player can use or collect in the game and describe what their function is. They can also be long lists of foes and their vital statistics. For flight-simulator manuals, they might include the essential mechanical characteristics of each available airplane so the player can know exactly how much fuel they can carry and what their flying range is.

Charts and tables are generally available to the writer so he can include them in the manual. Normally, the Lead Game Designer has created these charts in the game design doc (or on little sticky notes on his monitor screen), and you just have to go grab them. However, you'll probably have to reformat them so that they make sense to normal people. This is pretty straightforward: name of object in the first field followed by short descriptive text. If the item or unit has a series of statistics associated with it, discuss with the Game Designer or Producer what information should be available to the player (for instance, they might not want to tell the player how many hit points or what kind of armor a creature has, but they do want to tell the player what level of power it is).

Index

For long manuals, an index is a necessity. I know *you* know what an index is, but, just for that one person who bought this book who doesn't, an index is a list of important subjects and words (generally nouns) that comprise an alphabetical list at the end of the manual. This list also shows the page numbers where these words and subjects can be found.

Generating an index is a study in drudgery. Extremely organized people will, as they write the manual, keep a list of these words on a notepad, also scratching down the page number. Once the manual is done, they import the list into something like excel and sort the list in alphabetical order. They then collapse the list, putting all the page numbers of duplicate words next to one instance of the word. Then, after the manual is done, they go back and check each word to make sure the page number is correct. Then, they might reorder the index so that some words are headers for other words.

Unfortunately, we're not all that organized. Luckily, modern word processors have the functionality to generate an index from your manual. However, the process requires you to mark the words you deem important enough to be included in your index, so check the help menu of your word processor of choice and check out what hoops they'd like you to jump through to make the index happen.

5.4   In-Game Help and Text

Recently, game developers have realized two things.

1. No one is going to read the manual.

2. No one likes a game they don't understand.

This puts game developers in a bit of a bind. How do you teach the game to players who won't read the text that teaches them how to play the game? Luckily, the simple answer is in-game pop-ups that appear to help guide the player as he plays the game.

As the manual writer, it may fall upon your shoulders to help write the text that goes in these pop-ups.

Text pop-ups have a different flavor from manual prose. First, they have to be much shorter, especially for console games. In console games, text is much larger because of the lower resolution of the screen as compared to your computer monitor. For a quick demonstration, resize the resolution on your monitor to 640×480 to see how much desktop space you've suddenly lost. Normal TV is about 640×480, so the text you use has to be fairly big, or it doesn't come out at all. Some fonts also have problems with normal TVs, so you might be limited to some fairly boring choices. Depending on the artist that designed the fonts for your game, you may also not get a choice of having underlines, italics, bold letters, or even lowercase letters.

You may be wondering, "What about HDTV? It has better resolution than regular TV!"

Good question. HDTV does have better resolution. However, when game developers make a console game, they have to make it so it works on all TVs. It's part of the TRCs, or requirements that game developers have to achieve in order for a console maker like Sony or Microsoft or Nintendo to allow the developer to sell the game for their consoles. So, even if the game you are writing for is a spiffy hi-res next-gen monster AAA title, it still needs to play on Ma and Pa's RCA that they got back in '78.

This goes for PC games to some extent, as well. The artist has to make the fonts readable at the lowest resolution the developers want to support. This can make things a little cramped for your text, as well.

So, because of these size limitations, it is in your best interest to keep your in-game help text as short as possible. Maybe 15 words or less. Usually, the limitation is in characters and not words, so make sure you understand these limitations before writing all of this.

What to Write

Writing in-game help text requires an intimate knowledge of the game itself, not just how everything works but the order in which the player learns new things, where he is when he needs to learn them, and who is giving him these instructions.

If you haven't actually been designing and implementing the game, this can be a daunting task. So, the best thing to do is work right alongside the designers who have been doing the work and get them to show you exactly what they want and where they want it. Either they or a programmer will have to place the appropriate trigger to launch the text anyway, so working closely with them is paramount.

Next, find out if the developers want the in-game text to have character or not. Basically, find out if there is some sort of fictional mentor that is intruding on the character's play to give him hints on how to use his new battle armor or magic wand or obstacle course.

If the help text is suddenly turning into a full-blown tutorial, your job just got quite a bit bigger, as you have gone from dry teaching to actually writing narrative. Your script will probably have to be recorded by a voice actor playing the mentor, and you'll be taking over some of the duties of the writer for the game.

The good thing about this is that your word limit has suddenly gotten quite a bit larger. The bad thing is that your narrative will receive a lot more scrutiny, and you'll find yourself in more meetings with writers and designers all wanting to wordsmith how Igglzack the Old tells young Thorax the Mighty how to push the A and B button simultaneously to get the backswing combo to launch.

In-Game Tutorials

In-game tutorials are quite a bit different from manuals or in-game text. They generally take the form of a lesson being taught by a teacher. The teacher can take any form, from a mentor-type character to a generic block of words on the screen that pauses the game when it appears to give the player the next nugget of wisdom that will help him on his way to mastering the game.

Mentors are generally preferred, as designers feel that they are more immersive than the disembodied floaty text box of dullness. Here are some tips for writing this kind of tutorial.

Stick to the character. Make sure the character you write is also the same character that the player may encounter again in nontutorial missions. Make sure the "voice" is the same. It confuses the player when Sergeant Molson starts out being a kindly father figure in the tutorial and then becomes a hardened and abusive combat veteran thereafter.

Teach from basic to more advanced to advanced. It does no good to teach players how to create multinode waypoint paths for large groups of units when they don't know how to select a unit or move it in the first place. Work with the designers to create a waterfall list of skills, basically what is the most basic thing the player needs to know, followed by the next most basic, and so on.

Keep it understandable. Game worlds frequently come bundled with a lot of made-up words. Unit names, strategy names, functions that are only known to hard-core fans who have played these games before (know what a shmup is? How about a 4X game? A waypoint? Rushing in a real-time strategy game?) Character names, god names, place names, etc. are all likely to be unfamiliar to the new player. Keep the language simple and based in real English. If you need to introduce a concept or game item with a name that doesn't automatically tell the player about its nature, you'll need to define it somehow before going on. This is hard to do when you are trying to keep things short, which leads to the next point...

Know when to let the player go and let him learn by trial and error. Players don't want to be stuck in your crummy tutorial. They want to get to the action now! Make sure you get them there as quickly as possible. Remember that manual you've been writing and that in-game help you've been agonizing over? They can go to that if they want to know the specs on an A-10 Warthog. All your tutorial needs to teach them is how to choose a plane and get in the air. You can also spread your tutorial throughout the game, popping up only when a new gameplay mechanic is introduced or the character gains a new ability. See Chapter 12 for a more detailed look at this task.

In-Game Help

Let's back off a bit and say you're only doing help text and not the full-blown tutorial. Help text is short. Really short. And there's a lot of it, depending on the game. You may need a bit of text for each item and character in the game, as well as each distinct bit of the user interface. Some text may be as short as "Hit Points," while some may be as long as "Selection Interface: Use this to select individual units from your squadron."

As I've said, this job takes a lot of communication with the game development team. You'll need to find out every instance where a piece of in-game text is needed. Likely, you'll need to create a list in XML or Microsoft Excel that the programmers can call to pull the correct information to the right spot in the game. In-game text is also the easiest thing for testers to find errors with, so you'll end up having to learn the bug-tracking software the project is using and monitor that for the inevitable misspelling bugs (Bug 3456: Misspelled word: "L'ch'mok Du Aruk's Flaming Sword of Phlegm" should be "L'c'hmok Du Aruk's Flaming Sword of Phlegm") and wrongly attached bugs (Bug 3457: Lady's Purse is labeled "Dungeon of Horror" in pop-up text).

5.5   A Note about Credits

As mentioned earlier, credits are a big part of why manuals are the favorite part of the box for game developers. Most developers like recognition and are thrilled to have their name printed a million times in a million manuals showing off that they made this incredibly wonderful game. What they don't like is to be mislabeled or left out. There is nothing more sour and bitter than someone who has spent a good portion of their lives creating a piece of software and not seeing their name amongst the other people they worked with.

Unfortunately, the crediting issue is fraught with problems in the game industry. The credits section is the place where petty egos go to hurt the people who they feel slighted them during the development of the game. It's a place of low fidelity, of last-minute sign-your-name-here-if-you-worked-on-the-game list creation. In other words, it's a mess.

Further, the title for each role in the game differs from developer to developer. A "Lead Designer" one place may be a "Creative Director" another place and just "Game Designer" at still another place.

Lucky for you, the International Game Developer's Association has created a whitepaper to help you out with their attempt at standardizing the crediting process. If you are the person responsible for doing credits, you can access all the IGDA Crediting Committee has to offer by going to the IGDA wiki at http://www.igda.org/wiki/index.php/IGDA_Credits_and_Awards_Committee.

5.6   Conclusion

Hopefully, I've given you enough of a start that you feel better about writing a manual. If there are only two things you must remember out of this chapter, they are the following.

1. Keep it short.

2. Communicate a lot with the game development team.

Keeping to these two principles will go a long way to making a good, informative manual.

5.7   Exercises

1. Write a short manual on how to drive a car. Include pictures or drawings of the steering wheel, gauges, and foot pedals. Keep the manual fewer than three

pages using nothing smaller than a 10-point Arial font. What things must you include to make sure the driver knows everything about the controls. What things do you have to leave out in order to keep within the space limit?

(a) *Extra Credit:* Show your manual to someone who can't drive, preferably a 12-year-old boy. Test him to see how much he remembers and how much he ignores. The test should *not* include having him drive a real car.

2. Take the manual from Exercise 1 and write it as if you were an old wizard explaining the workings of the car to a young warrior in a fantasy setting. You may expand the manual up to six pages.

3. Find the manual for your favorite game and write a two-page critique of what it does right and what it does wrong in teaching the player how to play the game. Be sure to suggest ways that the manual could be improved.

6

Narrative Design

Jay Posey

6.1 What is Narrative Design?

The most accurate definition of "narrative design" is elegantly simple: narrative design is what Narrative Designers do. Unfortunately, for any practical purpose, this definition is also the most useless. Because the games industry has little standardization for titles, and the role of Narrative Designer is still an emerging one, precisely classifying what constitutes *narrative design* is a tricky business. With that in mind, this chapter will broadly outline core elements of narrative design and briefly touch on some specific tasks that may fall logically onto a Narrative Designer's to-do list.

For the purposes of this chapter, we will define narrative as "the story our game tells." (For simplicity, "narrative" and "story" will be used interchangeably, though in some circles of game writing this will surely cause mild spasms of philosophical outrage.) Narrative, then, consists of the setting, plot, characters, and themes within the game, specifically with the *player-character* as protagonist. By this definition, the narrative of *God of War* tells of Kratos and his journey to assume the throne of Ares; *Splinter Cell: Double Agent* follows Sam Fisher's dangerous infiltration of a home-grown terrorist organization. Though narrative can be defined much more broadly to include any number of elements (for example, a quest or series of quests in an MMORPG), this simple definition makes discussing practical details somewhat easier.

So then, if narrative is "the story our game tells," narrative design is the creation of that story and the design of the mechanics through which it is told. That is, narrative design encompasses not only the story itself but also how the story is communicated to players and how other game features support and immerse the player within the game world.

In some ways, a Narrative Designer might be considered to games what a Writer-Director is to movies. In film, the most well-written screenplay does nothing for the box office unless it is translated through the director's vision into images on the big screen. Though a Narrative Designer generally isn't going to have the level of project control of a movie director, narrative-driven games nevertheless similarly require someone to craft a narrative and then shepherd it through the development process, continually evaluating how features impact either the story itself or the game's ability to convey the story to the player.

Of course, the relative importance of a game's story directly affects the amount of input a Narrative Designer may have on any given project. Though *Doom* had a story (or at least a context), it did just fine without a Narrative Designer. In more narrative-centric games, a Narrative Designer may have a very high degree of decision-making ability, while in other cases, one may be little more than a sort of narrative conscience, constantly reminding people of story considerations (which may then be largely ignored).

6.2   So What Is a Narrative Designer Then, Exactly?

A Narrative Designer is what's left over when you smash a writer and a designer together. Rather than being part writer, part designer, the Narrative Designer is wholly both, devoted to story and storytelling, and equally devoted to creating the desired game experience. Ultimately, as specialized designers, Narrative Designers approach their tasks as viewed through the lens of the narrative and seek to balance the demands of gameplay against those of the story.

The "normal" Designer generally doesn't need to be concerned with the narrative implications of any particular feature. The Narrative Designer, on the other hand, must consider features and how they can be implemented to promote or enhance the game narrative, or at the very least not detract from it.

Take, for example, a save-game feature. When outlining how such a feature is implemented, a Designer is primarily concerned with functionality: how does a player access it, when is saving available, does the game use checkpoints or a save-anywhere mechanic, and so on. The Narrative Designer, on the other hand, must also consider how such a feature is presented in-game from a narrative perspective: does the user interface make sense in the context of the gameworld, does the saving mechanic need a "story" explanation, would a save-anywhere system interfere with the pacing of the narrative, and so forth. Though at first look a save-game feature may not seem like it needs narrative consideration, such details can make or break a player's buy-in to the game's narrative.

In the MMORPG *Star Wars Galaxies*, for example, when the developers announced that characters killed in battle could be brought back to life at a nearby cloning facility, many players were angered. Those upset by the announcement wanted to play the characters they'd created, not *clones* of those characters. In *Bioshock*, on the other hand, when the player-character died, he was "revitalized" in a nearby Vita-chamber. The underlying mechanics are essentially the same; the player-character dies, it reappears at a particular safe location. However, because of the narrative *expla-*

nation of those devices, players reacted quite differently to them. Balancing narrative explanation with player expectation is one aspect of Narrative Design.

The "normal" Writer, on the other hand, generally doesn't need to be concerned about the mechanics of narrative delivery. When writing dialog for the characters involved, Writers by and large leave it to someone else to see that those lines are properly delivered at the appropriate time. The Narrative Designer, however, must consider the method by which written words become in-game assets. Elaborate cinematics can convey a wealth of story information, but not in a game without cutscenes. Internal dialogue might be a fine method for adding depth to a protagonist, as long as he has a voice. The importance of understanding how a game will deliver its narrative content cannot be overstated. This is another aspect of Narrative Design.

6.3 But What Does a Narrative Designer DO? (And Can I Be One?)

The daily activities of a Narrative Designer can vary significantly, ranging anywhere from high-level meetings discussing overall vision down to sitting alone banging out hundreds of generic dialog barks, and everything in between. One day you may be helping design levels or missions, the next meeting with concept artists to discuss visual representations of story themes, and the next working on a document outlining the functionality of a narrative delivery feature. The work is varied and demands both artistic and logical faculties.

There are two main forces at work within the Narrative Designer. One is an unshakeable passion for story coupled with a thorough understanding of story mechanics. The other is an intimate knowledge of game design and the inherent interconnectivity of game systems. Simply put, games are big and complex, and when you change one thing over in feature A, it most likely will have some unintended effect over in feature B. Adding a layer of intricate narrative on top of an already complex system is asking for trouble unless someone is specifically paying attention to that narrative layer. Fortunately, such a person exists, and is embodied by the Narrative Designer. And yes, you can be one.

Though it may seem daunting at first, especially given the wide disparity of official responsibilities Narrative Designers may have, there's a simple mantra that can anchor the Narrative Designer adrift in the midst of their nebulous job descriptions: communicate, innovate, advocate. Just remember, CIA is your friend. Employing this mantra cannot only provide you with a plan of attack as a Narrative Designer, it can also serve as a sort of metric to gauge your own performance as one. But before you rush off to start your life as a Narrative Designer, let's look at the CIA mantra.

- Communicate! Communication is critical to success as a Narrative Designer. Narrative Designers must be bold enough to make their ideas known and secure enough to accept feedback of all sorts. Game narratives improve by iteration, and taking the best ideas from collaborative environments will not only create better stories but will also help teammates stay excited about getting your story told. No matter how brilliant your story is, it's no use to anyone if it's all locked away inside your brain. You need your teammates on board with the narrative if you hope to get it told well, and it's much easier to get that support when everyone understands the direction you're headed. By the same token, if you don't know what your artists or engineers or designers are working on or planning for, you could be in for a nasty surprise when your mind-blowing cinematic introductory boat chase has to make do without water physics. Or boats.

- **Innovate!** Innovation needs to occur on both levels for the Narrative Designer. From the design side, games are still in the process of figuring out how to tell a good story without becoming a movie or something other than a game. A Narrative Designer should actively seek new ways to deliver narrative content to players and challenge old ways of thinking. From the writing side, resisting the temptation to tell stories the way they've been done so many times before will help further elevate game writing as a whole. As the gaming audience is increasingly exposed to new and interesting narratives, developers will learn much more quickly what works and what doesn't, and how story can contribute to the overall success of a project.

- **Advocate!** If the Narrative Designer doesn't champion the story throughout the development process, no one else will. In the majority of the game development world, writers are generally brought on towards the tail end of a project, when many of the most important decisions have already been made and are unalterable. At those points, story must make do with whatever hand it has been dealt. The strength of the Narrative Designer lies in the ability to craft a narrative vision for the project and then see it through to the end.

Keeping the CIA mantra in mind, and putting it into practice continually, will maximize team buy-in and minimize disastrous surprises throughout the development process. In the real-world trenches of game development, however, there *will* be surprises that threaten to derail your beautifully crafted narrative. For those times, there is another three-word mantra that works just as well (as long as the US Marine Corps doesn't mind): improvise, adapt, overcome.

Mental (and emotional) flexibility and agility are highly desirable traits for the Narrative Designer to possess. Throughout the development process, at least one good crisis always seems to emerge. When developing the initial narrative pitch, or high-level story concept, it is wise to keep the inevitable crisis in mind. No one knows for sure what it will be, or when it will come, but every experienced developer expects it. As a Narrative Designer, developing a core vision or specific theme can serve as an anchor for your story when trouble hits. Rather than building your narrative on an elaborate and delicate web of game scenarios, first establish a central theme that defines your story. With that accomplished, as long as you hold fast to the heart of the narrative you are striving to tell, details can change without damaging the integrity of your overall narrative.

If you're a Writer working under the supervision of a Narrative Designer, you may face additional difficulties if expectations aren't in sync. Or if you're a Narrative Designer overseeing Writers, there is a strong potential for creative tension. If you find yourself in such a situation, regardless of whether you are the Narrative Designer or the Writer, try to keep the other perspective in mind when communicating. Most likely, the Narrative Designer has poured countless hours of life into the narrative and may find it difficult to let too much creative control get away. On the other hand, the Writer is no less talented and should be given freedom to bring a personal voice or touch to the work. Again, communication is key. Clearly delineating which aspects of the narrative are set in stone and which are open for tinkering can help avoid confrontation down the road.

Writers seeking to become Narrative Designers should immerse themselves in game design as thoroughly as possible. Additionally, as with any good designer, some familiarity with all aspects of game development should be cultivated. Knowing even basic terminology used by engineers, for example, can go a long way towards avoiding miscommunications with other team members. Also, taking every available opportunity to learn from other team members, offering suggestions boldly, and accepting feedback humbly will all provide valuable experience and education.

The emerging role of Narrative Designer is a new and exciting one. With the increasing capabilities of technology and the growing sophistication of the gaming audience, it is reasonable to expect an increased emphasis on narrative in games. The in-roads made by the many writers who have gone before are beginning to pay dividends for a new generation, as development studios begin to see the value a well-crafted and well-delivered story can add to games. This is an exciting time for the games industry and for anyone interested in exploring new methods of storytelling, and the future for game writers as a whole continues to brighten with each passing development cycle. If video games and story are your passion, now is the time to hone your craft and contribute to the rise of the Narrative Designer!

6.4   Exercises

1. In two sentences or less, summarize a high-level narrative concept for a first-person shooter, capturing the essence of the story arc. For example, "An ex-assassin reluctantly returns to his profession, targeting his former employers, in an effort to atone for his past." Except something much better than that.

2. Using a genre of your choosing, propose three different methods of delivering a game objective to the player without breaking narrative continuity. For example, in a real-time strategy game, a player may need to clear a particular area of an enemy presence. How would you convey this information to the player while remaining true to the tone and context of the game as a whole?

3. Using a genre of your choosing, create a narrative for a game with only three levels or missions where the story is progressed through the actions of the player-character. For example, in a platformer, your player-character may need to collect certain floating items in level one to gain access to a character in level two, who will then transport the character to level three for the climactic ending. Communicate the story through player-character action, without dialog or cutscenes.

4. Break out your current favorite game and evaluate its user interface (UI) in light of the game narrative. Does the artistic presentation of the main menu match the tone of the story? Do the names of menu selections fit, or do they seem at odds with the setting of the game? When cycling through menus, do you notice any connection between navigation and narrative? Are menu selections easy to understand, or are they obscure due to an attempt to maintain narrative tone (e.g., is the difficulty setting "easy" or "neophyte" or ".22 caliber"?) What does the UI do well, and what could be improved?

5. *Bonus:* Create an outline for your own game narrative no longer than a page that covers the beginning, ending, and the major actions the player-character undertakes through the course of the game. When complete, *verbally* pitch your story to a friend in a way that communicates the excitement inherent in the narrative. Repeat as necessary.

7

Game Writing at a Distance (aka Game Writing under Contract)

Chris Klug

Writing for games as a contractor off-site is, historically, the most common form of game writing. Very few companies think of hiring a writer as a staff member. More and more companies do so every day, but in the past, this has been the exception rather than the rule. This is true for many positions in the industry. After all, the game business has grown over the years from a single talented programmer working on every facet of the game into teams that routinely top 100 members, and many positions that initially were only considered to be part-time or temporary have made the transition to full-time (sound design is a recent example, but even someone classified only as a "designer" was once considered a luxury). With story becoming more and more important in games, more and more writers are moving on staff. One day, contract writers may be more the exception than the rule.

The guidelines in this chapter are presented from two perspectives: first, that of the Writer herself, and second, of the company hiring that writer. In my career, I have been in both positions. For many years, I worked as a freelance Writer/Designer. Then I made the transition onto staff, where I managed both freelance and staff Writers. I've seen this situation work and yield great results, and I've seen it go off the rails and become problematic for both sides. These ideas help to minimize the chance for failure and maximize the chance for success. As always, your mileage may vary.

7.1 Pros of Working Remotely under Contract

This type of arrangement mirrors the traditional writer's life. Get up in the morning, sit around in your pj's, drink coffee, and sit at the computer and type. Walk to retrieve the mail, go to lunch, come back, and write some more. You know, pretty much the kind of thing people like about making your living as a writer. For those so inclined, these lifestyle choices are their own advantage. Often the writer might need to talk to someone at the game developer on instant message or the phone, but the work can be solitary and productive. Following are some of the not-so-obvious advantages.

You Can Work on Multiple Projects at a Time

Since you are a contractor, your time is truly your own. The developer is not buying your time; they are buying your work product. Assuming you can handle the workload, you are able to work on multiple projects at the same time for multiple developers. In fact, I don't know of any contract writer who doesn't take advantage of this perk in some fashion. Most (if not all) the work you do is owned by the developer you work for, so you need to keep at least the semblance of a "clean room" approach to the work (meaning that you must be disciplined enough to not let the work you are doing on one project creep into the work you are doing for another). But with the odds being that the individual projects are different enough that the mental "gear shifting" won't be too difficult, this is fairly easily accomplished.

Note: I have seen contracts stipulating that the writer can only work on the contracted project and none other, or limiting the ability to accept a job in the same genre (preventing the writer from working on two MMOs at the same time, for example), but usually the developer understands this limits the writer's ability to make a living and compensates the writer for the exclusivity. For that reason, this is pretty rare in my experience. From the developer's point of view, the easiest way to do this, if you are worried about the writer becoming spread too thin, is to simply give the writer so much work and adequately compensate them that they don't have the time to do anything else.

Experience Different Development Methodologies

The game industry is very young, even compared to other modern industries such as the film industry. Our methodologies are changing and evolving at a rapid pace, and different developers will follow a very individual path to the finish line of a shippable product. If you are on staff, with games often taking two or more years to ship, it becomes easy to see the only viable way to the finish line as the one you're using.

As a contractor, in the same two-year period that your on-staff colleague has used only one development methodology, you might have worked on four or five titles and seen (for both ill and good) a corresponding number of methodologies, even as they pertain to your own job. This allows you to offer perspective and contribute in other ways besides the words you write. Even if a particular developer isn't interested, you have perspective on future job opportunities that allows you to be better at picking situations you want to be a part of and those you don't.

Multiply Your Network of Contacts

As contractors know, you spend 60% of your time actually working and 40% of your time marketing your skills. Working for multiple employers, assuming that they all love you and your work, increases your network of referrals and contacts that make landing your next job all the easier. But there is actually a multiplicative effect because of the game industry's gypsy nature. Doing good work for one company always spreads your positive reputation over multiple companies because by the time a year or two have passed, some members of that original developer are now working at other companies, and you can leverage those contacts into companies you've never worked for.

Work on Different Genres

This advantage falls into the category of "stretching your muscles." The kind of writing you might do for an RPG is fundamentally different from a first-person shooter. Developers certainly look for writers with experience in the genre they are building, but more importantly, they look for quality and dependability. You'll be able to experience different story problems and different styles, and it will be rare indeed that you find yourself working on the same genre of game two projects in a row.

Freedom to Work on Your Own Projects

You're a freelance writer, after all, and to some degree you are controlling your schedule. You want to write a novel? Go for it. You want to write a screenplay? Nothing stopping you. In fact, working on your own projects will make you a better writer. While it is true that this kind of outside work is often allowed when you are on staff (but staffers should carefully read their employment contract's non-compete clauses), working on staff is like a real job, and your own projects fall into the category of "when you get the energy and time."

Freedom to Work in Other Industries

This is a corollary to the previous advantage. Modern media is becoming a big soup (games become TV shows, which become films, which have derivative novels published about them), and as the writer, you may be the only member of the extended development team who has any experience in other media. The more you keep your chops in other forms of writing polished, the more you can become the bridge to those other media forms. In fact, if you keep active in other industries, you may become the instigator of business opportunities that raise your profile and could be very lucrative.

Sometimes a Little Distance Gives You Perspective

Most contract writers work off-site. Not always, but most of the time. Development environments can be emotional and political, and not always in good ways.

Sometimes being off-site allows you to maintain perspective about issues that, if encountered while on-site, can become webs of political intrigue that rarely do the writing any good.

You Can Be More Productive

Working on staff can be chaotic. Meetings multiply in a geometric pattern that can leave almost no time for actual writing. People not experienced in the pitfalls of our process can be ignorant of the flow of ideas and may think nothing of constantly interrupting you with what, to them, are innocent questions but, to you, cause you to lose track of the gossamer tendrils of that new plot thread. At home, you have to battle the demon Procrastination, but at least you can get into a mentally productive space without much trouble. For myself, for instance, rarely do great ideas come until I've gotten "warmed up," which for me means continuous writing for an hour or more. That kind of situation in an office can be rare indeed.

Ideas Can Be Fresher

In a similar fashion to the office politics alluded to above, ideas in a development office can become self-limiting. "Group think" can take over, and true "outside the box" thinking can be hard to come by. Development groups fight this by sometimes having off-site meetings, knowing that the change of environment can actually open up avenues for ideas that just won't come in the office environment. Working out of your space, you have access to thought patterns that don't exist in the office. Use that to your advantage.

You Can Be Near Your Own Workspace and Materials

We all have environmental "comfort food": music we like to listen to, artwork that inspires us, a chair we like to write in, keyboards that feel more like "us" than others. In an office, much of this can be out of your control, even in the most supportive environments. Many developers populate their office with cubes, and I don't know many writers who like cubes. For instance, I like to spread out my materials so that I have everything I could possibly want at my fingertips. To others this looks like chaos; to me it is a comfortable workspace.

Time Spent On-Site Can Be More Productive and Precious

Because you are not there every day, when you do visit (and I encourage visiting as much as you can; see Section 7.3), people will make time for you. Managers will inform their people that you're going to be in all next week, and they are willing to adjust their calendars so they make the time you need. This can be very productive and precious. Take advantage of this and appreciate it.

7.2 Cons of Working Remotely under Contract

You Can Become Out of Touch

Game development is a very slippery slope. By that I mean we have a hard time predicting such things as delivery dates, schedules, and features. We have all the difficulties of software development multiplied by the needs of a creative process. We have no equivalent to the film process of write a script, approve it, send it out for preproduction, and shoot it. The last two steps of that process are fairly predictable in terms of both how long the step will take and how close to estimated time and cost the step will take. The most unpredictable part of making a film is the creation of the script, and in that step, original estimates of six months can become years without any trouble at all. In part, that is because it is the part that involves the most pure creation, moving from a blank page to a dynamic story.

We multiply that by our process where we build the game engine from scratch almost every time. Thus, we take two uncertain variables and multiply them and then try to build a schedule. Because of this, schedules change, and products can change their fundamental core gameplay, genre, and even platform all on their way to production.

Because words are easy to alter, story can undergo countless changes even beyond the normal ones associated with our own creative process. For example: It will take longer than anticipated to animate the number of characters in your story; can you cut 25% without rewriting the story from scratch? Can you change locations here because we can't afford to put the scene in the nebula? We know we thought you'd have ten avatar types to play with, but we're only going to get six because the art won't fit on the cartridge; what can we do?

Few of these changes are made capriciously; they just happen as a part of the process. Each requires production, design, and scheduling to react quickly and decisively and choose a new direction. These meetings and discussions happen immediately after the decision to make the alteration. They often cannot be planned for or anticipated.

If you want to be part of that process in order to make your own concerns related to the change known, you almost always have to be on-site. But you're a contractor. You're not there, and you didn't know this was going to happen. And the people making the decision may not understand how it all impacts you, and you are left to pick up the pieces.

Because you are not there, it happens.

Projects Can Drift

Besides the dramatic changes noted above, the mindset of a project could drift. This change can be subtle, and it can be hard to identify exactly what has changed and when. You'll be on-site one month, everything will seem fine, then you go home for three weeks, return, and the sequence everybody liked now isn't a favorite any longer.

While you've been gone, dozens of short conversations can occur, on-site, off-site, in the hallways, etc., and these conversations become decisions without anyone formally deciding anything.

This one is easier to fix than the one noted above. You can minimize the gap that comes from drift by being on-site as much as possible as often as possible. The dramatic shift noted above is impossible to prevent.

Collaboration Can Be Less than Ideal

Story ideas come at all times. The World Builder is working hard on a map, building the latest point-of-interest (POI) that the two of you have carefully crafted, and she has an inspiration about how it can change for the better. If you were on staff, she'd just walk down to your desk and chat it out with you. But you're not there, you're not on IM, unavailable by phone (maybe you're at a meeting at another publisher), and so the World Builder makes a decision on her own and plows onward. By the time you see her next, she's possibly even forgotten that moment, and you only discover the changes she's made months later when you play the level. Hopefully her changes don't impact your story, but they might.

You go to her and ask her about the change, and she remembers the day she got the inspiration and simply says, "You weren't available, so I made a decision and moved on." It's a collaborative process. These kind of tactical decisions are made hundreds of times every day, and if you get upset by this kind of thing, you'll be labeled as "uncooperative" or worse.

Trust Becomes an Issue

As a contractor, you are an outsider. No matter what you do or say or believe, no matter how hard you try, you will always be viewed as someone who isn't as invested as the staff on-site is and may be viewed as someone who has less to lose, who might move on at any second, who views the project as "just a job."

Obviously, any of those emotions can belong to a staff member just as easily as a contractor, but their physical presence acts as a buffer against those assumptions. For example, given that most new job opportunities for designer/writers ask the applicant to move to the city where the game is being developed, the fact that the employee has relocated indicates a level of commitment that you, the contract writer, aren't being asked to deliver. So, can you be trusted?

The trust issue isn't expressed in the manner of, "We're worried that you'll violate your NDA and blurt what we're doing to the press," but rather that your heart and soul isn't in your work and thus when crunch time comes, will you be there along with everyone else trying to make this the best game possible?

You'll always be viewed as a visitor to the team until the day comes when you become an employee. There are ways you can minimize this, but none of them totally fix it.

Unfamiliarity with the Tools Can Lead to Dissonance

Every part of the story must be realized in some fashion: cinematics must be animated and rendered; levels and missions must be built in a tool or tools; dialog must be acted and directed and then placed in game. Just like you must understand what is possible with a film camera when you write a screenplay, you must fully understand the capabilities of all the tools the development team has at their disposal when you write your game story.

However, this is especially difficult because almost every dev team has their own custom set of tools, and being off-site most of the time, you really won't have much of a chance to use them. So, you may not really understand what is possible with this team's set of tools.

The danger here is simple: story beats written by you that cannot be built, and the odds are that you may be miles and time zones away when that part of the game is finished. The fundamental nature of the beat might change, the story might not make any sense, and you may get the blame. In this case, the blame is deserved because it really is up to you to make sure the story element is buildable as written.

7.3 Steps You Can Take to Minimize Your Risk and the Developer's Risk

In other words, steps you can take to minimize the feeling that you are being a pain in the ass.

Get Local Build of the Game

My most successful remote jobs were the ones where, every morning, I logged onto the developer's server and downloaded the latest build. I could play the game on my remote machine, see yesterday's changes, and react. Not all developers will trust you this way, because they may see letting their code base out of house as a security risk (they wouldn't be wrong). But if you can swing this, many of the cons listed above melt away.

Learn the Tools

Spend time while you are on site learning the tools the developers will use. Sit with the staff and learn what strengths the tool has as well as the weaknesses. If possible, write the final draft of any materials *after* you've had these training sessions. This will serve two functions. First, the writing will be better. Second, you'll be viewed as someone who isn't afraid to get their hands dirty, which always gains you brownie points with the team.

Provide Your Own Software

When you determine your run rate (see below), be certain to allow for the purchase, out of your own bank account, of any software needed for your job. Let's say they only want scripts in Movie Magic, and you are a Final Draft junkie. Some contract writers will say, "Well, if Movie Magic is your standard, I'll be expecting you to buy me a copy." In some circles, this won't be an issue, and you'll find one at your doorstep. But that may be viewed as an unexpected expense on your part and another reason why they shouldn't have used a contractor in the first place. Always offer to pay for the software, and that way if they don't want to pay, you've moved what could have been a sticking point into something that classifies you as someone willing to meet the company on their own terms.

Be in the Same Area Code as Much as Possible

This seems like a weird thing to say, but it will be echoed in some other suggestions below, and it goes like this: the onus to communicate is really on you. There is no set of circumstances where it is the developer's fault that communication breaks down, because part of what they are paying you for is to communicate. So, if you are in the same area code, stop by to "check in" as much as you can, even when not scheduled. If you are not in the same area code, make it feel like you are from the developer's point of view. Call, IM, and, if you are in town for some other reason, be sure to stop by. When I first started working as a freelancer, my agent told me that the *primary* factor when a developer hires a contractor is often the sense of security that comes with the ability to pick up the phone and ask the contractor, "Can you swing by this afternoon for a meeting?" It's always better to be close than far.

Take Some of the Travel Burden on Yourself

For most contracts, if you are off-site and must travel to the developer, call for a certain fixed amount of travel. I suggest, however, that when you determine what your run rate is (see the suggestion below), you build in travel that you will pay for. This not only demonstrates organization and planning on your part, it shows a willingness to meet the developer halfway as well as an enthusiasm for the project.

The developer is trying to control costs, and almost always a scheduled trip will come to its end and both parties will wish they had more time. It's very powerful when you say, late in the afternoon of your last scheduled day on-site, "Why don't I just stay through tomorrow and I can finish my talk with the animator? I'll take care of the cost." You become an instant hero.

Be sure, of course, to budget for this.

Load Your Rate Correctly

Okay, so this probably isn't the place to discuss how to determine your daily, weekly, or monthly run rates, but be sure to remember the following things.

- You are paying for your own health care.

- You are paying your own Social Security and Medicare.

- You are paying for and amortizing your hardware and software over time.

- You are paying for your office space, Internet provider, and utilities.

- You need to set aside money to pay for the time when you are marketing yourself to get the next job.

In addition to these things that you should already know, here are some things that are perhaps not obvious.

- Build in enough extra to pay for travel outside of the contract's definitions.

- Build in extra to pay for Internet service in unexpected times (sitting in a Starbucks, for instance).

- Find out what software they expect you to use and be ready to pay for that.

Regarding time estimates, boy, that is a thorny problem. What I tend to do is try to avoid specifying a time estimate for the work and look at the expected deliverables. One hundred dialog polishes is less time that an A-story treatment document, obviously. But this gets into the issue of what your strengths are, how fast you write, how many other projects you have going at the same time, etc. I suggest simply taking a look at what they expect for the next deliverable, and give your best estimate. Now, if they are under schedule pressure, that pressure is going to be transferred to you, so allow for it. Developers may not like to admit it, but they understand that work done under extreme deadlines is going to cost more than work done at leisure.

Lastly, never estimate by the word or hour. Always give them prices for each deliverable item.

Underpromise and Overdeliver

This time-worn phrase cannot be overemphasized. It is the key to all kinds of business relationships. But especially in a relationship that can be fraught with uncertainty and mistrust, if you do this with every deliverable, you will overcome both the physical and emotional distance.

Within Reason, Be Flexible on Milestone Definitions

Okay, so we all know that some game developers don't know what a "draft" really means. They aren't used to working with writers, and our language is different (I've worked on projects where there were writing milestones called "first viewable" and "first fun" simply because that terminology was already established for the world-building team. Everybody understood what was expected, there was no confusion, but to an outside writer, these milestones might be confusing). In this regard, be sure in your Schedule "A" to overdefine what will be delivered and when so you can be certain to keep on top of the "Underpromise and Overdeliver" suggestion.

Above all, be sure that you build in time to react to feedback and fix the deliverables they don't like. However, in this area, I also suggest some kind of guidelines for the developer, such as "deliverables not formally accepted within ten days of delivery become automatically accepted" and "deliverables rejected for corrections more than five days after delivery force the upcoming milestone deadline into the future a number of days equal to the delay."

Developers will fight these not-so-subtle reminders that they have some responsibility here to keep things on schedule in addition to your part of the bargain, but usually they will understand that it is all designed to keep the work flowing.

Lastly, always try to build a "draft-revision-final" approval cycle into the schedule. They may not think they have the time or inclination to read a draft, give notes, and then read a final, but you and I both know they will want to. Eventually, of course, you will have established a relationship with them where they sign off on your deliverables sight unseen.

One-Stop Shopping for the Developer

Make the most of your skills in order to make yourself more valuable. Many writers who have backgrounds in the performing arts (theater, film) are also capable of directing voiceover sessions. Some game writers also do website design or ARG design. Once the developer gets to know your abilities, play up the other things you can do for them. This increases your worth to them, and every task you successfully complete for them increases their trust.

Learn the Development Process

Some developers only want writers to fix their broken dialog. Some only want writers to craft their cinematics. Some want writers to set up levels in a first-person shooter or an RTS. Whatever they want, you will benefit greatly from a deep understanding of the development process and how you can best support that process. Don't assume that the developer knows all the ways you can contribute. Look for those opportunities and help lift the burden of the production team.

Be Flexible in Your Billing Methods

We all know that payments don't always come on time. Assume that you are probably going to have to chase after some of your hard-earned money. Don't let this throw you; it's almost never intentional. Most often, the cause is simply that overworked producers haven't had the time to follow up on your payment.

Be certain that you get your invoice in on time. There's nothing against sending in your invoice for the work before the work has been approved. Doing so functions as a gentle reminder that both approval and payment are due. If the developer wants to split your payment up in a way you're not used to or needs the invoice formatted in a manner you've never seen, just smile and do as they ask.

Build Travel into the Budget Explicitly

When your contract is drawn up, be certain that you have enough time called out for on-site visits. If you think you need more time, ask for it. All you are doing is making sure you have the time you need to sync up with the team. And, again, if the visits prove not to be long enough, offer to pay for some of the extra time yourself.

Don't Throw It over the Fence and Walk Away

After you make a deliverable, follow up with a phone call to see if it has been read and what people thought of it. Don't wait for them to get back to you. You're not asking here for approval; you just want to make sure they know you're concerned that the deliverable met their needs. Take extra responsibility for your work. The odds are pretty good that your work, once you hand it in, will not be gone over with a fine-tooth comb. People may not have the time to read it and appreciate the time you put into it. They may not see the effort as you do. Follow-up will help them see that as well as show you care.

Defining What a Draft and/or Version Is Accurately

Some game developers don't truly understand version control for creative writing. Don't make any assumptions here. Define drafts and sign-offs carefully. A project that has gone off the rails can most often be traced back to insufficient scrutiny paid to early drafts.

Here's a little story that gives you an example of what I'm talking about. A young producer I was working with was a big fan of "story," (right on!) but didn't really know how "story" got built. Nonetheless, we had lots of support for the story, and I got to hire my first writing "staff." Anyhow, we're sitting in a meeting building the master schedule, and we've got about 100 small cutscenes (done in the game engine), five major cinematics (two to four minutes each), and maybe 400 standard NPC dialogs. We build out the schedule to get these all written, and then we begin to schedule the second pass (call it what you will, but the pass where we go back in and make sure everything syncs up, makes sense, the reveals are set up correctly, etc.). The young producer literally asks me what I am doing, haven't we finished with the writing schedule? He had no idea that there was anything to be gained by going back over dialog after the whole thing was done "first-draft." So, I explained what I meant by that and why it would be a good idea. He agreed, but it was an interesting moment, I'll say that much.

Some other producers honestly believe that (and this is a quote), "What's so hard? Anyone who can type can write. Once is good enough. Just get it written." If you work for them, you have to build in time off the schedule on your own to do the rewrites you know will come. After all, if the writing stinks, they're going to blame you regardless of how the producer scheduled the project.

On my current project, we use language that comes out of the world-building arena (first functional, first playable, first fun, etc.). We do this because the studio head wanted all the teams to be on the same page with regard to terminology and milestones. This is fine, because the content team understands those mean "first draft," "final draft," and "polish."

Whatever your team calls these development phases, just smile and agree, but try to work into the schedule a time when you hand in something that allows the producers to review the work, give you feedback, and then gives you time to rework and polish.

Understand That the Game Industry Only Pays for "Approved" Work

Writers coming to the game industry from outside, especially film, may not be aware that simply submitting the work does not generate a payment. In film, if the writer delivers a draft, whether the studio likes the draft or not, the fact that the draft was delivered meets the contract requirement, and the payment for the draft is due.

In games, that's almost never the case. All work must be "accepted" before payment is due. Film writers find this bizarre, because the fear is it can lead to the developer playing with the writer and changing their mind about what they want and claiming the writing was "unacceptable" in order to avoid payment. In film, every draft that the studio asks for, even something as small as a polish, is covered under the basic agreement.

It just doesn't work that way in games, so if you want to work in the industry, you'll just have to get used to it.

Understand That They are Probably Behind Schedule

When you have any interactions with the developer, keep in mind they are most probably behind schedule. Filter all their demands on your time through that idea and try to help them meet your own schedule as best you can.

7.4   Conclusion

To succeed at contract life, make sure to do the following.

- Make yourself as available as often as you can.

- Overcommunicate.

- Offer to handle your incidental expenses.

- Expect the job and schedule to both change radically.

- Show them why they should always hire someone like you to write for them.

- Smile always.

8

Writing in a Team

Sande Chen, Maurice Suckling, and Anne Toole

8.1 Introduction

You walk into the room, sit down, and wait till the others file in. As everyone sits down, you can already feel a tingle in the air. Your lead maps out exactly where the writing needs to go, and, inspired, the group leaps into action. As each person offers up an idea, another person adds to it, or morphs it slightly into something bigger and better. Everyone feels included. Whenever a disagreement comes up, the group solves it quickly and with tact. The time flies by. Before you know it, you have a working concept that everyone is excited about. You can't wait to get to work!

... Okay, so this scenario doesn't always happen, but it's great to keep this vision in mind as you begin working with a team. You will need to do your part to achieve this ideal.

Every game you work on leads to a new adventure, with different rules and roles to fill. A game writer needs to be flexible enough to handle a number of different approaches to completing a game, including working in a team. Unlike other creative mediums, the quantity and complexity of content in games requires an even greater understanding of the fundamentals of collaborative writing. Furthermore, other game professionals often don't have the creative writing background necessary to support a game writer, so game writers on a team must work even harder to provide each other that support.

We're here to help. First, we'll explore the fundamentals of working in a writing team, managing expectations, and giving and getting feedback. We'll highlight the three collaborative writing processes of consensus, compromise, and ownership and consider a few case studies. We've also included a first-person perspective of respect when working with the entire development team.[1]

---

[1] Sections 8.2–8.6 were written by Anne Toole and Sande Chen. Section 8.8 was written by Maurice Suckling.

8.2   Working in a Team

No matter how your writing team is formed, two keys are essential: respecting others and managing your ego.

Respect

Respect has an inner component as well as an outer one. On the inside, respect involves not only respecting another person's strengths but also accepting their fallibility. If you don't respect the other person, it will appear in your verbal or nonverbal communication.

The outer component involves communicating this respect to your team members. *Listening* is just one part of the equation. An extrovert might find a quiet email critiquing an idea quite disrespectful, while an introvert would prefer this type of communication over a face-to-face conversation. Ask and learn as much as you can about how to show respect for your fellow writers, and educate them on how they can respect you.

For an inside look at respect and the rest of the game development team, see Section 8.8.

Managing Ego

The key in a team situation is not to eliminate ego but to manage it. Allowing others to discard your best ideas just to get along is no better than fighting for your every idea. Taking steps to maintain a healthy ego will avoid the dangers of extremes and help you choose your battles.

While you work on managing your own ego, you may be called upon to manage others'. Different people require different approaches. Even if you're not leading the team, getting a firm feel for your teammates' ego needs will come in handy when you need their help on one of your projects.

We would be going beyond the scope of this chapter by offering tips on managing specific personality types, but numerous books on the subject are available. If you're not a fan of the 16 Myers-Briggs personality types, consider exploring frameworks with only four basic personality types. For example, you may find helpful *More than Words: Nine Silver Rules for Powerful Yet Considerate Communication* by Edward Horrell. If you look, you're certain to find an approach that works for you.

8.3   Managing Expectations: Joining a Game-Writing Team

Upon joining a team, learning what the company expects of you is a crucial first step. Whether you are freelance or working on staff, you will be working for someone, so ask your team lead to clarify your role as the project moves forward. Questions you might ask include the following.

- How do you prefer to write? This question you can ask colleagues as well as your superiors. Do not assume everyone writes the same way you do. Some may prefer to start with a story premise and move forward. Some may start with gameplay. Others may start with theme. Knowing how your superior likes to develop a story can prevent misunderstandings going forward.

- How open are you to suggestions or comments at this stage?

- What is the vision for this project?

- What support do you need from me?

While asking these questions should smooth your transition onto the team, you should continue to ask these types of questions at each stage of the project. Always ask, "How am I doing?" Honest answers to these questions will allow you to correct problems before they become too hard to handle.

The second step to joining a team requires letting others know what to expect from you. You can answer some of the questions above or come up with your own. For example, a writer told his lead once that he wasn't good at pitching ideas orally and added, half-jokingly, that he was "never going to get better." This information helped his lead understand problems "in the room" and may have opened a door for this writer to pitch via e-mail instead. By taking a risk and being honest, the writer headed off a problem before it got too big.

8.4 Forming a Game-Writing Team

Forming your own writing team may take more work than you realize. You'll sort through writing samples, administer tests, and run a few interviews. When all is said and done, you'll have a writing team to be proud of. The End, right? Not exactly. As with joining a team, getting the team together is just the beginning. To get the team working together smoothly, you'll have to manage a few expectations yourself.

Many of the suggestions above about joining a team will be helpful to you when you work with other leaders on your project and when you're managing your own team as well. When a new members join your writing team, explore their expectations with a few questions. Be sure to explain in advance that you're supporting the writers; you want to put them in situations where they will excel. If you don't couch these questions in these terms, your new team members may wonder if they're in trouble and may unwittingly shoot themselves in the foot.

- How do you prefer to write? For example, collaboratively or alone?

- What is your goal on this project? How can I support you in achieving it?

- What are you most excited about in this project?

- What kind of feedback is helpful to you?

Naturally, you will want to tell your team what you expect from them and what they can expect from you. Even if your writers don't ask, you may want to answer the questions from Section 8.3. Not only should you be honest with them, you should be honest with yourself. If you want your team to check in with you every day, don't say "Check in with me when convenient." Both you and your team will benefit.

8.5   Giving Feedback on Game Writing

Feedback, or "notes" as it is called in Hollywood, is an integral part of the creative process. Everyone needs feedback, both positive and negative.

Ever heard of the feedback sandwich? It is the ideal structure for giving feedback. Positive feedback is the bread, while criticism is the meat. Feedback should be quite specific and relevant to the matter at hand. "You're a friendly person. Your writing needs work, but overall, good job" will only serve to confuse your writer. The feedback sandwich for this paragraph so far might be, "I like how you start out with a question to engage the reader. You do tend to use passive verbs like 'to be' a bit too much. Overall, it looks like you're on track." Simple, straightforward, and honest.

Despite the benefits of the sandwich, a few excuses do tend to crop up. If you encounter them, here are a few answers.

- "I don't have time to tell them what they're doing right." Well, do you have time to hire a new writer after this one quits? In the crunch of content development, the answer will most likely be no.

- "They know I like all the work I haven't specifically criticized." Oh, really? If your writer is half as neurotic as most, your writer may think you hate *everything* but only had the time to critique the most serious gaffes. This scenario rings even more true in game development, when you often don't have time to critique everything.

- "I don't want to step on the writers' creative toes." Unless you will lose your job because of it, step on those toes! This may come as a shock to you, but the game industry occasionally suffers from a lack of good writing. This problem may very well stem from the fact that no one had the guts to say that the story or writing wasn't working. Airing your thoughts earlier rather than later will save everyone a lot of time and anguish. If the story *is* working, your writers need to know that as well, or else they may change things for the worse.

Warning! While the feedback sandwich works, never use it in isolation. If you only give positive feedback moments before tearing into your writers' work, they will already be steeling themselves whenever they hear "I like how you..." Worse still, writers familiar with the feedback sandwich may think you're merely manufacturing positive feedback and ignore it completely in favor of the "real" negative feedback. Try to give positive feedback five times for each time you must use the feedback sandwich to serve up criticism.

8.6   Getting Feedback on Game Writing

You've mastered giving feedback, but did you know that *getting* feedback is another skill? While restraining yourself from throttling the person criticizing you may seem like a great skill, the subtle art of getting feedback leaves both parties better off and without the need for a sedative. First and foremost, remember that everyone giving notes on your writing has the best interest of the game at heart. They're not out to get you, and it's not personal. Try these four tips when getting feedback on writing.

- **Ask questions.** While many who give you feedback will give reasons for the note, their reason may not always be the right one. For example, a developer may say, "I don't like the word this character uses." You may dutifully change the word, but the real issue at hand may involve a misconception about the character or the style required for the world. Better to find this out earlier rather than later. This idea leads into...

- **Take the note, not the suggestion.** Often, feedback will come in the form of a suggestion: "Have this character yell at the player here." If you delve a little bit deeper, you may realize that the concern is not the yelling per se but the lack of drama in the scene. You may then change the scene to add more drama without any yelling. As long as you address the note underneath the suggestion, everyone should be happy.

- **Prioritize the notes.** For a number of reasons, you may not be able to incorporate all the notes you are given. You may be getting feedback from a number of people, or you may be pressed for time, even more likely in game development. Identify your priorities through speaking with your colleagues or leadership, then take care of the key issues first. Ideally, you shouldn't bother with typos, for example, when your story needs a major overhaul. However, for production reasons, you may indeed need to fix those typos for a demo or testing before getting to story issues.

- **Don't take every note.** Even if you have the time and ability to fix everything that was red-flagged, you may decide not to execute every suggestion. This scenario requires caution, a lot of diplomacy, and an honest evaluation of where you stand. Taking the wrong note may harm your work, and as the person hired for your expertise, you are responsible for keeping the story or writing on course. By the same token, you may not be in the position to make such decisions. Tread carefully.

- **Cool off.** If you find yourself feeling defensive, take time to cool off and appreciate the feedback for what it is—an honest effort to improve the game. Never forget that you work in a collaborative medium, and feedback is one of its joys.

8.7   Game-Writing Processes

When it comes to the practical organization of team writing, there are a variety of approaches in current use. Glibly put, you could say there are as many approaches as there are teams of writers. Learning every method would take a prohibitive amount of time, but luckily, they all incorporate a mere handful of fundamental models. Most writing teams use an integrated approach, choosing the process that works best in each situation. While majority rule and dictatorship can lead you to a finished game, try to familiarize yourself with the following three models to better collaborate with writers: *consensus*, *compromise*, and *ownership*.

Consensus

Merriam-Webster calls consensus "general agreement: unanimity" as well as "group solidarity in sentiment and belief." However, consensus is more than just an end result; it's a decision-making process. With a keen understanding of consensus, writers can improve not only the quality of their writing but relationships with their teammates.

In practice, consensus allows each team member to contribute to and influence the process. For example, most brainstorming sessions are run by consensus. Team members can offer up ideas, which the group explores for as long as it's fruitful. The goal is to settle upon an idea that excites every member of the team. Writers who have experienced successful sessions describe a lift in the entire room when they've hit on the right idea. The energy spikes and smiles appear, making it one of the most gratifying aspects of working collaboratively.

The goal of consensus is to reach this "lift," so it's important to move on quickly from ideas that just aren't hitting. However, sometimes you will need to plow through an idea before discarding it, and disagreements will arise. Fortunately, consensus allows for coming to a solution that literally makes everyone happy.

- **Identify the issue at stake.** No matter who disagrees with the direction the story is headed, make sure you understand what specifically is causing contention. "I don't know, that sounds dumb," is not helpful. If someone has a negative reaction to your story idea, ask, "What about this bothers you?" You may have assumed it had to do with the character you have envisioned, but your teammate may actually just have an issue with a particular plot point.

- **Allow everyone to describe their best-case scenario.** In order to make everyone enjoy the solution, everyone has to share what they enjoy. In the above case, your best-case scenario may involve a scene where your character has a change of heart, while your teammate's ideal scene would involve the character following the most logical path.

- **Find a solution that works for everyone.** At this point, brainstorm a solution that addresses everyone's concerns. If problems still arise, begin with Step 1, or try developing a new idea in its entirety.

For an example of consensus, see The Mustard Corporation and Writers Cabal's case studies in Section 8.9. Instances when the consensus model works best include the following.

- When you have few ego problems in your team.

- When you have a small number of people involved in the decision-making process.

- When the issue is integral to your project and/or will affect everyone.

- When a project is just beginning.

- When you have time and are willing to get to the root of each others' concerns.

- When team members prefer to work collaboratively.

Drawbacks. Consensus often works best with fewer people involved in the decision-making process, and a true consensus system may not give the recognition some writers need to manage their ego.

Compromise

Compromise has both negative and positive connotations. You can compromise your values, but being willing to compromise suggests you're flexible, open-minded, and a good team player. Compromise plays an important role in game development and can be an effective tool in a writing team.

According to Merriam-Webster, compromise results in "a settlement of differences by arbitration or by consent reached by mutual concessions." Like consensus, compromise leads to a decision that takes into account at least some of everyone's concerns. Unlike consensus, compromise often allows the group to make a decision quickly and move on.

The process for reaching compromise resembles consensus. However, compromise often means taking less time delving into the reasons why a team member objects to a problem. If concerns continue to arise, instead of working to achieve everyone's best-case scenario, a compromise allows everyone to agree to a scenario that works. Avoid time-delayed compromise, such as, "We'll do it my way this time; next time we'll do it your way." When next time comes, this compromise may be long forgotten.

An example of compromise. Joe and Sally are arguing over a character's dress color, which both agree should represent her personality. Unfortunately, Joe and Sally can't agree on the character's personality. Joe wants red to emphasize her seductiveness, but Sally wants to avoid depicting her that way. Sally wants black to emphasize her air of mystery, but Joe doesn't find the character is all that mysterious. While they do need to discuss the character more fully, they are pressed for time, and they would not be able to change much of the story if they revamp the character at this point.

Bob, another writer, suggests they compromise by emphasizing the character's role, rather than her personality. Since the character is a healer, they agree to dress her in green. The solution works, so they agree and move on to more pressing concerns. Although Joe and Sally didn't get what they were most passionate about, they don't feel like they lost more than they gave.

Instances when compromise works best include the following.

- When time is short but you still want others' input.

- When the issue is important but not a hill to die on.

- When you have no or low ego concerns on your team.

- When team members prefer to work collaboratively.

Drawbacks. After compromising, sometimes both parties are left feeling like they lost. When the compromise is imposed from somewhere up the chain of command, writers may be confused about what just happened, but complaining about it is counter to team-building. You want to avoid compromising your game into mediocrity, but remember to take changes as a challenge for excellence, not a personal insult.

Ownership

Ownership as a way to manage teams has yet to hit the dictionaries, but it is already a hallmark of the game industry. Also known as the "compartmental" approach (see Section 8.9), assigning ownership is the act of giving a project to one person who is ultimately responsible for its successful completion. Ownership allows writers to pour their passion into their work and take pride in it. For that reason, ownership is a great way to manage ego and makes it easy to track progress, because there's only one person to ask. Ownership allows a writer to tell his or her story without the drawbacks of working in committee.

A writer with ownership of a project may act like a mini-producer, making sure systems, level design, and art can support the story, characters, and dialog. Even if the writer isn't coordinating with other types of developers, the writer with ownership may very well need to enlist other writers to complete the task at hand. Here are a few tips on how a writer can do just that.

1. **Practice good salesmanship.** While you own a project, you will need to sell your ideas to everyone you enlist to aid you. The more excited you can get them about your idea, the more time and effort they will put into it. Remember, also, that good salesmanship does not end with the sale. Follow-up with thanks for their work speaks volumes.

2. **Ask for and listen to feedback from peers, with reservations.** No matter how fabulous your story is, you will want to get feedback from your peers. You

don't want to be making the big presentation when the company head points out the fundamental flaws in your story or character. That said, as you ask for feedback, give the caveat that you are simply trying to get people's impressions. If you don't take people's feedback, they may feel cheated or ignored unless you warn them in advance. These people may then be less inclined to help or give you feedback in the future. If someone felt particularly strongly about an issue, explain to the best of your ability why you have chosen the route you are on without discounting their ideas.

3. **Give as much as you receive.** While you may own a project, a team member may own another section. You will probably want help from them to complete your project, so make sure to offer help on other team members' projects. You want to avoid a situation where everyone is slammed with work because no one took the time to help each other in earlier stages. Worse still, you don't want to be the only team member who can't finish your project because no one will help you.

4. **Don't forget consensus and compromise.** Just because you have ownership of your project doesn't mean you can't use these other tools. Bolstering your position to the higher-ups with the comment, "We all agreed," can smooth the rough patches.

For an example of ownership, see Section 8.9, especially the case study from BioWare. Instances when the ownership model works best include the following.

- When time is short.

- When a lot of work needs to be done, and working on it concurrently makes sense.

- When most of the key issues have already been decided.

- When you need clear accountability.

- When you have high ego concerns on your team.

- When team members prefer to work alone.

Drawbacks. The biggest drawback of ownership comes from the term itself. "Ownership" is misleading, because it implies that you have final say, when that is often far from the case. When word comes down from on high or from another department that a change needs to be made, the "owner" may feel marginalized, frustrated, and stifled. On top of that, these required changes may occur more frequently, because a writer with ownership may not be soliciting, receiving, or accepting the peer feedback he or she needs.

An ownership system may also foster a tragedy of the commons. Teamwork best done as a group may fall by the wayside or may be done with less care while team members focus on "their" projects. Teammates, no matter how good their intentions, often end up putting less time into helping others, because their own projects take priority. If you own a project but are unable to enlist your teammates because they are busy with their projects, you are at fault. After all, you are held accountable for the outcome of your project, not they.

With a mastery of these three models of collaboration, a game writer should be able to integrate into any writing team or organization. Writers may also be called upon to use these tools when working with the rest of the development team. While writers share a common understanding of the writing process, both developers and writers often suffer from ignorance on how the other half works. How, then, can you as a writer successfully work with the rest of the development team?

8.8 First-Person Perspective: Working with the Development Team

"Happy families are all alike; every unhappy family is unhappy in its own way." So said Tolstoy in *Anna Karenina*. I hope he might allow me to invert that when I rather less succinctly say the following. Every development team and every project has its own unique relationship with its writer or writers, and when things are working, chances are they're working in their own particular way—a testimony to all the individuals and all the processes that form that particular "family." But when they're not working, the reason is invariably the same thing.

Aretha Franklin summed it up in one word in 1967: R-E-S-P-E-C-T.

With the industry still growing up and interactive narrative still in its infancy, the place of writers in a development team is often under dispute. There are people in studios who still remember when they got to do all the fun stuff like dialog and naming characters and trying their hand at storytelling, and they got to do it as a treat, a reward for all their hard work designing, doing art, programming, or producing. It can be hard for these people to take kindly to seeing a freelancer unconnected to the project for the first months of development walking through the studio to take a meeting with a view to being hired. Who are you? And what happened to the good old days? You can feel the thoughts being pumped round the semi-silence of each air-conditioned office. And in any case, how hard can it be to write? Everyone's seen movies and everyone can write, right?

As a game writer, sooner or later you'll meet coworkers from other disciplines who take a less than enlightened view on your value to the industry—or at least their project. These are the "stories are anti-game-matter" fraternity, the people who take the view that stories and gameplay are fundamentally opposed and anywhere you have story is a place where gameplay can't be, and vice versa. Games are for gameplay and stories belong elsewhere.

This is clearly a huge issue in its own right. However, let me say here that every game has its own particular story requirements—ranging from nothing at all at one end of the spectrum to it being fundamental at the other. The trick is to be clear about what kind of game it is you're trying to make at any one point and who you are trying to make it for. That will tell you the place of story in any particular game. In any event, story versus gameplay is a false match-up. In truth, everything is subservient to the game experience—story, gameplay, physics, art, music. I've played *Silent Hill* late into the night, and the thing I most remembered the next morning was the fantastically evocative sound effects.

You should expect designers, programmers, producers, artists, musicians, and execs to respect the contribution you can make on a project, just as you should respect the ability of everyone around you to deliver the work expected of them in their own fields of expertise.

You should still expect people to ask you to explain your opinions when they're puzzling or when they impact on other areas of development, just as you should also feel entitled to ask others to explain their opinions when you find them puzzling or when they give rise to decisions that impact on the story.

There's a degree of essential mutual education that needs to go on. There are people who simply won't understand what it is you do, and part of your responsibility is to help them. And you also need to take responsibility to get yourself educated about what it is that other people do and why that has an impact on your work.

Respect is the bedrock you need if you're going to make a game together. Story is constantly crossing over into other territories of game development, just as those areas cross over into the realm of the story.

This can inevitably give rise to a kind of "us versus them" mentality. Without the expertise of everyone involved being respected, this mentality soon leads to everyone picking up shovels and digging trenches—and everyone remembers from history how difficult and bloody it is to get through trench networks. (Even if you get hold of tanks, it's still bloody—and the whole thing is still an extravagant waste of time when you could've been standing on bridges together looking at the view.)

Respect your craft, too—remember that writing is essentially a craft of logic. Of course there's imagination, but without logic a story just implodes under its own weight. The best solution is usually the simplest. Be logical and you'll be persuasive. Even if it's not always possible to ascribe reason to your views—like, for example, why you might prefer Otis Redding's 1965 original of "Respect"—you need to engage in the collective debate, and you have a responsibility to try to guide the discussion toward a productive conclusion. After all, as a writer within a development team, you're a card-carrying member of the unofficial Logic Police, helping to look after everyone else and making sure they all get home safely to the place where things make sense.

When all else fails and arguments seem to be going round in circles, respect can come to your assistance yet again—respect for the original vision of the game, what its creative core is, and who it's for.

Of course, if you're working on a game that doesn't have a vision document of some kind, or at least a vision keeper, then you're in serious trouble, and it might be time to respect yourself and see if there's another company needing a writer.

8.9   Case Studies

Mike Laidlaw, Bioware

The approach taken by Mike Laidlaw, Lead Writer at Bioware, is a good example of ownership.

> [I]... make sure writers complete a "unit" of work, be it a plot, planet, romance... Ripping people away from their work arbitrarily does nothing but crush morale and remove investment. "Why should I bother writing this if I'm just going to be ripped off of it half way through?"

But he clarifies this further.

> ...I wouldn't take a single person and task them with the same type of plot writing over and over. Variety is the only way to keep things fresh, so you can't expect... someone to only write funny plots, because it won't be long before their stuff isn't funny any more.

Mike ensures the tone of voice is kept consistent by utilizing Lead Writers or Editors as the "arbiter and enforcer, respectively, of the game's voice."

He recently decided to change the process a bit.

> I used to think that the best way to maintain consistency was to divide the game into large sections and let each writer work on a broad swath of story, to create a large area that's masterminded to hang together. Recently, I've begun to question that wisdom, and I'm preparing to try an approach that throws the entire writing team together to tackle areas as a group. So, instead of tasking one writer with the Imperial Arena from *Jade Empire*, I'm looking at saying: Writer A, can you take the announcer? B, I'll need you on the weakling guy you face first. C, can you handle the gruff veteran? It will be an interesting experiment. It will either be an organizational nightmare, or a way of making sure all of the writers are familiar with all parts of the game. My suspicion is that it will be a little of each.

Maurice Suckling, The Mustard Corporation

"Mike's experiment more closely resembles what I would term an 'integrated' approach. This is the approach taken by my own company, The Mustard Corporation.

"Our usual complement of writers on a project is a team of two, or a team of three. Our usual practice is to ensure all the team is involved in early conceptual discussions, so high concepts, outlines, character profiles, and treatments are all built by the team in close discussions. Essentially, at this stage there is just lots *and lots* of talking, thinking, more talking, research, some drawing of story structures on whiteboards, more talking, more thinking, and yet more talking. Our intention is to work through the issues to a point at which we form a kind of unified opinion, backed up by the conclusions from our discussions and deliberations—and we can then present this opinion to the developer. When a developer brings six or more personnel to a meeting, including designers, producers, and execs, and these people are often approaching a problem from multiple perspectives, it can be extremely beneficial for a project to have at least two or three people with a unified vision.

"It is only after a treatment is signed off that the team separates to write up individual scenes or chunks of in-game text. For us, a signed-off treatment is the essential blueprint that ought to tell us everything we need to know to set about writing the actual script—it's as much a blueprint for the developer so they know what to expect from us as it is for ourselves, so we know what to expect of each other. It's like being an architect, and if the blueprint isn't built right—if the structure isn't sound—then the story isn't going to work no matter what frills you're capable of in the dialogue. If you've got cool art on the walls of a building that's going to fall down, it's hard to care that much about the cool art—people probably won't hang around in the building long enough to see it.

"Having written a first draft of our respectively allotted scenes, our usual practice is to review them all face to face over several hours. We will then either take back the scenes we wrote, or, if someone gets excited by the potential within a scene and sees a way to unlock it, we might swap the scenes over.

"We'll rewrite and review scenes and in-game scripts as many times as a deadline allows before presenting a complete script to the developer to review.

"Once we have their feedback, we will then begin the process again of internally reviewing the feedback, rewriting and reviewing it amongst ourselves before resubmitting.

"Although our approach is what I would term 'integrated,' there are still points at which writers have to buckle down and write a pass of a scene or an in-game script on their own—perhaps it's really just a question of when you blow the whistle and send people to their own keyboards.

"Because of the intense and highly integrated manner in which we work, we've found from experience that two or three writers working closely together is about the maximum number that works well on any particular project. Any more and we've found that there's a tendency for the group to all have a slightly different vision in our heads of what we're trying to build. The group can tend to split off into subgroups. In addition, from about four writers up there needs to be an undisputed lead writer—and there's nothing wrong with that—it's just a question of what works for you and generates the quality of work to satisfy yourselves and your clients to a timescale acceptable to both of you.

"As a general rule, the longer you work closely with other writers, the more likely it is that things will end in tears if you bring your egos with you. Team writing requires trust and professionalism, and it will all go a whole lot more smoothly if you can work with people who remind you that what we do is actually fun."

Sande Chen and Anne Toole, Writers Cabal

"As a partnership, we typically resort to consensus throughout the game writing process. We may each prepare ideas ahead of time as a launching point for our discussions. Once we start talking, however, the ideas morph and grow, and we begin to articulate our goals for the story, keeping in mind the developer's vision. With our goals in place, our story proposals incorporate concepts from both of us.

"Once we're actually writing the game, we divide the work evenly between us but still rely on consensus. We look over each other's work and may reassess how to approach certain sections. Even so, there is a bit of ownership. When we review our partner's writing, we are less likely to make creative edits to preserve our distinctive voices. Since we know each other well, we often divvy up the work based on our particular strengths.

"Even the best writing partnership may occasionally call for compromise. We typically make compromises on thankless tasks that neither of us enjoys. Most of these tasks involve the business end of our partnership.

"Over time, we've remained flexible in order to incorporate our process with those of different developer teams. Each time we are reminded of the importance of understanding the fundamentals of working in a team and how they apply not only to writers but to all game developers."

8.10   Conclusion

The game is over, the product has shipped, and now you are moving on to a new project, a new company, and a new adventure. Fortunately, you are armed with the tools you need to succeed in any team environment. You remember the importance of respect and managing egos; you've learned to ask questions of your colleagues as both team member and lead; and you've mastered the fine art of giving and getting feedback. Your understanding of the models of consensus, compromise, and ownership has prepared you for whatever new development process may come your way, and you're ready to use these tools to educate your development team about your needs and to learn about theirs. Known as a flexible, easy-going writer, you're an ideal addition to any writing team. As such, there's only one thing left to say. . .

We look forward to working with you!

8.11   Exercises

1. If you were on a writing team, how would you answer the questions in Section 8.3?

9

Getting the Work Done

Wendy Despain

You've got one of the most exciting assignments of your writing career. It's cutting edge, it's interactive, it's new. Now what? Well, now you've got to get the work done. Video games may be notorious for slippery deadlines, but nobody (especially not the new writer) wants to be responsible for that calendar creep. And you're probably not going to have a huge team to spread the blame over. Quite often, if the script is late, there's nobody to blame but you.

Worse yet, in video games, they'll move ahead without you. If someone needs your dialog and they don't have access to it, they'll put "dummy text" in so they don't miss their deadline. Sometimes this is as basic as "blah blah blah," but usually they try their hand at writing dialog (because, come on, everybody can do this) and will show you exactly why they needed to hire you. And there's always a danger that some VP will read that dummy dialog and think it's the final dialog coming out of your office. In a project where so many people have their hands in the mix, the best thing you can do to avoid any confusion is to meet or exceed your deadlines.

9.1 It's a Matter of Scope

When facing your enemy the blank page, or even worse the blank spreadsheet, don't underestimate the scope of the battle ahead. Most writing projects are scoped by words. An hour-long episode of television is somewhere in the range of 12,000 to 13,000 words. A two-hour feature film is roughly 20,000 to 30,000 words. A novel, which every writer would consider a big project, is anywhere between 50,000 and 100,000 words.

Video games blow all of these out of the water. They often have 100,000 words of dialog alone. This isn't counting character or scene descriptions, notes to the voiceover artists, or trigger notes so the programmers know which line should be played when the character trips over a crate. This is a big job. You're not going to write three novels in a month and a half, and you're not going to write one video game in that time, either. Respect the enormity of the task and scope your projects realistically.

9.2   Eating an Elephant One Spoonful at a Time

The only way to tackle something this big is to break it into smaller pieces. Otherwise, you'll face an initial project paralysis and a final frenzied kamikaze attack at the end. Don't try to do everything at once. Every project is different and every person will split things up differently. When I worked on *Bratz: Forever Diamondz*, I worked on one level at a time, then on the mini-games within each level, and on barks last. On *ArchLord*, I edited all the quest dialog and broke it up by the average length of the lines. There were 1500 short ones, 2500 medium-length ones, and 1200 long ones. The short ones were fewer than ten words, the medium ones were between ten and twenty words, and the longer ones were, well, longer.

When you've divided the overall project up into smaller pieces, make a task list. Consider using a spreadsheet or project-management software. It will be most useful if you include the following specific information about each task.

- **Detailed descriptions of each task.** This task list will be with you a long time. Don't let a vague description cause confusion down the road.

- **Time estimates.** Guess how long you think each section will take to complete. As the project progresses, compare your estimates with actual hours spent and adjust future estimates as necessary.

- **Approval/edit lists.** If anybody needs to look things over and approve them— or if you're lucky enough to have someone editing your work—provide a place in your task list to specify which day feedback and approval was requested and when it was given. If more than one person gets approval, provide a slot for each person on each task.

- **Their contact information.** Sure, you have it written down somewhere else, but when you realize it's been three weeks since you sent in the last segment and you haven't heard anything back, the last thing you want to do is go find that phone number in that email they sent three months ago.

- **Deadlines.** Set specific deadlines for each task and hold yourself to them. Remember to check your estimates to make sure you're not working 30-hour days. Don't give every task the same deadline and give yourself some wiggle room. Nobody estimates perfectly.

- **Collaboration details.** If you're working with other writers, include their contact information and a description of what they're contributing.

An example of my own task spreadsheet is included in Appendix C as an example you can use as a starting point for your own project management plan.

Also keep in mind that the best way to get the work done may be to share. Many game writers freelance and may be available to help out with one or two of these sections if it's just not possible for one person to meet the deadlines. Chapter 8 in this book addresses techniques for working in a team. Consult that chapter for advice on how to make this work.

9.3   The Basics Can Save Your Backside

Remember that pep talk every Obi-Wan mentor ever gave the plucky young hero facing their worst fears? Remember your training. Don't abandon the fundamentals under pressure. When you're facing a huge project, the only way to get through it with any elegance is to remember the basics of the writing craft. They apply to game writing as much as anything else.

For example, fully realized characters write their own dialog. Cardboard characters are hard to write for. I was really worried about this when I started *Bratz: Forever Diamondz*. I didn't realize detailed character descriptions had already been written for each doll/character. When I turned these up in my research, I knew my job just got much easier.

I made one-page character sheets for each of the main characters, including their image, brief description, and personal quirks. I hung these up around my office and really got to know them. I knew how each character would respond in a given situation, and that made writing dialog a breeze. Take a look at the script sample in Appendix C to see how it worked out.

You may have your own shortcuts, but one I use is personality theory. I'm a fan of Carl Jung's personality types, a system also known by the names of the creators of the sorting test Meyers-Briggs. It's a way to categorize different personalities with shortcut acronyms. I use them often enough that I know how effervescent an ENFP will be when she wins a game, and how embarrassed an INTJ will be when she's the center of attention. The dialog in those situations comes to mind instantly, whether it's for a video game or a TV episode. Faster dialog writing will more than make up for the time it takes to breathe life into your characters.

Another truism writers in other media hear is that to be a good writer, you have to read a lot and you have to write a lot. This is just as true for game writing as long as you also include playing a lot. Playing video games should be a regular habit. It sounds crazy at first, but when you work on games and get caught up in your job, it can be easy to stop immersing yourself in other games and media. Don't let that fade out. You don't have to be the best gamer ever, but being literate and caught up is important, and you can learn a lot from your peers.

One of the fundamentals often overlooked in the games industry is editing. Editing and rewriting are the bedrock of writing. Do your best to include this step in your video game work. You may have to fight for it, but it will turn mediocre dialog into lines people won't mind hearing every time they replay the game. Try to get another pair of eyes you can trust to give honest feedback on your work. At the very least, read your dialog out loud before you turn it in. The line that sounds hilarious in your head may not be so great when it's said out loud.

Tips for Staying Organized

Organization can rescue a project in peril and avoid deadline slippage. By now I'm sure you've noticed how much I enjoy making lists, so here's a list of tips for staying on top of your projects.

- **Write things down.** Use whatever system works best for you. If you don't know what works best, try color-coded sticky notes, day planners, to-do lists, wikis, spreadsheets, email, text documents. You're a writer; use the written word to your advantage and don't depend on remembering important details.

- **Communicate with others.** Even the best planners sometimes need someone to say, "Wait, weren't you writing a script that week?" Beyond that, the creation of an interactive narrative is a group effort, and your teammates will appreciate knowing how your part of the project is going.

- **Use folders to organize files.** Both digitally and in real life. I've got a different folder for each major project both on my hard drive and on my bookshelf. They're not exact copies of each other, but I have backups of important documents, and I can lay my hands on them at any moment.

- **Use a calendar.** There's nothing like a visual representation of time to help keep you on track.

- **Learn your pace for this job and work to that pace.** They call this a job for a reason. If you know you can edit 500 lines in one day, sit down and do it. In a similar vein, don't schedule 3000 lines in a day if the best you've ever done is half that.

- **Institute some form of version control.** This doesn't have to be complicated. Simply saving a file with a new name including the date could be enough. Whatever works best for your own system, you need to be able to instantly bring up the most current version as well as several previous drafts. You never know when you'll need to step backward a bit, and you definitely need to be confident you're working on the most up-to-date file.

9.4   Strategies for Freelancers

Freelance game writers often work removed from the development team and sometimes have to keep on task from the comfort of their own living room couch, surrounded by the distractions of housework, movies, and family. I've found a personal schedule and routine is critical to getting work done. I have a personal schedule each day and each week. So I know at 10 a.m. on Monday I need to have the dogs walked and the spam cleared out of the inbox so I can get to work on research. I don't always stick to my schedule, but at least I know what trade-offs I'm making when friends want to take me out to lunch at 11:30 a.m. on Thursday.

Also, do everything you can to have a separate, dedicated office in your home. Not only is it beneficial for tax purposes (at least in the United States), but it also provides some separation from work and home life. I've found that if I'm not careful, I'm not working from home—I'm sleeping in my workplace. Sure, sometimes I work best on the couch with the TV on, but sometimes I need silence with project-related inspiration around me. I have to change it up sometimes, and it's a lot easier to get up and go in the other room rather than redecorating the dining room. Get to know your own quirks and make them work in your favor.

Finally, go ahead and acknowledge the fact that you're working from home sometimes. One of the perks of freelancing is throwing a load of wash in the dryer between conference calls. Taking breaks and feeling productive can help you avoid writer's block and burnout as long as you don't go overboard and lose focus.

9.5   Strategies for In-House Staff Writers

When working as a staff writer in-house, the biggest thing I have to watch out for is losing focus. It's easy to get caught up in the excitement of everything going on with coworkers. Of course, being connected to the broader development of the game is very important, but writing takes focus and concentration, so be aware of how your time is being spent. If you're always getting pulled off task by something shiny across the cube farm, you'll find yourself missing deadlines. Little things and interruptions can nibble away your day into nothing.

Chris Klug is Creative Director for *Stargate Worlds*, a story-heavy MMOG from Cheyenne Mountain Entertainment. He's worked with in-house teams of writers in games and television and had several tips to share about getting the work done while on staff. One thing to remember, he says, is that many game developers aren't familiar with the way writers work, so there may be some resistance to some of the strategies writers see as beneficial. They may not understand why you want to take over an entire wall with index cards and string. Don't let that stop you. He says that the most important thing for writers on staff at a developer is to take charge of their own work process. If you need some uninterrupted time to focus on a tricky plot problem, ask if you can work from home one morning. If you want a whiteboard to break down a story into beats as a group, ask for one. Of course, you don't want to be a diva about it, but know the circumstances where you work best and do what you can to make them a reality. Don't expect the developers to set things up for you without being told.

In-house writers should also take every opportunity to learn the tools other departments use to do their job. One of the benefits of sitting right there in the office is a chance to integrate narrative more closely with gameplay, but this can be an uphill battle unless writers step out of their comfort zone and learn about the other game-development systems. The more you know about the tools Level Designers use to build the game, the more you'll be able to make narrative easy for them to implement. Don't be afraid to get your hands on the more technical side of game development.

9.6   Beating Writer's Block with a Clock

There's never enough time in this business. You're always trying to beat the clock, and you never have the luxury of indulging in writer's block. That thought alone can be enough to send me into a mini panic attack, shutting down all progress. I know it doesn't sound logical. There's a reason writers have a reputation for being heavy drinkers. It's easy to give up and wallow in paradoxes. At some point, you're going to face writer's block on this job, and I hope I can provide some strategies you can use rather than turning to alcohol.

First of all, work on what you want to work on. Just sit down and get your fingers moving. If you feel like writing dialog for one particular character rather than the voiceover direction editing you had scheduled for today, go ahead and write the dialog. Progress is progress, and the scheduled work will come when it's ready. Just remember to reschedule it if you don't get it done that day.

Interestingly enough, this strategy applies to non-writing tasks as well. I sometimes hit a block, and if I'm not careful, I'll sit staring at my computer all day, doing nothing. In the back of my mind, other tasks nag at me. If I stand up and go work on them, I get myself moving both figuratively and literally. Currently I work from home, and sometimes doing the laundry is exactly what I need to do to get past my writer's block. I'll be folding socks, and the solution to the writing problem will just come to me. The trick is to get up and go back to the computer the instant that happens. Don't get sucked into the other work so entirely you forget what pays the bills. If inspiration isn't striking when you're away from your desk, set a timer. Work on the other tasks for 15 or 20 minutes, then go back to the blank page and see if the momentum carries over.

Another way to get yourself moving past a block is to edit some of yesterday's work—or better yet, last week's. It can get your brain into the right space and push you forward. Be careful not to edit and re-edit just to look like you're doing something, though. Use that timer again if necessary. Edit for 20 minutes, then write new material for 20 minutes. It doesn't matter if it's no good—you'll go back and edit it when this happens again next week.

And while we're on the subject of being good, nurture your inner cheerleader and recruit a real-world cheerleader. We writers have a host of demons in our heads telling us we'll never measure up to Shakespeare, so why bother? Often, they're at the root of writer's block. Don't let them win. Hemingway doesn't measure up to

Shakespeare, either, but he did okay. You're cultivating your own voice in a whole new media. A few mistakes are allowed along the way.

Another strategy for dealing with writer's block is to call in some reinforcements. You're not alone in this. Talk to someone else about why you're stuck. Putting it into words will clarify the problem and help you find solutions. If you don't know why you're stuck, try telling someone specifically what you're trying to write and brainstorm a little with them. There are always multiple ways to say whatever you're working on. Try batting a couple of approaches around verbally and see if it goes over the block. The wackiest brainstorm ideas sometimes turn into just the unexpected twist you were looking for.

Finally, remember the fundamentals. Write an outline. It may be as simple as, "Get stick. Beat Black Spider with stick. Bring Spider's legs to Grog." It's not pretty, but it's a start. Now you can edit each of those sentences into the right voice and tone. Voila! You've made progress.

9.7   Exercises

1. Brainstorm seven different ways of having an NPC orc tell a player they've taken a wrong turn and need to go back.

2. Spend ten minutes editing a writing exercise you produced from a previous chapter.

3. Write a basic outline for a collection quest.

4. Estimate how long it takes you to write 12 lines of dialog for one of your favorite characters (an original character or one you know well from another property). Now time yourself writing 12 lines of unique dialog for that character and compare the actual time with the estimate.

5. Write a list of ten positive things about yourself and your writing for use when the demons start shouting you into paralysis.

10

Writing for All Audiences

Beth A. Dillon

As the game industry grows, the new line is "games are for everyone." This doesn't just refer to housewives playing casual games on the Web. The 2007 poll data from AOL Games and The Associated Press revealed that 80% of kids between the ages of 4 and 17 play video games, 38% of adults play video games of some form, and 42% of self-described "hardcore" gamers are female. Well, so much for the 18–25 male target audience in North America. Of course this audience still dominates the market, but there are many opportunities to work on games for other types of players.

As a writer, you should consider a multifaceted audience. Although the kind of players you're writing for will likely depend on the genre of game, you have a role in pushing a game beyond its typical genre limitations. Often, you'll enter a project after design decisions have been made, but there are still steps you can take. If you're fortunate enough to be a full-time team member who gets design input or even if you're brought on later in the project, you'll get mileage out of audience-based research.

For insight on meeting player expectations and how an audience generally evaluates a game, read Rhianna Pratchett's "The Needs of the Audience" chapter of *Game Writing: Narrative Skills for Videogames*. For specifics on writing for localization, which has its own challenges considering the very differences behind cultural concepts of play and transferability of language, see Tim Langdell's "Beware of the Localization" chapter in the same book.

In the meantime, there are several points of advice to take from game writers who have been there and done that. Above all, research, research, and research some more. Whether you're writing a tutorial or dialog for a character, take the time to know who you're writing for and about. If you have the resources, hold mini focus groups with your audience or people who can inspire your writing content and style.

10.1   Age

Don't assume you know what you're talking about or what's considered cool to demographics you don't belong to. In my case, I don't even know if it's still cool to say "cool." Game writer Eric Hull worked on a cell-phone game targeted at teenagers. After taking some wrong turns, they figured out that they need to fill the writing with self-conscious humor and a casual tone, but they avoided using slang, knowing it would seem out of date quickly. The team also found they had to avoid anything in the vein of marketing or self-promotion, since kids these days are increasingly conscious of being sold to. They ran a focus group to weed out the flat jokes from the ones that hit with their audience, and they noticed a considerable thunk with anything based on pre-90's popular culture.

When writing content for games directed at teenagers, you'll need to immerse yourself in their popular culture—everything from movies and television to music and clothing. This is very important for games that use humor to nail jokes, but also for character development. Your audience should identify with the player character. This can be said for any target age group.

For audiences over 35, character development is often left by the side because many of the games fall under the casual genre. Web games such as the classic *Bejeweled* have created a standard for playability. The hugely successful Nintendo DS series *Brain Age* focused mainly on the game mechanics and quick fun activities that promised to increase brain activity. However, games like *Diner Dash* and *Puzzle Pirates* have shown how to merge narrative elements with casual game mechanics. The characters are easily understood, and the gameplay relates to a larger theme.

Hull also worked on a game for this audience, but the demographic was specifically predominately female, and more rural than urban. Right away, the term "casual" seemed useless—many players of casual games are actually hardcore about their play. They had no desire to know or learn technical jargon or a complicated user interface. He took some helpful advice away with him. First and foremost, present the gameplay in the first three minutes—no paragraphs of intro text setting up the story and no extensive cutscene dialog to wade through. Let your player leave at any time—give auto-saves and exits at the players' whims without a user interface to negotiate with or penalties for leaving. Players may be there to play and win, but they aren't necessarily there to beat each other—avoid teasing and aggression, and instead provide cooperative mechanics and supportive, funny, self-deprecating text and characters.

On the other side of the age spectrum, the same can mostly be said for young children. Cooperative family gameplay is preferred, with humor both for the child and the possible adult playing as well. Simple characters and dialog make for a fun experience. Write characters that can work together and keep the emphasis on straightforward progression with flexibility in the selection and re-playability of levels. Although these are matters of game design more than game writing, your writing can influence how the game is perceived. *Lego Star Wars* is a prime example of a fun game that parents can play with their children. Ultimately, games for this age aim for immediate visual and audio reactions to controller functions and forgiving gameplay with abstracted player character health that never ends in "game over." You're responsibility is to find ways to keep the writing simple and fun, such as in the *Dragon Tales* hide-and-seek game or *Winnie the Pooh* on Gameboy. You'll also want to find ways to justify the player being able to replay levels or choose any level within unlocked tiers.

A real task is getting together a game that appeals across several ages. I've seen a 7-year-old girl, 13-year-old girl, and 14-year-old boy all playing *Fusion Frenzy* and equally enjoying it. In the game, you get to choose from different pre-made teenage-looking characters of different genders and compete in a tournament of fast-paced casual games. The context of the competition and the ability to test play a game with simple instructions before playing it for points seemed to be the most supportive features to cross the age divide.

For age-oriented games, the trick is to get the point across quickly and accurately, to not waste anyone's time or lose anyone's attention. A little bit of humor doesn't hurt either, so long as you're not making jokes only you find funny, and you can localize easily.

10.2   Gender

As of the 2005 Independent Game Developers Association (IGDA) demographics survey, 88.5% of game developers are male. It should be no surprise, then, why game titles still tend to favor the male demographic. Even when females are acknowledged as a market, again, it's the "middle-aged rural housewife" targeted for casual games, understandably so, though, since publishers like PopCap Games say 60% of their players are female.

Simple steps can be taken in any game typically targeted at the male audience to make them more accessible to females. Repeatable tutorial levels can be one possible key to give female players, and players new to the controls in general, a chance to learn the technology without fear of affecting the saved game. If you can't get that change made in the design, then at least think about the wording of the manual. Freelance game writer Wendy Despain recommends using "her" instead of "him" occasionally, when referring to the player in text found in the manual or promotional materials, or avoid assigning a gender at all.

In games intended to appeal to both genders, it can simply be a matter of including more material with female representation. Interactive music-based games such as *Guitar Hero* and *Rock Band* include songs by female artists but could add even more, at least as extra downloads. Here again is a genre of game where it's safe to refer to the player as female. Slanting some of the clever quotes on loading screens toward females will tell them the game is acknowledging them as players as well.

Often when young girls are given the opportunity to design their own games, they're mostly concerned with narrative. In my own workshops with indigenous

First Nations and Native American youth, the girls have been more enthusiastic about game engines that allow them to make role-playing games, so much so that they often don't bother with the technology but instead spend most of their time writing out the characters and story of the game. Similar points have come up in workshops by academics such as Magy Seif El-Nasr and Mary Flanagan. This can be particularly helpful for game writers to know, since all of that dreamy writing you do will get read by someone out there if it's put in this audience's hands. This is not to say that the same doesn't apply to some male audiences as well, but young girls consider it a requirement. Writing can be cleverly embedded as optional reading on objects placed throughout a game. The trick is to be non-invasive so that players can choose if they want to spend the time reading all of the personal diaries of the characters.

This can also be the case for other game genres. *Click! Urban Adventure* is a mixed-reality game that was developed by Carnegie Mellow University in 2005. Betsy DiSalvo and other team members wrote a narrative that the girls would uncover, or not, built around a pop-star high school student who is involved in a battle-of-the-bands mystery. When girls were brought in for playtesting and participatory design, the game took a new direction to concern real-world issues such as water quality and interpersonal relationships between the characters. Most notably, the personal histories of each character were at the forefront of the story.

Certainly, most female characters in games aren't given much of a story, so much as cleavage and tight clothing, and probably a wicked weapon or fighting move. Most are stuck in the sidekick role, such as the eerie virtual projection of Cortana in the *Halo* series. The tradition of *Tomb Raider*'s Lara Croft has continued in games such as *Blood Rayne* and *Heavenly Sword*. Chances are you're not going to have complete control over the physical appearance of characters like these as a writer, but you can at least make her sound smart. Humor is often the best medicine.

So what are females looking for in a player character anyway? When I asked a 13-year-old girl if she always chose the girl in the pink outfit on *Fusion Frenzy* because she wore pink, she practically scoffed at me. "No, I don't like pink. I play her because she looks edgy and I like her hair cut," which was, notably, a short punk spiked style. So there you have it. Not all females like the color pink, and putting a game in pink wrapping isn't going to change its inaccessibility to female players.

Furthermore, shooting isn't a no-no for girls; they just want a good enough reason for why they're doing it. One of the members of the Terra Nova blog game researchers guild brought up why he couldn't get his wife to play *World of Warcraft* (*WoW*). Her first quest was to go kill animals and collect a body part from them, a very common quest type in *WoW*, but when she killed her first one, it didn't have that body part to loot. She didn't get why the animal wouldn't have that very necessary body part on it and why she had to kill it if it didn't have what she needed anyway. Moments like these are in part due to the wonderful programming that goes into random item spawn. It's not that killing is an issue; it's that it just doesn't make sense to do it without purpose. As a writer, you get to see to it that if the player has to kill someone or something, there's a good story why and adequate follow-up afterwards.

In addition, be conscious of how the wording turns out in any game you work on, particularly those with Barbie-like imagery or activities such as exercise and locations such as gyms. Games that could potentially add to body-image issues are not fun to play. Games like *Wii Sports*, particularly the Wii Fitness test, incorporate exercise in a way that's not gender-specific. The writing mostly relates to instructions and responses to your standings in the activities, which are always supportive, even if you miss ("Homerun!" and "Nice try").

Really, here, the key can be not trying to write specifically for females, but rather to write in a way that remains open to everyone and doesn't turn gender into a fetish to be exploited. If your game doesn't have the room for characters to be at the forefront, then consider small ways you can add to the overall experience of the game that will appeal to all genders.

10.3   Ethnicity

During the "Top Ten Game Research Findings" session at the 2007 Game Developers Conference, a study titled "Self-Portrayal in a Simulated Life" pointed out that the majority of players polled had a desire for more diverse game characters in positive roles. Certainly, commercial games are not completely devoid of diversity, but when you look closer at the roles of these characters and the writing that goes into them, it's hard to find a racially diverse player character *hero*.

If you're all for players making their own choices, try working on games that fit into genres with character customization. Just make sure that someone on the team asks for a variety of physical builds, facial builds, skin tones, hair colors and styles, eye colors and styles, and so on. The most ironic part of the Electronic Arts *NHL* series is the apparent lack of First Nations-friendly skin tones, even though hockey is very popular among that demographic in Canada. *Saints Row* features several options, understanding it's a gang game set in a city based on Detroit and Chicago. *Oblivion*, a role-playing game in the *Elders Scrolls* series, has the widest range of options and also includes fantasy-based races.

Races (or rather species in some cases) that are fictional are often still based on real races. *World of Warcraft* draws from several ethnicities, incorporating everything from trolls with Jamaican accents to dwarves with Scottish accents. *WoW* can get away with this usage because the characters are cartoons and the representations create ethical implications of the killing and gathering quests that remain a staple for fantasy-themed massively multiplayer online games. You'll face limitations in creating your own fictional language or accents if your game includes voiceovers or special fonts. Even using existing languages can be a strain, but there are clever devices such as opening dialog in the heritage language and then gradually shifting to the main language of your audience, which will depend on your game's localization.

For games with multiple character-selection options for cooperative or competitive play, you can include diverse characters, but this use of ethnicity is often tied to character skills, abilities, traits, stats, and so on. Examples of this can be found in the past with games such as *Gauntlet* and *Diablo 2*, but also in more recent titles including *The Warriors* and *Tony Hawk's Pro Skater 2*. Although the lead character in *Obscure* is a Caucasian teenage male, some of the other characters are left open-ended. When you determine aspects such as a character's appearance, background story, and interests, you're also going to identify what makes them different from each of the other characters. Players end up choosing the value of a character's play on what they're able to do. It's easy here to fall into stereotyping abilities based on race, so carefully consider the implications of your writing. Find real people to inspire your characters.

Even when writing sidekicks, where most racially diverse characters get slotted, take care in rounding out their personalities. Of course, don't expect the programmers on the team to read your lengthy background stories. However, taking the time to work on the context of a character even just for you will make writing dialog and actions more natural later on. Sergeant Johnson in *Halo* is remembered as a solid heroic sidekick, in part due to the decisions he makes and his honorable assistance up until his death in *Halo 3*.

The overall cast of characters can also influence impressions of sidekicks. In *Darkwatch*, the juxtaposition of Tala, the femme fatale Native American, and Cassidy Sharpe, the good-willed Caucasian blonde cowgirl, creates a very apparent good vs. evil/white vs. Native simplification of the characters. If you choose to side with Tala, who you've been seduced into biting, you end up remaining a vampire, but if you follow Cassidy, who tragically dies and continues as a spectral guide, you redeem yourself. The actions of the characters are just as important as their appearances and abilities.

In some cases, character appearances can lend to racial ambiguity. Particularly in Japanese games, such as the *Pokemon* series and *Oni*, the characters tend to lean between Asian and Caucasian features and draw from manga-style modes of expression. This is certainly a style in and of itself, but ambiguity dips into other games as well. Torque in *The Suffering* is left anonymous in his background, other than that you as the player determine whether he murdered his family or was framed based on your negative or positive actions throughout gameplay until the revealing cutscene at the end. Throughout the *Halo* series, the main player character Master Chief is fully covered in armor with his face covered. However, in an excerpt of a book based on the games, one of the writers described him as "white" beneath the armor. This is a case where the character could have been left completely ambiguous, but writing had a direct impact on the character's racial representation. With characters that are left ambiguous in their appearance, it is up to the writer to make the decision whether to maintain ambiguity or determine ethnicity. In some cases, ambiguity is a preference. Master Chief may have been better left ambiguous so that players could identify closer with him if race impacted that connection.

In any genre you're writing for, it's certainly viable to look back at stories told before us and find ways to transform them into games or take methods of telling stories and use them in games. In this way, ethnicity can be represented beyond characters. In *Okami*, for instance, you play as a wolf from Japanese myth. The cultural inspiration enriches the cutscenes, interactions with non-player characters, art style, and game mechanics. Ethnicity is naturally embedded when it is approached holistically and has an opportunity to influence every feature of a game rather than simply serve as a layer over some of the characters.

Tips

- **Consider every aspect of game writing.** What game writers are tasked with can change from project to project. Think about what you as a writer are likely to be able to influence.

- **Follow script and design document templates.** Check out other chapters in this book for insight on how to structure your documents.

- **Try different audiences.** Don't just go with an audience you know you're already prepared to write for. Push yourself to research a new audience and see where it takes you.

- **Go for one game that appeals to multiple audiences.** Push yourself to change the writing of a game so that it works for different audiences without creating a narrowed niche market.

10.4 Accessibility

Game accessibility in regard to players with disabilities often hinges on interface and hardware design. *Game Over*, put together by the University of Crete, was developed as the most universally inaccessible game to provide insight on 20 suggested guidelines for making games accessible. Just some of these guidelines include adjustable game speed, enemy speed, game graphics, sound effects, music, and speech, as well as captions using text and graphics. Although fully redefinable controls and compatibility with alternative controls for players with mobility impairments will likely be the main factors for accessibility, there are still contributions you as a writer can make. For example, you may be involved in joining audio and visual writing in both the game space and in manuals.

As has been brought up before for other audiences, you should use simple wording and easy-to-understand directions both in the game and in the manual. This is relevant to all players, but it takes on new meaning when approaching, for example, cognitive disabilities such as dyslexia. Attention to detail is essential in game menus but also adds to enjoyment in dialog and cutscenes. Michelle Hinn, who heads up the IGDA Game Accessibly SIG, adds, "You'll want to allow someone to *easily* turn these features on and off. So you might consider tying in game menu navigation as something that is even more important so that gamers can know that these features are in the game and that they can turn them on or off. It doesn't make sense to add accessibility when you make it impossible for people to find out about the features."

Place your dialog to give audio cues during gameplay, but also have text written as subtitles. You'll want to consider how a voice actor can concisely alert the visually impaired of actions and locations relative to what they're doing in the game at any given moment. Hinn advises giving attention to "the differences between subtitling and captioning. Captioning includes all ambient sound (especially when hearing what is going on is the only way to know what to do) and captioning through the cutscenes. Subtitling is just concerned with the dialog." Both will be relevant but should be considered separate efforts.

Additionally, you will need to think about how choices made to support blind players may affect the accessibility for the hearing-impaired. There is much room for creativity in this field as it grows, but in any choice you make, it will be essential to playtest and put the gameplay (the fun part) at the forefront of any game.

10.5   Conclusion

Attention to your audience's needs and taking the time to research or work with focus groups and playtesting groups can make the difference for an enriched game experience in any genre and for any audience. Whether you're writing to address a specific audience or appeal to all audiences, your focus will be on honing your craft and understanding your audience.

Your role as a writer is ultimately to communicate with the players and add to the design in a way that makes the game more enjoyable for them.

10.6   Exercises

1. Take one of your favorite video games and imagine it in light of a different audience. Rewrite anything you want to—from character background stories to dialog to player tutorial text. After you do this, ask yourself: Has the genre of the game changed? If so, in what ways? What does this mean for an audience-specific game?

2. Take a video game that you feel has poor localization, low-quality writing, or a general lack of appeal to multiple audiences. Go step by step identifying each aspect you as a writer would be able to change and rewrite the game without changing the genre or overall story.

11

Writers in the Recording Studio

Haris Orkin

11.1 Does Good Voice Acting Even Matter?

Nintendo's *Zelda* games tell their stories with text. There's no voice acting other than the occasional grunt, groan, or strange excited fairy laugh. Yet the stories are still epic, emotional, and immersive. If those games are just fine without voices, why do we need voice acting in games at all? Well, to be honest, we don't, just like silent films don't need sound to be funny, moving, or exciting. But times change, technology continues to march forward, and different kinds of games and stories require different techniques in the telling. As games become more like films in the complexity of their characters, they require a greater sophistication in the writing, the dialog, and especially in the voice acting.

The days of drafting voice actors from the ranks of artists, programmers, and level designers are long gone. To spend millions of dollars developing a game, creating a story, crafting the artwork, perfecting the programming, and then spend too little money and time on the voice acting is more than counterproductive; it's a disaster. Yet, that is exactly what many developers have done over the years.

So why does it really matter? After all, we've all played popular best-selling games with horrible voice acting. We grit our teeth and get through it because the game itself is so much fun. But who knows how many more units they would have sold and how many more people they would have reached if the acting and the story rivaled the quality of the game play.

The best designers have always known the importance of good writing and voice acting. Their mission is to create immersion. Games can achieve this in ways movies can't even begin to dream of. With atmosphere, environment, sound, and most importantly, interaction, the player becomes a participant, not a viewer. One way to help this process along is to create strong, complex, and engaging characters. We want the player to form an emotional attachment to the characters, just as they would watching a movie or reading a novel.

Good voice acting can instantly create indelible characters. Bad voice acting can have exactly the opposite effect. Nothing can wrench a player from the reality of a gameworld faster than a beautiful elf princess who sounds like she grew up in Newark, New Jersey (unless, of course, it's a fantasy adventure set in Newark, New Jersey).

11.2   Why Do So Many Games Have Such Terrible Voice Acting?

Audio Atrocities is a website dedicated to "the study and enjoyment" of terrible video game voice acting. Clearly, this has been a problem since the first audio file was inserted into the very first video game. Sometimes the problem is the dialog itself. If it is stiff or stilted or awkward or just plain embarrassing, not even a great actor can save it. For the purposes of this particular chapter, we're going to assume that the dialog in question is snappy, witty, believable, and smart. So, if the dialog is serviceable, why is the voice acting in games so often less than stellar? Well, for one thing, quite a few game developers and producers aren't experienced or educated in the area of acting, directing, or drama. It's possible that some of them literally can't tell the difference between good and bad voice acting. Or maybe they don't believe it's all that important. They know people don't buy games for the voice acting, so why sweat the small stuff? Of course, the biggest bugaboo is probably the budget. Many publishers only allocate a tiny part of the budget to this part of the process. They don't want to spend the money necessary to hire union voice talent. They don't want to hire a casting director or a professional voice director, so they'll make do with either the audio engineer or one of the designers. Once in the studio, they'll go with the first or second take, whether it's working or not. All those decisions affect the final product. Of course, you can hire a slew of Hollywood stars, rent the best studio in town, spend a fortune, and still end up with lame voice acting. Blowing money doesn't necessarily guarantee quality. So what *can* developers do to ensure that the voice acting in their hot new game doesn't cause players all over the world to wince?

Before we get into the specifics, I'd like to give some props to games that do have great voice acting. There were a few early games with fantastic voice acting. Some of these include *Fallout* (Interplay, 1997), *StarCraft* (Blizzard, 1998), *Wing Commander II* (Origin, 1991), and *Sacrifice* (Interplay, 2000). Luckily, the tide is turning and voice acting in games has improved dramatically over the last few years. Publishers are beginning to understand its importance, because they know it affects their bottom line. And because the bar has been lifted, players are demanding better voice acting as well.

Whether a game is realistic sci-fi, fantasy, contemporary crime drama, or whimsical comedy, they all have one thing in common. The acting is authentic, truthful, real. This chapter will examine how to raise the level of acting above the majority of games.

Here are some recent (and fairly recent) games that were praised by critics and players alike for doing it right. Play them if you haven't already. Listen to the voices.

- *Half-Life 2* (Valve, 2004)

- *Kingdom Hearts* (Square, 2002)

- *God of War* (Sony, 2005)

- *F.E.A.R.* (Monolith, 2006)

- *No One Lives Forever* (Monolith, 2000)

- *Splinter Cell* (Ubisoft, 2003)

- *Knights of the Old Republic* (BioWare, 2003)

- *Indigo Prophecy* (Quantic Dream, 2005)

- *Psychonauts* (Double Fine, 2005)

- *Company of Heroes* (Relic, 2006)

- *Dawn of War* (Relic, 2004)

- *Max Payne* (Remedy, 2001)

- The *Grand Theft Auto* series (Rockstar North)

- *Gun* (Neversoft, 2005)

- *Dreamfall: The Longest Journey* (Funcom, 2006)

- *Bioshock* (2K, 2007)

These are all games with inspired voice acting. I'm sure I neglected to mention many other fine games with great voice acting, but at least this list will begin to point you in the right direction. It's hard to know how to judge your work without a standard to measure it against.

11.3 Casting

George Lucas said, "The most important part of directing is casting." Academy Award–winning director John Frankenheimer said, "Casting is sixty-five percent of directing."

Pick the right voice actor and you're most of the way home. But where do you find the best voice actors? Hopefully, the producer will hire a qualified casting director to facilitate the process, but the writer still needs to be involved. No one understands the characters and tone better than the writer.

Union or Non-Union

Professional voice actors in the United States belong to the Screen Actors Guild (SAG) and/or the American Federation of Television and Radio Artists (AFTRA). Both SAG and AFTRA have interactive agreements. In the United Kingdom, Australia, and New Zealand, voice actors belong to Actors' Equity. In Canada, they're members of the Alliance of Canadian Television and Radio Actors (ACTRA).

For union members to work for your company, your company needs to be a signatory to the union. This costs nothing in itself, but down the line, if for any reason your company decides to use non-union talent, they could eventually find themselves in hot water. For this reason, game developers/publishers often contract with production studios/entities who are themselves signatories. You can contact SAG or AFTRA (or ACTRA) directly for information on rules and minimum fees for actors.

The biggest benefit of using union talent is probably obvious. The best voice actors in the business are union actors. This includes, of course, stars and celebrities. Union members aren't supposed to do non-union projects, so if you want to hire a star or a celebrity, every other voice you cast will have to be union talent as well. Union voiceover actors are consummate professionals. They're quick and they're good and you'll be out of the studio much faster than you would if you used less experienced talent. They can usually play multiple roles, and the chances of having to re-cast or re-record will be greatly reduced. So, even though you may have to pay union talent more up front, you could conceivably save quite a bit of money on the back end.

The other benefit of using union talent comes during the casting process. For the most part, voiceover agents only handle union talent. Agents make the entire casting process much less work intensive. You can email them audition scripts (also known as sides—a sample is included in Appendix D), and they will take care of the auditions. They will audition the actors they feel will best suit the roles. They will then put all the auditions on a CD or email them to you as an MP3. There are voice agents all across the country (and the world) and in most of the major cities. The largest agencies with the top talent, however, are in Los Angeles, New York, Chicago, Vancouver, Toronto, London, Sydney, and Auckland.

There are a number of online services that allow you to audition union talent (and non-union in some cases). One of the largest and most successful is http://www.voicebank.com. You simply go online, select the talent agencies you desire, and upload the sides and any casting specs (casting specs are documents that describe who the characters are: age, sex, accent, all the details). This service isn't free, but it can be cost-effective when you consider the price of renting a recording studio and holding your own auditions.

If you decide to use non-union talent, the casting process is quite a bit different. First of all, you need to find actors to come in and audition. In Los Angeles and New York, you can place an ad in one of the local casting publications. Currently, the most well-known are *Back Stage* and *Back Stage West*. Both have online sites. There are also a number other online casting resources. One of the most well-known is http://www.breakdownservices.com. Then there is always the ubiquitous http://www.craigslist.org.

You will have no problem finding willing actors by going this route. The problem will be separating the wheat from the chaff. One way to do this is to hire a casting director who is knowledgeable in this area. They do charge a fee, and in the end, it may make more sense to go the union-talent route.

Handling Casting and Audition Materials

Whether you hire a casting director or handle it all on your own, you're going to need to do the proper preparation and put together an information package. This should include the full script and a breakdown of the script. The breakdown delineates the number of characters in the script and the number of actors required. Many times actors will play multiple roles. The current AFTRA interactive agreement allows actors to play three roles for each half-day they are contracted (with additional fees for additional voices). Unions in other countries have their own rates and rules. For instance, in the United Kingdom, voice actors are hired by the day, not by the voice.

You'll need to figure out how many lines each character has and whether they will be doing them alone or as part of an ensemble. This will help determine how long you'll need each actor in the studio and how much he or she will need to be paid.

This information package should also include detailed character descriptions and artwork to show the talent what the characters look like in-game. A short biography of each major character is essential. If the character is supposed to sound like a particular star or celebrity, put that down as well. You will also need audition scripts (sides). These are monologues that bring out all facets of each character. No more than one or two monologues per character should be included. Keep the monologues fairly short. The longer each audition is, the more time it'll take you to record it and listen back.

Choosing the Talent

As the writer, you may not be consulted as to the final casting decisions (especially if the publisher wants to go the celebrity route), but if you are, here are some things to keep in mind.

You should be there for the callbacks. Have the actors show you all the different characters they can do. You're usually not casting one actor for one part but for multiple parts. You'll want a vivid contrast between different characters and different voices within each scene. Keep in mind what the in-game characters look like. You want the voices to match the artwork. But remember that these are voiceover actors: they don't have to look the part and, in fact, rarely do. Young can play older, old can play younger, women can play boys, and men can play women. The only limit is your imagination.

Since you know the script, you know which characters interact with each other (something the casting director may not be cognizant of). You don't want to cast an actor in two roles where he has to perform against himself. Occasionally, because of logistics, there's no way around it. Hopefully, the actor's various voices are different enough, but this is never an optimal situation. Also, ideally you don't want the same actor playing different characters in contiguous scenes.

So how do you choose who to use in the end? If your casting or voice director has worked with the actor in question and recommends them for their professionalism and talent, I would take their advice. In the end, it's all subjective, a gut decision. Just as you have to trust your gut when you're writing, you have to trust your gut in terms of casting and acting. Do they feel right? Do you believe them? When you close your eyes, do you see the character you imagined in your mind's eye? Or maybe the voice talent is doing something far different from what you imagined, but much, much better. Be open to that as well. In the final analysis, it's a leap of faith. When you've had more experience, it's less of a leap, but casting is not an exact science. Until you're in the recording studio, all bets are off.

11.4   Creating Scripts for Voiceover Actors

Most contemporary game writers/designers work in Microsoft Excel to create their scripts. Every line has its own specific code number, to facilitate placement by programmers and the audio team.

Some developers have their own proprietary software for creating game scripts. BioWare uses a conversation scripting tool that keeps audio tracks of all the thousands of words they use in their NPC conversations. They're in the form of dialog trees and allow comments that delineate the character's emotional state. The *Neverwinter Nights* toolset also allows for the creation of dialog.

Voice actors will need their own version of the script. It should be in a format actors are more comfortable with. The script should be clear, simple, and easy to read. It's possible to reformat an Excel script and enlarge it to make it more actor friendly. The IGDA Game Writing SIG has a sample of how to do this and still keep the script in Excel. It's included in Appendix A, and for more discussion of this topic, see Chapter 2.

For cinematic scripts, many writers use a commercial screenwriting program such as Final Draft or Screenwriter. Whatever format is used, the point is to make the recording process easier for the voiceover actor. The recording session will move faster, saving both time and money. This script is also intended to facilitate the voice director's job. There should be areas where the director, the audio engineer, and the writer can make notes on each take.

11.5 Working with a Voice Director

If the developer/publisher hires a professional voice director, there's still an important place for the writer in the recording studio. Some developers, publishers, and voice directors prefer not to have the writer present. They're afraid the writer will complain and ask endless questions and request useless takes and basically slow the whole process down. Don't be one of those writers. If you do your job correctly, the recording process will go smoothly and quickly, and the quality will improve exponentially.

First, remember that you are not the voice director. If you have a note or a concern or a suggestion, give it the director. The director should be the only one who talks to the actors. It's confusing for actors to hear notes from multiple sources. Let the director do the directing. You should be making notes on each take and marking your favorites.

So, if you're not doing any directing, why are you even there?

Because you are the guardian of the truth, the tone, and the story.

Ernest Hemingway said, "The most essential gift for a good writer is a built-in, shock-proof shit detector." As a writer, you need to know when your writing isn't good enough or rings false. You need that same internal compass when you're listening to actors deliver your lines. Academy Award–winning actor James Cagney once offered a nervous young actor the following advice. "Walk in, plant yourself, look the other fellow in the eye, and tell the truth."

Acting is about truth. Whether the actor is playing an alien from another planet, a dwarf with a battle axe, or a fairy princess with a lisp, the player wants to believe. As the writer, one of your jobs is make sure every line rings true. Yes, it's subjective and you can't get obsessive about this or you will be booted out of the studio, but you can definitely help keep everyone on the right path.

One concrete way you can help is to give the voice director and the actor the context of the scene. The basic context and intent for every line should be indicated in the script, but often it's helpful to offer more detail. Make sure the actors understand exactly who they are, where they are, who they're talking to, and why they're talking to them. Are they outside? On a horse? In a saloon? In a bathtub? Are they talking to one person? Are they are talking quietly, so as not to be overheard? Or are they addressing a crowd? Are they chasing someone through a forest? Through a sewer? How far away is the person they're addressing? Five feet? Ten feet? Fifty feet? By setting the scene and describing the context, you can help to ensure a more believable and powerful performance.

Some actors, especially older actors, aren't very video game savvy. They have no clue what the finished product will look or sound like. As much as you try to explain it, they can't quite grasp the context. The best thing to do is to show them videos, trailers, and an actual game demo, if it's available. If not, you can demonstrate (and show them how to play) a similar game. This can get them excited and help them to understand the final result everyone is working towards.

Beyond the truth, the writer is also the guardian of the tone. What exactly is the "tone"? It's the story's personality, and it's reflected by everything in the world. Usually the lead designer, lead artist, and writer will come together to collaborate on a consistent tone. If the tone changes through the game or movie or book, the effect is jarring. It pulls the player/audience out of the story and derails the suspension of disbelief. Consider the tone of *F.E.A.R.* (Monolith, 2004) compared to the tone of *Serious Sam* (Croteam, 2001) or *Call of Duty* (Infinity Ward, 2003). All three are first-person shooters, but each has its own specific tone. *F.E.A.R.* is a supernatural horror story mixed with a military action plot, while *Call of Duty* is military action in a realistic historical setting. *Serious Sam* is anything but serious. The wild, speedy gameplay matches the screwy dialog and characters. Your job is to make sure that each voice actor is playing a consistent part in the same story. If the performances are getting too maudlin or too broad, too silly or too serious, you need to let the voice director know. A good voice director should already be on the same page, but sometimes an actor can be so entertaining and charming that the voice director is seduced into accepting a performance that doesn't fall within the tone.

As the writer, you are one of the few people keeping the entire equation of the story in your head. The voice director only knows what you tell him and can never know the script as intimately as the writer. At all times, you should know what is happening visually, physically, and emotionally. Since in most cases, you're only recording one voice talent at a time, the actor needs to know not only who they're playing against but the intention and emotion of each line. When all the audio is inserted in the game, you want the characters who are conversing to sound like they're in the same room... or cave or submarine or rooftop. They need to inhabit the same physical and emotional space.

It's also important to make sure the characters stay consistent throughout the length and breadth of the story. Sometimes an actor is playing multiple parts, and it is easy for them to let their accent slip and become some other character. The voice director obviously needs to be cognizant of this, but so does the writer.

You also need to be vigilant in the area of relationships between the various characters. All the relationships must make sense and stay as consistent as the individual characterizations. If Bill hates Sally at the start of the story and always gives her an attitude and that attitude changes as he learns to respect her, that change needs to be reflected in the performances. As the writer, you know better than anyone how each relationship changes and grows, and you need to make sure that it all stays on track.

Every story has its own rhythm and momentum. Excitement builds. Characters change. They grow braver. Or more cowardly. They pull together. They splinter. Your job is to make sure that the actors are reflecting the reality of the story as it progresses. Since most of the dialog is recorded out of sequence, it is easy for everyone involved to veer off the continuity highway. If that starts to happen, you need to grab the wheel.

Occasionally, actors will improvise additional lines, and that's to be encouraged. When actors make the lines their own, they often make them feel more real. This is great, as long as they don't derail the story or turn a three-word exclamation into a long monologue. It is the writer's job to note the changes and include them in an as-produced version of the script. In most games, dialog is not just spoken but shown on the screen in subtitles. The subtitles need to reflect any changes made during recording.

For all those reasons, the writer's presence at the recording session is essential. The writer can often be an exceptional resource for the voice director and the recording engineer. Just remember that as the writer, you're not the one running the show. Time is money, and your job is to help speed things up. If your presence starts to slow things down, next time you may find yourself persona non grata.

When the Writer Is the Voice Director

Occasionally, the writer may also pull double duty as the voice director. Sometimes they have experience in this area, but for the purpose of this chapter, I'm going to assume that the writer reading this knows bupkes.

David Mamet, the award-winning playwright, screenwriter, and director, had this to say about directing. "What is the scene about? What does the protagonist want, what does he or she do to get it? The scene is over when they get it."

To play a scene properly, the actor needs to know what the character wants and needs. Someone only says or does something when they want something specific. It doesn't have to be a selfish want, though it often is. It doesn't even have to be concrete. The character could want revenge, a cup of coffee, a legendary treasure, acceptance, sympathy, love, or a bathroom. Whatever it is... every word, every statement, every action is made for a reason. Even if a character only says, "Hello," he or she says it for some purpose. Maybe he wants the person he's greeting to like him or fall in love with him. Maybe he wants to sell the person a used car. Maybe he just wants to capture the other character's attention at a party. Every word needs to be motivated. If the actor is doing a monologue, he needs to know who he's talking to. Give him someone specific. Or let the actor choose someone specific. His mother. His brother. Whoever and whatever will elicit the proper emotion. The actor needs to know his motivation before he can begin to deliver a believable performance.

Tips for Eliciting Believable Performances

Constantin Stanislavski, co-founder of the Moscow Art Theatre and one of the fathers of modern acting technique, said, "The language of the body is the key that can unlock the soul."

Stanislavski focused on the development of artistic truth onstage by teaching actors to "live the part" during performance. He created a system designed to train actors to work from the inside outward. One way to find this truth is to physically manifest actions, and those actions in turn elicit emotions. This is a very effective technique for voice actors. Voice acting is not just about using the voice but the entire body. The best voice actors are very expressive and physical. They bring that physicality to their performances.

You can help a voice actor by telling him where the character is located, where the action is taking place. Give him a physical space that he can create in his mind's eye. If he's on top of a mountain, he needs to feel the cold, hear the wind, and experience the sensation of standing over the edge of a precipice. If the actor uses his senses (or sense memory), the truth of the situation will come across in his voice. If someone is chasing him, he needs to run in place, get his heart racing, create the physical sensation of fear and flight. If he's supposed to be eating, give the actor something real to eat. If he's supposed to be reading, give him a book. You don't need him to create the actual sound effects; what you need is verisimilitude.

Sometimes an actor will get nervous and tighten up and fall back on his bag of facile tricks. Every actor has them. Sometimes they can be useful, but often they can become a crutch that causes the performances to become less visceral and more superficial.

If an actor is tense, you want to help him to relax. A relaxed actor is more likely to be in touch with what he's really feeling inside. And those emotions are the gold you are trying to mine. There are numerous relaxation techniques, and most experienced actors will know the ones that work for them. Some of the most helpful are vocal exercises, focused breathing exercises, and physical movement. Stretching. Running in place. Rolling the neck. Anything to loosen up and relieve the tension.

How you communicate with an actor will have a direct bearing on his level of relaxation. The director should always stay calm. Keep a sense of humor. You want to keep all pressure out of the recording booth. If you're frustrated, if you're nervous, don't let it show. Be positive. Be encouraging. Try to keep negativity to a minimum. Don't frown when the actor delivers something that isn't working. Everything you say or do will affect his confidence and tension level.

The exception to this is when you purposely act a certain way in order to elicit a specific response from the actor, for instance, if you purposely try to anger the actor in order to elicit believable rage. This can often work, but it can also be difficult to bring the actor back from that emotion. The technique should be used very sparingly and judiciously, if at all, especially if you don't like getting punched in the nose.

You want your actors to be good listeners. Whatever they say needs to reflect the imaginary conversation they are having with either another character or the player. You want their responses to sound spontaneous. This requires the actor to play moment to moment. He shouldn't anticipate what he's going to say next. "Happy accidents" are when the actor veers from the text, or even flubs a line, and creates a genuine emotional moment. The actor has succeeded in elevating his performance beyond the page. You want to encourage those happy accidents by not always being a slave to the text.

Improvisation can also be a great tool to help your actors to relax. They'll try the unexpected and may just come up with something brilliant. The end result can be a more believable, vulnerable, and emotional performance.

As the director, your job is to tell the actor what to do, but this must be done in an oblique manner. You need to direct... indirectly. The idea is to lead the actor towards his performance, not push him. If you give him line readings or tell him how to say it, all he'll do is mimic you. You want the performance to come from an authentic and emotional place within the actor. Every writer hears a line a certain way in his head when he writes it. As the director, you have to let that go. You have to be open to a fresh approach. If that actor can do the line as you imagined it and still be believable, then great. But prepare to be surprised and be flexible enough to be okay with that.

Most voiceover actors use headphones, but a few prefer to avoid them. They'd rather not hear their own voice in their heads. For some actors, hearing their own voice as they perform can be a problem. When you hear radio broadcasters with that deep studied and clearly phony announcer voice, you are hearing someone who spends too much time listening to themselves annunciate. Sometimes simply asking an actor remove the headphones can really bump up the performance.

George Burns said, "Acting is all about honesty. If you can fake that, you've got it made." He was being funny, but facetious, because it's not hard to tell when actors are faking it. You don't want them pretending to be afraid, you want them to literally be out of their mind with terror, and it's your job to take them there.

A good voice actor will ask you a lot of questions. "Who am I talking to?" "What do I want?" "What is my subtext?"

Don't panic if an actor asks you that last question. As the writer, you should know the subtext better than anyone. Good dialog often has another level to it, an underlying or implicit meaning. For example, a woman could ask a man to come inside for some coffee after a date, when in reality she's asking him to come inside for a reason that has nothing to do with hot caffeinated beverages. A scene in Woody Allen's movie *Annie Hall* (United Artists, 1977) in which subtitles explain the characters' inner thoughts during an apparently innocuous conversation is an example of the subtext of a scene being made explicit. As the voice director, you want to make sure that the subtext is coming through.

How to Direct Celebrities

Celebrities come in all shapes and sizes and temperaments. Some are just regular folks who want to be treated like everybody else. They'll stay and work until the job's done and will give you no attitude at all. Others are *all* attitude. It's always good to be deferential without necessarily being an ass kisser, but always be prepared to pucker up. Celebrities usually come with handlers or an entourage, so be prepared. It's often helpful to befriend the handlers. If you get them on your side, they'll do a better job of helping you out with their meal ticket. Some celebrities are a little prickly about being directed. You need to handle celebrities with a large and cushy pair of kid gloves. Often you may not be able to request many takes. Be prepared to get what you need in one or two. A few celebrities regard video games with disdain, like they're slumming. Don't take it personally. Stay professional. The more you can get them excited about the game, the better their attitude will be. Show them videos, artwork, and the actual game if it's available as a demo. Mainly, you just want them to understand the context of the gameworld and the character they'll be playing.

Usually, you can't expect that celebrities will return to make any corrections, so you need to be especially diligent to get it right the first time. Don't act like a fawning fan. Don't invade their personal space. Personally, I don't even think you should ask for autographs. If there's a voice director there, you may not even need to engage the celebrity at all, except perhaps to offer to answer any questions they may have about the script.

Just remember that they're just people. If you find yourself getting nervous or flustered in the presence of a star, try the old trick of imagining them without any clothes on. Unless you're working with Jabba the Hut. Then you probably don't want to do that.

How to Direct Non-Actors

Non-actors require the same kid gloves you were using for the celebrities. First of all, they'll probably be very nervous. Step in a recording booth sometime with ten people watching you through the glass. It's intimidating. So you need to relax them. Take the pressure off. Talk to them for a bit. Show them artwork. Show them the game. Get them excited about the process. Sometimes it's helpful to direct them from inside the booth, so that you're not talking to them through the glass. This is especially true when you work with children. With young children, it's sometimes helpful to arrange the microphone very low, so they can stand or sit on the ground. Sit next to them. Have their parents in there as well. If the kids are too young to read, you're going to need to read to them and have them repeat the line back to you. With preschool kids, it's perfectly acceptable to give them line readings.

It's often helpful to have non-actors turn the script over and forget about it. Have them ignore the words on the page and simply talk to them. This is a very useful technique when you're working with professional athletes. Basically, all you're doing is interviewing them. Subtly steer them towards the main ideas in the script. Get their responses in their own words with their natural inflection. (This technique can also work well with regular voice actors who are having a problem sounding natural.) Sometimes after they've done this for a bit, they can bring that same attitude to the words on the page. You usually won't be able to do many takes with non-actors. The more takes they do, the less spontaneous they sound. Plus, they just start getting nervous, because they feel they're screwing up. You will either get what you need quickly, or you won't get it at all.

Microphone Techniques

Professional voiceover actors already know most of the microphone techniques. If you're directing a novice or a non-actor, you may need to offer a little instruction. Here are a few of the more basic techniques to remember.

Actors should stay fairly close to the microphone (between four and six inches from the mike). If they're too far away, you'll pick up too much ambient room noise, and the actor's voice will sound thin, distant, and hollow. The closer on the mike, the more intimate the sound. The exception to this is when the actor isn't talking directly to the player but to another character on the screen. If a character is supposed to be shouting to the player from a distance, they need to back off the mike and turn their head slightly before they shout. This will create the impression of calling to someone from a long way off.

They should not position the mike dead center in front of their lips. It needs be slightly to one side or the other. This helps reduce breathing into the mike and the dreaded popping of the P's. (It also allows a clear view of the script.) Certain words that start with a P or a B can create a popping sound. The actors need to be conscious of this and so does the recording engineer. Some microphones will have a wind screen to help reduce popping. The actor can move his body all he wants as long as his mouth stays the same distance from the mike and his head remains relatively stationary.

Directing Barks without Killing Your Actors

No, I'm not talking about directing the actors to bark like dogs (not that there's anything wrong with that). I'm talking about unit responses in real-time strategy games, taunts in first-person shooters, or death screams in virtually any game. Those short interjections like "Attack!" "Pull back!" "Head Shot!" "Enemy spotted!" "Regroup!" "Arrgggghhh."

The simple rule for directing barks is this: save your screaming for last. Don't fry your actor's vocal cords until the end of the session. Do the in-game dialogs or monologues before you get to the shouting. You can actually record these "barks" very quickly. Just make sure you identify each one as you proceed. Actually, the audio engineer should be putting an identifying tag on every take of every line you record. He or she will be taking notes as to favorite takes, and you should as well. This will prevent having to listen through every single take from every single session again. You'll be able to quickly play everyone's favorite takes and then make a decision.

11.6   Editing and Post-Production

Once the recording is finished, the job isn't done. Editing and post-production are required, and though writers are rarely present for this part of the process, they can contribute quite a bit. All the best dialog takes have to be chosen and edited for insertion into the game. Often, two or three different takes can be combined to create the best take of all. The writer should be there to double-check everything and make sure no words or dialog is dropped or missing. When you're dealing with thousands and thousands of recorded lines, it's very easy for something to be lost. If the character is a machine or some fantastical creature, sometimes dialog needs to be processed with a special effect. The writer can help determine if this effect adds to the performance or fits within the overall tone. Even though very few companies will pay for the writer to be involved in post-production, the writer's presence can end up being very cost effective. It's often said in Hollywood that a movie is written three times: once when the writer creates the pages, once when the directors and actors collaborate to create the scenes, and a third time, by the editor, when he cuts it all together.

11.7   Acting 101

Since this is just one chapter, I'm not about to get into a detailed description of all the schools of acting. But the more you know, the better you'll be able to communicate with actors. If you really want to direct voiceover, it's important to learn something about acting. I advise every would-be voiceover director to read books on the various schools of thought and take acting classes. Here are some recommended books on the subject written by some noted teachers.

- *Acting: The First Six Lessons* by Richard Boleslavsky.

- *Respect for Acting* by Uta Hagen.

- *An Actor Prepares* by Constantin Stanislavski.

- *Sanford Meisner on Acting* by Sanford Meisner, Dennis Longwell, and Sydney Pollack.

- *Audition: Everything an Actor Needs to Know to Get the Part* by Michael Shurtleff.

One reason it's helpful to learn about acting and directing and its particular language and jargon is so that you can effectively communicate with your voiceover talent. You need to speak their language. There are words and directions specific to acting, a shorthand that facilitates the directing process.

There is also jargon specific to recording studios and directing voiceover actors. The website http://www.voiceovers.com, an online marketplace for voice talent and another resource for casting, has a glossary of voiceover terms that would be helpful for a novice to look over. It'll help with directing the talent as well as communicating with the audio engineer.

11.8   Conclusion

There's an important place for you as the writer in the recording studio. Whether you are doing the directing or assisting a voice director, your job is to be the guardian of the truth, the tone, and the story. To hear your words finally come alive can be inspiring and exciting and sometimes horrifying. It's the moment of truth, where the rubber meets the road. You'll see what works and what doesn't, and by you being there, you'll be able to fix things on the fly.

It's one of the more gratifying and terrifying parts of the writing process. And since it's all part of the process, the writer belongs there as much as anyone. I'll close with a quote from Stanislavski. "In the creative process there is the father, the author of the play; the mother, the actor pregnant with the part; and the child, the role to be born."

11.9 Exercises

1. Pick two or three characters from a book, a movie, or a game and create casting specs that will explain the characters to actors auditioning for the part. You'll need to include basics like sex, age, and accent as well specifics like point of view and personality. It should be no longer than five sentences.

2. Find a game (or movie or animated film) that you believe has bad voice acting. Pick out a particularly egregious character and write down directions you feel would help the actor adjust their performance. Be concrete and specific. Find the language and those metaphors that will illustrate what you're looking for and get your point across. This is exactly what you need to do when you're in the studio.

3. Take one of the script samples in the appendices and create a breakdown for a voiceover recording session. List all the characters in the script. Then list the number of actors you'll need to play those characters. (Remember that SAG/AFTRA actors can play up to three characters for the same fee.) Figure out how many lines each character has and create a rough recording schedule.

4. *Bonus:* Go to http://www.voicebank.com and find actors for the roles in Exercise 3. (You'll need to pick actors who can play multiple parts.) Select House Reels, click on an agency, and listen to voiceover demos. Make a list of actors you feel would be perfect to play those particular characters.

12

Writing Tutorials, or Press Start... to Start

Andrew S. Walsh

12.1 To Begin at the Beginning—What Is a Tutorial?

A tutorial is the section of a game that teaches the player how to play. So, what does this have to do with a writer? Surely teaching the player about gameplay falls into the purview of the game designer. Well, you're a writer,[1] so put yourself in the player's shoes for a moment.

You're Tommy, a twelve-year-old male and gaming newbie. You like skates and have only ever kissed one girl in your life.[2] Finally, after months of pestering, you have a shiny, new, exciting console that your one parent, waitress mother, has scrimped and saved to buy. You're excited. You're ready to play.

The game opens, and the tutorial throws fifty control sets at you, which your hormonally overdriven, uncoordinated fingers will take a week to grasp, the controls are described in on-screen text that you don't read (because (a) you're twelve and (b) you're male), and fifteen seconds in your dream has turned to a nightmare. The game's not fun, and your minimum-wage mom won't be able to get you another one for six months without sacrificing food, or turning the heat off. The gamer has had a bad experience. The tutorial has botched its job. The game has failed. So, how can this be prevented? It's obvious, really: the game designer makes the opening level really easy, adds tutorial elements slowly, and gives the player the chance to learn at a steady, basic rate. There. Simple. Only... it's not.

Empathy exercise number two: meet Kevin. Kevin is 34, married,[3] and has been playing games since two paddles moving simultaneously made the moon landings

---

[1] If you're not a writer, pretend you are... you have to start somewhere, right?

[2] And she was your cousin, but you were six and only playing doctors and nurses...

[3] For four years. He loves his wife, but forced to choose between making love with his beloved and playing level six, then hey... his wife lives on this planet, too, and she's not going to like alien occupation, so he's going to finish this level, give her a quick squeeze, and hope she doesn't steal the duvet again.

look technologically primitive. He's played more tutorial levels than the number of millimeters middle-age spread has added to his midriff. He's spent $50 on this game, and he's going to be really unimpressed if he has to do yet another "drag yourself through baby school" tutorial.

Then in box three we have Julianne, a bored housewife, and in box four a college student called Bob, and in box five...

This is the challenge for tutorials. They must teach the player how to play, but they must do so in a way that is fun for an increasingly diverse pool of players. Aha! I hear some of you cry.[4] Aha! But all that *is* the job of the *game designer*. However, while other writers need to know their medium, to be aware of technical limits, appreciate budgets, etc., game writers really need to cozy right up to the technical aspects of games. Good game writing demands a close relationship to the game design if it is to produce a meaningful experience. If the game's design and the game narrative aren't intertwined, then the game will produce the sort of experience games are trying to put behind them, one where the narrative is meaningless to the player.

Similarly, if the game's narrative and design aren't harmonious then the game's design risks being unengaging, bland, and dull. The game narrative can help the game designer, and it can overcome the problem of introducing both Kevin and Tommy to the game by making the introduction fresh and entertaining to all parties.

So, while at the start of a narrative the writer must introduce the player to the plot, the characters, and the world, set up the protagonist's goal, create conflict, and produce a measure of narrative drive—and do all this as quickly and invisibly as possible—a writer cannot wrestle with these ingredients without taking the needs of the game designer into account.

Meanwhile, the designer's shopping list of needs requires that at the start of the game they teach the player to play, establish a difficulty curve, demonstrate the game-play style, and get into the action as quickly as possible. They must do this in a way that is clear and represents the style of gameplay found throughout the game, and they must make this experience fun.

With these competing needs it can feel like conflict will result; however, if each party supplies the other with solutions for the other's challenges then the process can be a rewarding and creative one.

12.2   Learning to Play—The Needs of the Game Player

At the start of the game, the writer's natural priority is to establish the narrative world. On the other hand, the primary aim of a tutorial is to teach the player to play. The writer's role in this is to make this experience engaging by making the learning less visible. This means that at the point a game writer is facing perhaps the trickiest section of their story, the opening, the game's design's needs will often place a large

---

[4]Yup, I'm breaking that fourth wall and reaching right out to you.

number of constraints and a stack of exposition onto the writer right at the point when the writer is trying to get the narrative out of the starting blocks.

Teaching the Player to Play

Play is composed of action, and the player's priority is to get into this action as quickly as possible. Remember that this is a *game*, so the start is not a chance to present the world's longest cinematic because you can't get a job in film. Frustrating a player's desire to play is not a good way to engage them in your story. If you choose to use a cinematic, do not forget the tutorial's main aim: to get the player playing.

The first slice of interactivity the designer serves up introduces the player to the basic controls and the effect these controls have on the gameworld. Action games, for instance, regularly open with tutorial sections where the player learns to walk then run then fight. Role-playing games often open with sections that teach the player to search their environment for objects and then how to interface with the objects they discover. This introduction is often via a series of on-screen instructions paired with in-game encounters designed to allow the player to practice. This process of instruction is often framed within an objective, something the player is told they need to achieve. This objective could be a level-design objective—do something within a time limit, travel from one place to another, or talk to some character. Such objectives are often cloaked within the narrative. While the controls are taught through text, the description of the objective is often done through dialog, in-character and cloaked by narrative. Such descriptions could take the form of a military objective presented in a briefing (*Metal Gear Solid*) or the need to get somewhere presented by circumstance (*Grand Theft Auto: San Andreas*).

Game objectives are limited. Any player who's played a number of games from the same genre will begin to notice the old favorites that come around again and again—get here, get there the fastest, blow this up, stop that getting blown up, etc. Such recognition risks making the missions both repetitive and abstract. The writer's job here is to find a way to give value to the gameplay information, thus diverting the player and creating a meaning and legitimization of their gameplay actions. So, while CJ starts with a gameplay objective—"get here"—he also has a narrative objective— "return home to meet his family."

Pressing All the Right Buttons—Controls

Put your hand up if you've played games before...okay, okay...and who's played a couple of console games that involve shooting? Aha, aha, so...put your hands out in front of you, put the book down, and imagine you're holding a controller. Now...start firing. Chances are that an exercise like this would see most people twitching the same finger. This is because designers have learned the value of continuity of controls. As such, many players who have played similar games will instinctively know the controls of another game in the same genre.

This is one reason that while a beginner needs a gentle introduction to a game, a hardcore gamer will find relearning controls to be a dull affair. The game's narrative, on the other hand is a fresh, entertaining experience for both sets of players. For the beginner, such a narrative screen is a valuable immersive tool hiding the artificial task of learning the controls. For the more advanced player, it is a lifeline that helps engage and entertain through a section of the game that would otherwise be dull.

While the writer is focused on this aspect of the game, the game designer needs to determine a beneficial pace and order with which to teach the control structure. Making such an introduction too fast or too slow will damage the game, making it frustrating to one group of players. Frustration is, obviously, bad. Frustration destroys immersion, and a joint objective of the games designer and the writer is immersion.

Difficulty Curves and Learning Curves

Aside from thinking about controls, the designer will also be concerned with establishing the game's difficulty curve. Difficulty curves are a way of plotting the way that gameplay challenges that the player faces are distributed through the game. Getting this distribution right creates a sense of progression and a balanced series of gameplay challenges. This is the reason games are generally easier at the start than the end.

At the start, the player needs an environment that allows them to learn the controls without becoming frustrated. However, once the player has learned how to interact with the gameworld, the challenges can become more difficult, thus offering an increasingly interesting and rewarding experience.

Difficulty curves are comprised of a wide range of game elements. Depending on the style of game, these elements can include challenges such as enemy types (defined by ability, weapons, moves, or relative level of intelligence), the speed of the game, or even the combination of controls a player will need to utilize to progress successfully.

Taking enemy type as an example, the table below illustrates the sort of difficulty curve to be found in a first-person shooter (FPS) title.

Weapon	1	2	3	4	5	6	7	8	9	10
Pistol	S	S	F	F	F	F				
Machine gun			R	R	S	S	F	F	F	F
Rocket launcher					R	R	S	S	F	F

R = Rare, S = Some, F = Frequent.

In the early levels, a player will have to fight a small number of enemies armed with pistols. By the middle of the game, the player will be fighting against larger and more heavily armed soldiers.

It is worth noting that in many difficulty curves, the learning and teaching does not stop at the end of the formal first-level tutorial. Instead, the player will discover new moves and opponents as the game progresses. As such, the techniques used by the writer in the tutorial section need to be taken into account by the game writer if their plot is likely to encompass evolutions of the gameplay.

The Immersion Equation

The pace and complexity of a game's tutorial is important because it relates directly to how quickly and effectively a player becomes immersed in the game world. The speed the player masters the controls = the speed they can enter the gameworld = the speed of immersion. The writer has a complementary equation: The player's lack of consciousness of learning = the depth of immersion = the success of the narrative.

The writer and designer's jobs are to frame the teaching mechanisms so that the player can learn while being entertained. Whatever the writer's and designer's choices, they need to ensure that the tutorial's style doesn't put barriers between the player and the game or the player and the story.

12.3   Opening Your Story—Narrative Concerns

This is a book on writing, so why is the writing section after the design section? This question plays into the ongoing debate about story and gameplay. How do they work together? Which is the servant of the other? Most of this debate is semantic twittering. Essentially, gameplay and game design must come first. A game is defined by gameplay because it is a game. Note that this statement says that gameplay comes first. Note that this statement does not say that story should come last. Sidelining the story will damage the design.

For a story to work in a game, the gameplay and narrative must function as intertwined entities and in harmony. While a game writer must work their story to fit the design, a designer who does not take narrative concerns into account will produce an inferior experience lacking immersion.

Gameplay comes first, but a well-constructed narrative can be its best friend.

What Makes a Good Opening?

Talk to writers in any medium, and they will tell you that a good opening is essential. First impressions count, and if the player doesn't like the story's start or their first glimpse of the characters, the writer will need to work incredibly hard to get the audience to change their minds later. This does not mean that a writer should start to write final scenes and implement dialog straightaway.[5] Writers must ignore this temptation until they have properly developed a number of key plot elements. These elements demand that the writer establish the world, the characters, the protagonist's goal, and the conflict they will face then back these with narrative drive. Fail to plan and establish these areas and no amount of sparkling dialog will save the narrative.

Establishing the World

Before character, before even plot and story, comes the narrative world. This is because the story's world not only defines everything that will take place within it, but it also tells the player what sort of experience they can expect. Defining the narrative world starts with game genre then narrative genre.

---

[5]And that means you, bub.

Game genre tells the player what the rules of the world are and tells the writer how a story is to be told. This is because game genre determines the game's engine and, therefore, the technical tools a writer will have at their disposal. Genre also tells the writer what the game's audience will expect (there is a reason many FPS titles have interesting story engines and sports titles don't).

Second to game genre is narrative genre. Just as with game genre, this tells the player what to expect of the story and tells the writer the tools they will have at their disposal. Genre dictates certain narrative conventions that define that what makes a story fit under its umbrella.[6]

A genre's rules and conventions also give writers many narrative shortcuts that will allow a player to quickly immerse themselves within the gameworld. Knowing that they are entering a romance allows the player to quickly recognize who the hero is[7], what his quest is likely to be (to get the girl[8]) and how to recognize the antagonist.[9]

Once a writer has considered genre, setting comes next. Setting comprises location and time—where and when is the story set? Is it the claustrophobic setting of a 1940's science-fiction world gone mad (*Bioshock*), a modern football stadium (*FIFA 08*), or a modern fantasy fight arena (*Dead or Alive*)? While the game genre tells the player whether they will be running, shooting, and fighting for survival (*Bioshock*) or seeking to annihilate Chelsea's defense with a well-timed chip (*FIFA 08*), the setting and period will tell the player the sort of equipment, characters, and story dressing they can expect.

Once the writer has established the game's setting, they can move on to deeper points. What is the character's place within the world? What problems do they face, and who is responsible for these problems? In a game such as *Grand Theft Auto: San Andreas* (GTA), while the game's period sets a style for clothing, music, and attitude, the game's locations present the variety in gameplay and narrative objectives the player will face.

In the opening areas of GTA, the player faces urban gang violence in a stylized city that bears a passing resemblance to Los Angeles. As the game moves out of the city into the country, the player will meet farmers, cultists, and hippies, and their gameplay objectives will switch to wrecking crops and stealing combine harvesters. The gameplay objectives do not alter vastly from those found in the city, but the change of narrative creates a fresh experience within these familiar gameplay constructs.

Deeper into the game, the protagonist enters a casino-lined Vegasesque city. Now, the player must plot heists from casinos, steal armored cars, and run mobsters out of town. Again, there is little change in the actual gameplay mechanics, but

---

[6] For example, the sort of character archetypes, story ingredients, and plot structures a reader will expect from a genre that defines the story as a detective, action hero, or love story.

[7] The guy with the wavy hair.

[8] Or boy, or goat, depending on the sort of love story this is.

[9] The rich guy who really only wants the girl for her, um, assets.

the change of location gives an impression of progression and a fresh feel to the game design. Subtler still, each area expects the player to be better dressed, and the generic characters respond to the protagonist as suits their locality. Setting defines character, narrative/gameplay objectives, and the player's expectations.

The writer's job of establishing the world is easiest when the narrative fits the look and feel of the world.[10] The right choice of visuals will instantly show the player if the genre world they are entering is one set in science fiction, fantasy, or sports without the need for a single spoken word. Taking this idea further, the writer can also use visuals to establish character, setting, objective—in fact, pretty much everything. If the area the protagonist lives in is a rich neighborhood or a poor one, then this choice will allow the player to draw conclusions about the character. Indeed, it is what they player sees and interacts with that has the most affect on them, so a writer has to use more than just dialog to tell the story. As such, liaising with other departments to make sure that each shares a common vision is vital to successful game storytelling. Done properly, a world can be established in a split-second visual, allowing the writer to spend their limited resources on other areas of the story experience. Carefully matching a narrative objective with gameplay can mean that more of the story can be told within the gameworld. In other words, using visuals does not necessarily mean resorting to cinematics.

The use of visual storytelling should extend into the gameplay itself. *God of War* sets a number of its levels against a mythological background of gods and monsters that stride through the gameworld, not just the cinematics. Remember that while the start of a game can certainly be a good place for an establishing cinematic (years of game narrative form have led players to expect a narrative cinematic at the start, making this is one of the less punishing places to put one), the point of the opening is not to spend an hour discussing the finer detail of the character's soul but to get the player into the action as quickly as possible.

Establishing the Characters

Many problem scripts can trace their weaknesses to a failure to properly establish interesting characters. To create characters with more life and impact to them, the writer must craft them so that they are instantly recognizable but also surprising. They should have a sense of life beyond the central plot and an interesting story to tell within it. Each character should be distinct from all the others in the piece. Finally, when constructing such characters, the writer must also ensure that each character is believable.[11]

The most important characters to establish at the beginning are the protagonist and the antagonist. This might seem obvious, but it is quite common to find a story that develops a believable protagonist and then forgets the antagonist. Without a believable and interesting antagonist, the protagonist's story will not be compelling.

---

[10]That is, the graphics, sound, and animation.

[11]That is, believable within the gameworld they inhabit. Sonic is "believable" in *Sonic the Hedgehog* but would not be a believable character in *Assassin's Creed*.

The antagonist and protagonist are who the story is about, so the player needs to know as quickly as possible what the characters want, what makes them want it, and how are they going to go about getting it. Without these key pieces of information, the player can't understand what the story is about.

Just as with the world, establishing a character begins with appearance. However, the most important way to define a character is not how they look but what they do. If the opening of the game is a WWII beach landing then is the protagonist hanging back and panicking? Brave, but just a foot soldier? A strict commander? Action speaks louder than words, meaning that a writer must *show* not tell.

In a game, though, the writer doesn't fully control the character—the player does. While the writer can give parameters and objectives that define the character, each player will play that character in their own way. Does this render the writer's choice of character action meaningless? No.

While it is true that players do take a measure of control over the character, a look at most game forums will show that players rarely make a distinction between the writer's definition of a character and their own actions. Just as with other media, if the chemistry is right, players will suspend their disbelief. They accept the rules of game narrative and will take their character cues from the behavior the writer and designer place upon the game's characters.

Establishing the Situation—Goal and Conflict

Drama equals conflict.[12] Conflict stems from anything that prevents the protagonist from reaching their goal. As such, the narrative cannot make sense until the player understands what the protagonist wants and who or what is going to stop them.

The Getaway starts with the protagonist's wife being kidnapped in a violent manner. This incident sets out what will follow, as the central protagonist is forced into a series of criminal acts to save his wife. For the player, the bad guys are bad because we've seen them being bad.[13] We know instantly what the protagonist is doing (trying to save his wife) and why (because the bad guys are no-nonsense violent thugs who will kill her in a very painful manner if he doesn't). This clear goal instantly places the player in the narrative and tells them what they need to do. It also helps create narrative drive.

Creating Narrative Drive

Narrative drive isn't the street in Hollywood where all the writers live; it's the force that pulls a reader into the plot and makes them want to keep going. If the player doesn't feel an urge to discover more about the story, it might not stop them from playing the game, but it will lessen their sense of immersion.

A simple way to create narrative drive stems from the selection and arrangement of narrative information—what a player is told and when they are told it. Wondering

---

[12]Drama without conflict: Kratos and the Gods have a picnic, everyone likes each other, the end. It is unlikely that *God of War* would've garnered so much praise if this had been its story.

[13]"Show not tell" in action!

what someone is doing, why they are doing it, or what will happen next leaves the player wanting to know how the story will unfold.

All stories have suspense and mystery within them; the difference between genres is what the suspense and mystery is about. Will the boy get the girl?[14] Will the detective find the murderer? Will ultra-machine-soldier-man escape the enemy-filled nuclear reactor? There is often pressure, particularly from non-storytellers, to explain the whole story in the opening.[15] Not only don't you need to do this, you shouldn't or you will leave the story nowhere to go.

Project Zero/Fatal Frame starts with the mystery of what happened to the protagonist's favorite writer. Entering an old creepy mansion, the story's hero Mafuyu begins to search for the writer, only to disappear himself and leave the player with the game's true protagonist—Mafuyu's sister Miku. As in turn Miku searches for her missing brother, the mystery unfolds by feeding the player scraps of research detail and short, scary encounters with the undead residents of the house. These give the protagonist increasingly detailed flashes of imagery that tell her what happened in the house both recently and in the distant past. With each new revelation, as many questions are asked as are answered, characters are introduced, then their fates revealed, but not the complete picture of what happened and why. Gradually, the past and present begin to tie together, and at every stage the player is left satisfied that they have learned something and so are making progress. However, they are left with questions so that they want to know more—"Just what is going on here?!"

Keeping information from the player is tricky, however. A writer must be careful that they don't cheat the player. Characters failing to reveal information at points where they would naturally disclose it or a writer simply excluding information for no valid reason can lead to frustration rather than narrative drive. The writer and the characters must have a reason for their reluctance to speak.

12.4 Design Models

With the basic design and narrative elements laid before us, let's turn to the forms that a tutorial can assume.

The Classic Tutorial Design

The classic tutorial design is to take the first level, or a level designated "Tutorial," and to use this to teach the player how to play. Such a tutorial is often set in an area removed from the main gameplay area. The design then sets out the learning process from the most simplistic to the more difficult—walk, run, jump or run, pass, shoot, tackle—with small, simple, and "safe" gameplay sections surrounding these.

---

[14]Or guy or goat.

[15]"But won't people wonder why he's doing that?" YES! That's the point (mimes pointing a gun to his head).

Integrated Tutorials

The integrated tutorial takes the principles of the classic model but rolls them into the game. Such tutorials seek to hide the break between the teaching elements and the game by placing the player right into the middle of the game experience and allowing them to learn as they play.

In *Grand Theft Auto: San Andreas* the player is dropped directly into the gameworld after the opening cinematic. Prompted to walk, the player is then given the option of riding a bike. However, as this is an open-world game, the player can ignore this suggestion and go off to explore the world, leaving them free to discover the game's basic controls in free play.

Separate Tutorials

In an effort to maintain the story and gameworld's integrity, some games teach the player the basic controls in a section that is totally separate from the rest of the game. This gives the player a choice of whether to enter the tutorial or not. Such a choice removes some of the pressure to cater to both the beginner and the expert. RTS games, such as *Medieval II: Total War*, often use separate tutorials. Here, the player learns troop types and how to control them in a series of exercises before moving on to basic battle scenarios set aside for use only in the tutorial. This approach isn't limited to the RTS genre. Atari's *Fahrenheit* uses the same approach only in an adventure game, featuring a bizarre tutorial where the game's auteur personally introduces the player to the game's unusual control set.

However, whilst such separate tutorials can solve the problem of teaching a player within the gameworld, removing the tutorial from the rest of the game can create a false situation, distancing the player from the game and story before it has even started. Separating the tutorial also risks making the tutorial feel more like a chore that the player must complete before they get their reward, gameplay, a reward they've spent their hard-earned cash to have right away.

The Invisible Tutorial

Some games appear to have no tutorial at all. Designed with the idea that many players know the basics and that those who don't will experiment and discover the controls, the invisible tutorial removes the classic tutorial's overt instruction, building instead a series of level-design features that teach the player through exploration and experimentation.

The much celebrated title *Ico* introduces the player to the world and the character via an opening cutscene—a boy is dragged to a castle, sealed inside a stone sarcophagus, and abandoned. Once the guards have gone, the boy manages to make the sarcophagus fall on to the stone floor below it, spilling the character (and the player) into a large room. The player receives no instruction as to what to do; it is up to the player to use the control pad and find their own way to explore the room and to discover the problem (how to escape) and the solution (pull a lever). The next sealed room presents another problem that requires the player to discover how to climb and jump. In each case, the player is restricted to an area that requires them to complete a stage of learning before moving on to the next.

In *Ico*, these problems not only teach control and game style, but they also present the protagonist with his goal (the need to escape) and the world (a large, forbidding, and hostile temple) without a single word being spoken or displayed.

Once the player has learned the basic controls, they encounter a girl imprisoned in a cage whom they must free and then protect. The antagonists are made clear by action and appearance—shadowy, evil-looking creatures that arrive to take the girl and frustrate the boy. We see that they are evil as they attempt to carry the heroine off to her doom.

Ico's story is simplistic and draws heavily on story archetype, but it succeeds because it shows rather than tells the story, combining game and narrative in a way that prompts not only a basic level of immersion but genuine emotion for the characters contained within its story world. This process begins at the first moment of the tutorial.

Ongoing Tutorials—Spreading the Teaching Load

Many games add new elements throughout the course of the game. When a writer works on a game with such an extended learning experience, the writer must consider how to introduce these new elements. While not all such elements need to be commented on by the game's characters, some will demand an explanation either to tell the player how to use the new gameplay, or simply because it would be natural for the game's characters to comment on what they are experiencing.[16] Game characters don't need to jabber away through an entire game, but they do need to feel real.

In *Harry Potter and the Order of the Phoenix*, the player is able to learn new spells throughout the game. Each of the open-world missions in the main section of the game requires the protagonist (Harry Potter) to persuade a character to join Harry in the Room of Requirement to practice spells. Once a character goes to the room, the player can then choose to meet them and learn a new spell. This hides the artificial "power-up" process by using people as well as creating a separate, safe tutorial area within the game itself. This idea is taken even further in *Tomb Raider*. In this game, the player can go to Lara Croft's mansion throughout the game, allowing them to self-select ongoing tutorial and training elements and providing a continuous safe environment to experiment within.

Ongoing tutorials don't have to be limited to one location, nor do they always require on-screen text. *Half-Life 2* introduces a number of weapons throughout the game. One technique the game uses to handle these new ingredients is to have a new weapon introduced by a character who not only hands it over but also explains how to use it.

---

[16]If a large monster with flaming breath and a magic axe tore part of the city down and slew a hundred people in front of you, chances are you'd comment on this. If this is true for you, it can feel right for the game's characters, too—if this fits in with the game's genre and design.

12.5   Narrative Models

Whatever the medium, writers face the same challenge—creating a memorable opening that grabs the player and throws them into the story.

Grab Them by the Nose

The Hollywood-blockbuster approach starts a story with spectacle. A plane blows up, a huge space battle announces the start of an alien invasion, or a car crash smashes the main character's world to pieces. This sort of spectacular opening puts the player on the edge of their seats, feeding the player promise of more action and spectacle to come. Action RPGs regularly employ video cutscene openings to achieve this.

Onimusha 3: Demon Siege opened with a huge cinematic that at the time was one of the most expensive ever seen, while other action series such as *Metal Gear Solid* use spectacular cinematics throughout. More recent games such as *King Kong* have made these fabulous cutscenes partially interactive, allowing the protagonist limited control as the cinematic unfolds. The thing all of them have in common is that the visuals paint in a larger world beyond the levels the protagonist inhabits while highlighting the narrative's genre, setting, characters, and conflict.

Writer beware! Remember that when planning a big opening, the energy at the end of such an opening should carry into the first interactive section. A game that has a huge opening then drops the player into a lethargic, slow-paced tutorial risks not only a sense of anti-climax but also risks alienating the player from the game and the story.

The Slow Burn

In contrast to the spectacular opening, the slow burn gives the player time to orient themselves before presenting the moment of change that pushes the protagonist into the central plot.

X3: Reunion starts with an integrated tutorial where the protagonist takes a group of rookie pilots on their first training flight. This level gives the player a chance to learn about the universe, the lead character's place within it, and the antagonist (an alien species invading the universe) before beginning the main narrative in the second mission.

This slow-burn approach gives the player a chance to learn details and become comfortable before the moment of major change. Just as the player can need time to take in the game's controls, if the game's story is complex and requires the player to take onboard a large amount of information, spreading this information allows the player more chance to take these details in and means there is less chance of bulky chunks of exposition damaging the game flow.

The Retrospective

The retrospective creates narrative drive by beginning the story at the end (or partway through a story) and looking backwards. Often beginning the story in a perilous, mortal, or bizarre situation, the retrospective hooks the player in by asking the question "How did we got here?" *Heavenly Sword* opens at the end of the story with the protagonist close to death. The player watches her die and be taken to purgatory, setting the player the question of how she got to that point and whether they can change this.

The Prequel

While the retrospective looks backwards, the prequel sets out events that precede the main action (often prior to the introduction of the main character) and pushes the player forward into the narrative. Such an approach is often used to set up suspense, leaving the player wondering what happened and/or how the events they witnessed will link to the main plot. This tool can also put the player in the position of knowing things that the character doesn't. This was the approach utilized in *Project Zero*.

The Arrival

Story is about change, and so a common way to fundamentally change the protagonist's world is to send them somewhere at the start of the story. A character's arrival somewhere not only has the advantage of clearly establishing a change for the protagonist but also allows the reader to encounter new things at the same time as the character, therefore justifying the need to explain them within the plot.

Arrival can mean the protagonist coming to a new location, such as a new school (or summer school in the case of *Psychonauts*), or it can mean placing the character in a familiar location but with a changed situation (CJ's arrival back in San Andreas after the death of his mother in *Grand Theft Auto: San Andreas*).

The Narrator

Narration, either via a narrator or through text, is a popular way to introduce stories. There is often no need to explain how a narrator has the knowledge they have. Narration can give information quickly in a concise way and, depending on the type of narrator selected, can allow for neutral commentary on the action. That said, the use of narration also carries many pitfalls. It is very easy to fall into lazy writing when using narrators because narration tells rather than shows. This can separate the player from the narrative and lead to them ignoring what the narration has to say.

Named and unnamed narrators. A voiceover narrator can be a character from the story who introduces the story, a character from outside the story, or an unnamed voice. Voiceover delivers the information in a dramatic way.

The joy of text. Narration does not have to be voiced. *Lego Star Wars* starts not only the game but each level with a scrolling synopsis of what has happened prior to the gameplay. This orientates the player and allows the levels to focus on only one or two narrative moments per level, i.e., freeing Princess Leia or meeting Yoda for the first time. The narration also helps set up the Star Wars story world by aping the text used in the films.

The hidden narrator. Recently, more and more games are using "hidden" narrators. Instead of an external voice, the game puts the narrator right inside the game. *Half-Life 2*, for example, uses a public-address system to provide the player with narrative information as they pass through the world. Similarly, *Max Payne 2: The Fall of Max Payne* uses programs shown on strategically placed televisions to not only provide a feel for the gameworld but, in some instances, to talk directly to the protagonist. This means the information provided by the narration is experienced by the player rather than forced upon them, making it feel more real, more relevant, and therefore more immersive.

12.6   Getting the Writing Done

There are some aspects of tutorial design and narrative construction that go beyond the basic models and that need the writer to consider the points where the story and the design, the narrative and gameplay exposition, meet.

Merging Design and Narrative

While the writer's aim is to obfuscate the artificiality of the learning process, they must do so in a way that does not obscure the lessons the player needs to learn. It is easy for the tutorial to become congested with too much information, so when planning their narrative structure, the writer must ensure that they do not overload the player.

Remember the equation: The speed the player masters the controls = the speed they can enter the gameworld = the speed of immersion.

It may feel frustrating to a writer if the game design reduces the amount of narrative information that can be placed in the game's opening, but it is in the writer's interests to make this work. After all, immersion is the aim of both the writer and the designer, and the way a writer decides to present narrative material also affects the speed and depth of immersion.

Dealing with Backstory

When putting story concepts, outlines, and development documents together it is common to create backstory.[17]. Backstory can allow the development team to see who the characters are, predict their behavior, nuance their actions, and make the characters feel fully rounded. The art department can use backstory to create the character's look, the animation department can use it to define how a character is animated, and designers can use it to think about ways the characters can interact. These attributes make backstory a useful tool.

Once created, though, backstory can be incredibly seductive. While background information can illuminate characters and enrich the narrative, it is easy to bog a story down in the past. The player wants to experience the now. The now should be

---

[17]Backstory being all the guff that happened before the player, protagonist, and writer enter the time the plot takes place in.

the most interesting part of the story and should not be overshadowed by a fabulous backstory that is more interesting than the story the player is playing. If the backstory is more appealing than the game story, then why didn't the writer set the story then?

Overshadowing doesn't always mean that the backstory is more interesting than the narrative. It can also mean that the game narrative has been overloaded with information from the backstory. What is relevant to the player is what they are experiencing in the game. Backstory that does not shed light on the present is redundant.

Military games seem to fall particularly foul of the trap of redundant information. Many such games mistake elaborate, unbelievable biography for character. "Lieutenant Bostain played professional football for the Cowboys and took part in the Olympics as a pentathlete before serving with the Green Berets, SEALs, SAS, CIA, and becoming the first man to climb Everest carrying a grand piano." Worse still, such biographies are often the cue for the entry into the game of a mindless drone who occasionally shouts "Huh!"

Backstory is there to help the development team, but it must remain relevant.

Expert Characters

While a game character may be a trained FBI agent, hitman, space pilot, or footballer, the player could be a schoolgirl, plumber, or a microbiologist from Swansea. While the character is an expert, the player might not even know how to make their character walk around.

It is possible to ignore this problem. The player knows they are playing a game and are sometimes prepared to suspend their disbelief to a degree. That said, the smoother the writer can make this process the better.

Removing a character's powers. One simple way to level the player and the character is to remove the character's skills or their equipment. *Far Cry* opened its story by sinking the character's boat and stripping the character of their equipment. Such an approach doesn't alter a character's physical powers, but it does allow the player to be gradually introduced to weapons in the game, thus helping with the game's difficulty curve.

Removing powers is more difficult when dealing with physical powers or knowledge. A hackneyed and overused method for removing knowledge is to give the main character amnesia. This removes the character's skills and also presents an opportunity to fill the character and therefore the player in on the back story, but the overuse of this technique renders it hackneyed and so will damage the player's interest in the story.

Physical powers often require a physical explanation for their removal. In *Metroid Prime 2*, Samus suffered battle damage that resulted in the loss of her extra special abilities. This can be a useful technique, as long as the method used to remove the abilities is believable.

The player as tutor—teaching others. When creating *Harry Potter and the Order of the Phoenix*, the development team faced the problem that while the central character was an established wizard, the players were not, and there was no allowance in the franchise for the character to lose his powers. The solution was to use a sub-plot from the book that put Harry into the position of teacher. Putting the character in the position of a tutor meant that when the protagonist "taught" other characters how to cast a spell, they also taught the player. This kept the character in line with the existing franchise fiction, taught the player, and maintained the character as knowledgeable.

12.7   Making a Tutorial

Contrary to expectation, tutorials are often tackled late in the game development process, as they can be the most difficult part of the game to get right. They need the team to balance difficulty curves, cope with the concept of players with different levels of gaming experience, etc., which makes the tutorial a strange beast. This does note mean that the writer can leave it until last. While the rest of the development team can leave the tutorial until last, the writer will need to make crucial decisions about the distribution of narrative information early in their process. This will still give the writer a chance to make alterations later on, but chances are the cinematics they planned will already have been made, and the later levels will be in place when the writer comes to deal with the more detailed implementation of the tutorial.

12.8   Conclusion

Tutorials provide game writers with a number of challenges that go to the heart of game writing. To create a successful tutorial that not only teaches different players how to play the game but immerses them in the gameworld, the writer will need to work closely with the game designer and pay constant attention to the game design. The writer can make their job easier while both creating narrative drive and clearing space for tutorial information by thinking very carefully about what information is needed and the fastest way to introduce this information. Where possible, show don't tell; let the imagery and action do the work. Come into the action as quick and as late as possible and focus on an active way to establish the characters, their world, and their situation. Succeed at this and you're away. There's only the rest of the game to write, but that should be a breeze...

12.9   Exercises

1. Examine the tutorial section of a game you like to play and consider how it would seem to the players from Section 12.1: Tommy, Kevin, Julianne, and Bob.

2. Write a plausible narrative explanation for why an experienced firefighter would need to go through the basics of how to use his equipment and move around. Do not include amnesia!

3. Come up with a clear goal that can be quickly introduced to the player and function as a hook to get them into the tutorial level of a game.

13

Writing Strategy Guides

Alice Henderson

A good strategy guide can be the ultimate guide to a game, revealing all the best strategies, treasures, hidden areas, and more, all presented in a glorious full-color format. The task of the strategy guide writer, then, is to create as complete a guide as possible, even adding background information and other extras that allow the player to experience far more than the gamer who does not possess a guide.

13.1   Creating a Solid Foundation Before You Start

During the days or, if you're lucky, weeks you spend writing a strategy guide, the contacts you build at the publishing house and the game company can be your lifeline. You've gotten the green light to write the guide, and you're likely waiting for the dev kit and game to arrive. This is the perfect time to build a solid foundation with your contacts.

Your Editor

Before you begin writing the guide, ask your editor some key questions. Your publisher may want you to write the guide in a specific in-house code that makes it easier for the layout people to read. They'll likely give you a printout of code words for different console buttons, sidebars, hint callouts, and more. Be sure to follow this code, as it will improve your chances of writing future guides for them.

Ask your editor exactly when each portion of the guide is due, if they are wanting you to turn it in as you go, or when you have written half, and so on.

Getting copies of strategy guides to similar games can also prove helpful. It will show you exactly what the company is looking for, and your editor should be able to provide you with a stack of them.

Game Company Contacts

These people will be vital to the completion of an excellent strategy guide. If you aren't already familiar with the testers and game designers at the company then ask your editor to put you in touch. Be sure to get contacts for both designers and testers, as each can provide you with different information should you need it.

Once you have their info, contact each one and introduce yourself, saying that you are writing the guide for the game they're working on. These people can be incredibly helpful. The testers have played the game over and over, and the designers know where hidden areas are and might be able to provide maps, secret codes, and more.

13.2   What Makes a Good Guide

A successful guide will have a number of key components. A succinct, detailed walk-through of the game is, of course, essential. You should create easy-to-follow maps that show the locations of key items. Take clear screenshots of enemies and important locations. Compose appendices with character and opponent stats and lists of items, spells, weapons, and so on. Interesting sidebars about characters and locations can spice up the guide. Cheat codes and guides to hidden areas can go in the back, as can interviews with game designers.

13.3   Getting Through the Game

One of your first tasks as you begin writing is to play through the game, making notes as you go. If you have a short deadline, quickly obtaining working copies of the game can prove difficult, and you will have to be on top of it constantly.

Getting a Copy of the Game

You can either do this through your editor or your game company contact. Ask your editor which one is more appropriate, as it can change with different companies. If you don't receive a copy right away, get proactive. Unfortunately, getting a copy to the strategy guide writer is sometimes not much of a priority for the game company, and every day you lose will be felt toward the deadline.

Getting the Most Current Copy of the Game

Of course, the game you're working on hasn't been released yet and is likely still full of bugs. You may get a version that has unplayable levels or isn't complete. Perhaps they haven't finished balancing the game, and a boss is undefeatable or defeated too easily. These factors will change by the game release date, so it's vital that you keep getting updated versions of the game. Keep asking your contact who provides you with copies of the game. If it isn't your editor and the person is slow to respond, get your editor involved.

Playing with a Buggy Game

This is a standard struggle for any strategy guide writer. A few things can help, though. Ask the designers and testers for shortcuts like in-house codes that allow you to jump from level to level automatically. You may find a level completely broken, locking your system up every time. A level-jumping code allows you to get working on later levels while the game company fixes the broken one. Other codes like god-mode will make the screenshot phase of your guide go a lot faster. It's not fun trying to screenshot an enemy who keeps killing you when you pause for the image.

13.4   Screenshots

This step can be one of the most time-consuming processes in writing the guide. As mentioned above, if you have a god-mode code from the game company, that can simplify the process. You can then take screenshots of AI villains and locations without having to worry about your character constantly getting killed while you're setting up the shots.

Taking Screenshots

Before you take any screenshots, ask your editor what resolution, file format, and so on she requires. Take two or three samples and send them to your editor for approval before you go ahead and take the bulk of the shots. Many times your editor will change her mind and want a different resolution or format after seeing the sample. It's good to know exactly what will work for them before you spend a lot of time taking screenshots.

PC Games vs. Console Games

On a PC game, you may have to use the Print Screen button and then paste the image into an image-processing program like Adobe Photoshop to crop it or get it at the right resolution and file format.

For a console game, a few different options exist. Again, ask your editor if she has any preferences first. You may need to invest in a video-capture device like the Dazzle Video Creator. This will allow you to take screenshots right off your TV if you're dealing with a PlayStation, Xbox, Wii, or the like. These are relatively inexpensive and will be a good investment as you write more and more guides. Since console technology is constantly evolving, you may be able to take screenshots by networking your computer to the console itself.

When to Take Screenshots

Depending on your preference, you can either take screenshots as you first play through the game or take them when you've finished writing the guide. Some writers may find pausing to take screenshots too distracting when formulating strategies. Others may find it convenient to not have to backtrack through levels.

Ultimately, it might be the shortness of your deadline that dictates the method. Taking screenshots as you go can save valuable time you may need at the end.

What to Take Screenshots Of

You'll want a thorough representation of game elements in your screenshot collection. This will not only help the player but will add to the visual appeal of the guide itself. You will definitely want to get images of the following:

- the heroes in action;

- all villains;

- important items to complete quests;

- key story points (like meetings with quest-giving NPCs);

- key locations;

- strategic locations to stand or hide during boss fights;

- confusing areas the player must navigate through;

- hidden areas.

Acquiring Art to Accompany Your Screenshots

To further jazz up the visual appeal of your guide, you'll want to acquire some concept art from the game company itself. Sometimes your editor will send you sheets of sample concept art, allowing you to choose the pieces that would fit your guide best. Other times you may be talking directly to the artists at the game company.

Choose pieces that will fit well with sidebars you have written, pieces that are dramatic, and pieces that show off areas or characters that don't come through as sensationally in the screenshots.

13.5   Maps

Time and game design play important roles in how your maps turn out. A writer with a longer deadline (a month or more) will likely have time to send maps to the layout people in time for them to add stylized icons, depth, shadows, and so on. A book with a very short deadline will end up using maps no different than how the writer turned them in.

The ease of map creation will vary depending on if there is an existing in-game map or not. Many games have maps built into the HUD, while others use separate map screens. These you can adapt for use in the guide. However, some games will have no maps at all, and you'll have to create them from scratch.

Most publishers will want you to turn in a digital version of the maps, so if you create them yourself on paper, be prepared to hunt down a scanner if you don't have one.

Where you place the maps in your guide is a subjective choice. You may want the map for each level to be included with the walkthrough, or you may prefer to have an appendix just for maps at the back.

Creating Maps from Scratch

If the game has no map screens or map in the HUD, you'll have to create them yourself. Your first step might be to contact the game level designers and see if they will take screenshots of their level layout for you. They may have to turn off excess geometry before doing so to make the image easier to follow. You can then take these screenshots into an image-processing program and clean them up.

If the level designers can't do this, you may need to sit down with the game and draw out the levels by hand. Using graph paper with blue non-reproducible lines, map out all the levels manually. Note where items, enemies, entrances, exits, and important locations and NPCs lie. Since you'll need a digital copy, scan your hand-drawn maps into an image-processing program. Clean them up and add colors.

Adapting the In-Game Map

If the game has a map in the HUD or, even better, a separate map screen, you are in luck. Take screenshots of the maps on each level and import them into an image-processing program. Clean up the images, especially if it is a HUD map. HUD maps usually lie in a transparent layer over the game action, and you'll want to remove those background images.

For All Maps

Whether you've created the map from scratch or have adapted an in-game map, you will need to add elements to it.

- **Title.** Title the map so the reader can see at a glance to what section of what level it pertains.

- **Legend.** Create a legend for each map with icons for items, weapons, enemies, quest-giving NPCs, treasure locations, and any other information the player will need. If there is more than one typical common item the player might find, then create a separate icon for each item.

- **Labels.** Label entrances, exits, routes to take through mazes, and any other important locations.

- **Multiple maps for each level.** You may find that you need to create multiple maps if a level has more than one floor or has a vast series of rooms.

13.6   Writing the Guide

Be as thorough and specific as possible when writing the guide. Among other things, the guide is the source for frustrated players who just want to get past trouble spots and enjoy the game again. The guide also serves players who want to get the absolute most out of the game, finding all its secrets, items, and opportunities to gain XP.

Introduction

In the introduction, set the mood and atmosphere for the game. Whet the player's appetite for the adventure that lies ahead. Be creative. You'll also want to include a rundown of the game basics. It may feel strange to you to repeat some of the information that will undoubtedly be included in the manual that comes with the game, but many players find it handy to have all the information in one convenient place—the strategy guide.

- **Game controls.** Diagram the console controller or keyboard and label what each key does.

- **Game modes.** Describe different modes, such as single-player or multiplayer, and how each mode differs.

- **Characters.** Get screenshots or, even better, concept art for each of the main characters. Describe their histories, what drives them, their temperaments, and what players can expect by choosing to play each character.

- **Common enemies.** If players will encounter common enemies throughout the game, such as different monsters, describe them, using art to add visual appeal.

- **Common items and weapons.** List the common objects a player will need, including what they do and their advantages and disadvantages.

- **General strategies.** Finally, in your introduction, include any general strategies that apply throughout the game. For example, perhaps it's a survival horror game in which shutting off your flashlight or ducking down behind boxes will cause monsters to pass you by without attacking.

The Walkthrough

The walkthrough is, of course, the heart of any strategy guide. You'll likely want a separate chapter for each level. In each, a number of game elements should be addressed.

- **Objectives.** Describe the goal of the level and include any optional objectives and miniquests as well.

- **Rewards.** List rewards for objectives completed, again including optional objectives.

- **Map.** Clearly label all items, weapons, enemies, and quest-giving NPCs on the map.

- **Enemy rundown.** For each level, list what opponents the player will face and to what attacks or weaponry they are most vulnerable. You can also add any treasures or XP the player will receive from dispatching them.

- **Hints.** Throughout the guide, provide callouts for trouble spots. For example, "If you shinny up the left set of vines, you won't drop into the vat of acid as easily."

- **Warnings.** Warn the player of any areas where they could be killed or suffer loss to their inventory. For example, "Watch out for the sniper on the ceiling beam to the left." Or, "Don't enter the cave, as a thief there will seize all your healing potions."

- **Step-by-step instructions.** And of course, you'll need to provide very detailed instructions on how to not only make it through each level but come out with a high success rate. Let players know where crucial spots are to get the most XP or loot.

- **Strategies.** As you play through the game and develop the best strategies for winning each level, talk to the testers, as well. They will have added insight to levels and might have some interesting strategies that come from playing a game for months and months.

- **Sidebars.** As you play, you may encounter interesting cultures, places, or characters in the game. Likely other players will feel the same way. Including interesting sidebars (preferably with some concept art or screenshots) will jazz up your walkthrough. Providing backstory for a strange alien outpost, for example, will add dimensions to the game that players without the strategy guide might never know.

13.7   Appendices

The appendix section of your guide is a great place for all the stats and charts for game characters, items, weapons, enemies, and spells. The type of game will determine what you need to include in the appendices. An RPG should have a spell appendix, for example, but this likely won't be applicable for a first-person shooter.

Sometimes these stats will be available in-game, and other times they'll function more behind the scenes. If your game is an RPG, there will likely be screens listing the strengths and weaknesses of characters, items, weapons, and armor. Usually, though, this information will not be so readily evident. The easiest and most efficient way to obtain these stats is to ask the game designers. Usually they'll have an Excel document that lists these numbers. Another reason to get these numbers straight from the designers is that stats keep changing up to the last minute before game release. When you create tables and charts with this information, be sure to use the layout code mentioned earlier to create your appendices.

Appendix Topics

Depending on the type of game, the following categories make good appendices.

- **Character stats.** List each player character's strengths and weaknesses, ability to upgrade, and so forth.

- **Enemies.** Include all enemies encountered, their stats and weaknesses, and which levels they occur on.

- **Items.** All items collected throughout the game, their function, and which levels they are found on.

- **Spells.** Describe where the characters learn the spells, their function, and their cost.

- **Miniquests.** If the game has miniquests, list where the player acquires them and what the rewards are.

- **Hidden areas.** These places are great fun to find and are one of the main reasons readers purchase strategy guides. Talk to game designers to be sure you haven't missed any, and include them on the maps for each level.

- **Easter eggs and cheat codes.** These little extras are another reason readers buy strategy guides. However, the game company may be reluctant to share these with you. This is where a good rapport with the designers comes in very handy. You can also ask your editor to do some convincing for you.

Including Optional Cool Extras

To add even more depth to the player's gaming experience, you might want to include some game background. Interviewing a game designer or artist could prove fruitful. Another cool addition would be a glossary of game terms, especially if there's an alien language involved.

13.8   Turning In Drafts

Hopefully before you embarked on the project, your editor gave you firm dates for turning in each section of manuscript. You might be turning in each chapter as you go or turning in the manuscript when you finish each half. Be prepared for these dates to change. Strategy guide publishers must release their guide to coincide with the game's release. If that date changes, you may find your deadline suddenly shorter.

Turning In Your Draft Chapter by Chapter

If you have a short deadline, you'll likely be assigned this method. The layout people do a lot of work to transform your manuscript into the full-color glossy format it gets published in, so they need those chapters as soon as you write them. You won't have the luxury of being able to go back and add to chapters, so you'll have to get organized quickly right from the start. Carefully think out what you want to include in every chapter. The good news is that if your editor wants you to change something about how you'll write subsequent chapters, you can do so early on in the process.

Turning In Your Manuscript One Half at a Time

If you have a month or longer to write the guide, you have more breathing room. You can go back and add bits to chapters, perhaps inserting sidebars. Still, it might not be a bad idea to send your first chapter to your editor, just to be sure your vision jives with hers.

The Game Company Review Process

After you've turned in your manuscript and the layout people have made it beautiful, the game company receives a copy. They mark corrections and send it back to you. Set aside ample time to make these changes. By the time you've written the guide, the layout people have set it up, and the game company has received and reviewed it, many changes will have happened to the game. Perhaps you described defeating a boss using fire arrows, and now no fire arrows are available on that level. Or maybe you told the player to use a shortcut through a cavern that now no longer exists because the designers had too many collision problems with it. This stage may be time-consuming, depending on how much the game changes prerelease.

13.9   Deadlines

Deadlines can vary greatly, depending on when you are brought on board. If you're the initial writer assigned to the project, you might have six weeks or more to write the guide. But if you're filling in for a staff writer who had too many projects, you might find yourself looking at 10 to 14 days. Depending on the type of game, you may want to request more time from the get-go. Writing a guide for an RPG in that limited time will be very difficult, and you likely won't get much sleep. The nature of an RPG, with all its quests, miniquests, spells, magical items, and so on, makes it a very complex game to write a guide for. A guide for a survival horror game or first-person shooter will be a little easier to pull off with a shorter deadline.

If you have a very short deadline, keep in mind the following time-saving tips.

- Do your screenshots during your playthroughs, instead of taking them all after you've finished writing the guide.

- Ask designers early on for the stats you'll need for the appendices.

- Set up a system, either with the editor or lead tester, where you can receive the most recent build of the game as soon as it's burned.

- Be sure you're always working with the most current version.

13.10   Conclusion

An excellent strategy guide is the product of several factors. The writer must not only write a succinct guide, but it must be engaging, adding dimensions to the game that players without the guide will miss. It requires good communication with the game company and the editor at the publishing house. But mostly, it takes a determined writer who not only wants to help players navigate through trouble spots but wants to write the ultimate guide to the game itself.

13.11   Exercises

1. Pick out a level in a game that you found confusing. Write a walkthrough of the level, explaining the most efficient way for a player to get through while picking up any necessary items and treasure.

2. Play through a recently released game. Develop strategies as you play and write them down. Give these to a friend who hasn't played the game and see how they fare. Can you hone the wording? Are your strategies clearly communicated to the player?

3. Draw a map for a level of a game you like. Add locations for items or quest-giving NPCs. As in Exercise 2, give the map to a friend who has never played the game before. How easily were they able to follow the map? Are there parts you can improve?

14

Writing for New IP

Rhianna Pratchett

14.1   The Game Writer and New IP Creation

New intellectual properties (IPs) in the game industry have become very much of a double-edged sword. They are eminently desirable from a player's perspective and to an industry press that often rails against sequel-itis. But in this still relatively risk-averse publishing climate, new IPs often struggle to be born. Even if they manage that and wobble, Bambi-legged, out onto the market, they're all too often crushed by the same press and consumers that demanded them in the first place.

According to Steve Allison, Midway's Chief Marketing Officer (not to mention their Senior Vice President), "93 percent of new IP fails in the marketplace." Allison, in an interview with N'ai Croal for *Level Up*, went on to claim that, "While the 90-plus review scores and armfuls of awards create the perception that titles like *Psychonauts*, *Shadow of the Colossus*, *Okami* and other great pieces of work were big successes...they were big financial disappointments and money losers. The truth is that there is no correlation between review scores and commercial success."

So it appears that even if you are greeted with open arms, the chances of an IP making it to financial success, and more importantly (as far as publishers are concerned) making it from IP to franchise, are incredibly slim. But even with Electronic Arts starting to support new IPs (of which *Mirror's Edge* is one of the first), they still clearly need all the help they can get. This chapter is aimed to help professional game writers reduce the failure rate cited by Allison, or at the very least, make sure their titles fall into that eminently desirable 7%.

The need for coherent worlds and, just as importantly in an industry that loves its icons, magazine covers, and front-page stories, the need for strong characters (that are actually characters with *character* rather than just pretty avatars) are more important than ever. *Bioshock*, although it certainly borrowed a lot from *System Shock*, was a new IP with a strong emphasis on storytelling (as much through its world as its dialog) that was very successful both in scores and sales. Likewise, an emphasis on

Figure 14.1. Thwarting rock giants and dwarves—all in a day's work for the Minions in the world of *Overlord*.

narrative and storytelling certainly haven't hampered the fortunes of *Portal*, *God of War*, *The Longest Journey* series, *Destroy all Humans*, the *Neverwinter Nights* franchise, or *Heavenly Sword*.

Okay, let's get down to the nitty gritty. As writers, we all want to contribute as much as we can to the narrative development of a new IP. Unfortunately, the point at which you're brought on board can have a big impact on how much you can bring to the party. Whilst sadly this factor is often in the hands of your employers, here's a guide on what to expect and how to make the most of it.

The Starting Line—In-House

So, a writer in on the ground floor, eh? Can't get much earlier on than that. Oh, the bliss! Get ten writers in a room, and although they might differ on everything from story implementation to interactivity versus cutscene to character development, the one thing they'll agree on is that the sooner a writer is brought on board, the better.

If you are an in-house writer (and to be honest, those are sadly few and far between) then you're probably used to being there at the start, ideally taking an active role in concept meetings, brainstorming story and character ideas, and liaising with the other teams on a regular basis. Lucky you! This is an ideal situation to be in, as long as the studio you're with values your contribution and ideas. And the fact they've employed a full-time, staff writer (or team of writers in the case of companies like BioWare) in the first place is a pretty good indication!

The Starting Line—Freelance

Freelance writers, on the other hand, won't be quite so accustomed to this luxury. This is mainly because a depressingly large amount of freelance game writing is still comprised of projects that fall into the we-didn't-think-we-needed-a-writer-but-now-we-do-and-we-have-no-budget-left-and-two-months-until-we-ship category.

If, as a freelance writer, you find yourself being included in original IP creation at the start of a project, it's usually because (1) the game in question is part of a would-be franchise that you've previously worked on in some capacity (i.e., staff-to-freelance gig, freelance-to-freelance, or work within the same development studio or publisher) or (2) the right people have realized they need a writer at the right time and actually found through random googling, an agency, or merely through positive word of mouth, you. Either way, it's still a fantastic opportunity to help shape a gameworld, get involved in narrative design, and generally prove that writers, even freelance ones, can be a valuable addition to a game project in its early stages.

The Golden Window

It can often be the case that developers who know they are going to need a freelance writer will choose to bring them onto a project during what I call the *golden window* phase. This is a period that usually falls somewhere between story pre-production and first-draft script. In this window, certain elements of the gameworld will already have been decided—certainly the core gameplay, and often many of the environments, levels, and even some of the characters (at least visually). Yet in many cases, these elements are not joined together to form a coherent story or a complete world. It's rather like a half-completed jigsaw puzzle.

In this situation, the writer will be expected to work within the given boundaries and often retrofit a story around what has already been established. Despite sounding quite restrictive, these boundaries can actually allow for a lot of creativity and often filter into the various facets of IP itself—especially elements that are likely to spill over into possible sequels and downloadable and expansion content (something a new IP writer always has to keep in mind). In short, this is where a freelance or possibly a short-term in-house contractor can still make a real and lasting difference. The following are a few things to keep in mind to make the most of your golden window.

- Get to know the team, particularly the level designers. You will need to work with them quite closely to get the most fluid and well-executed level dialog. If your employers aren't encouraging this then gently suggest it.

- Make sure you focus a lot of time on getting together a strong story doc and world vision. This will not only help you when you come to write the nuts and bolts dialog but also be informative for everyone else, from production to design to marketing.

- Become familiar with every one of your characters before you even write a line for them. Profile your characters—their journeys, their backgrounds, even the way you imagine them walking and talking. Most importantly, think about how elements of their character can further the gameplay and story themes.

- Focus on looking at the different ways that narrative can be embedded in the world, from interactive and noninteractive cutscenes right through to ambient and level dialog. Also, think about how visual aspects of the world might further the story—newspapers, letters, billboards, TV spots, radio/TV broadcasts, etc.

- Make sure your employers are aware of your range of skills. If you have experience with localization prep, casting, audio direction, manual writing, marketing, or writing advertorial copy, then these can all be utilized to strengthen the narrative production.

Parachuted In

We're not just writers when it comes to games, you know. We're narrative paramedics, parachuting in with our magic word bandages to patch up an ailing story. Outside of the golden window, there's no guarantee just how much influence a writer will be able to have on a new IP. At best, you might get a couple of months in which to polish a game's story and dialog, possibly sew up a few plot holes, and if you're lucky, turn no-necked space marines or buxom, sword-wielding wenches into actual characters. At worst, you'll have a couple of weeks to merely polish up the dialog.

In either case, you can usually still do some good with honest, diplomatic, and constructive feedback. Most developers/publishers will listen, but you still do get the occasional case where they just want you to tick off the story they've already written, rather than actually put your writer's skills to good use. My personal motto used to be that of Commander Peter Quincy Taggart in the very fine *Galaxy Quest* "Never give up, never surrender," but now, after more than a few headbangs against walls, it's more like "Pick your battles!"

You should also be aware that many writers do hike up their rates for short-notice, short-running gigs, as the stress and turnover rates are greatly increased. This is up to the individual writer to decide, based on a client-by-client basis.

Overview: The Role

Whether you're in-house or freelance, the tasks that await the game writer when working on a new IP will be more or less the same. Where it differs from other forms of game writing is that you don't just have the challenge of building the narrative world but also helping create the bricks you're going to use. It's a task that is as much about narrative story design as it is about dialog creation, namely defining how and where narrative is dispersed through the story, as well as the content of that narrative.

More often than not, there will be ideas for the central gameplay already in place (even for an in-house writer), and the writer will have to work with the design team to create the best story and characters to complement and enhance the gameplay. Ultimately, although the needs of narrative and gameplay rarely run along exactly the same path, there needs to be that fusion there to avoid the feeling that the story has merely been poured on top of the gameplay like some kind of narrative custard.

What you're really looking for is a narrative trifle, where the player is equally invested in both story and gameplay, and gameplay challenges and losses are reflected in story challenges and losses, bringing the player and the player character more in-line.

Overview: The Scope

Perhaps more than any other kind of game writing, working on new IP requires a good working knowledge of game creation and the development cycle. Whilst external writers with little experience with games can wing it as long as they have firm briefs and good lines of communication, anything that requires story design, pre-production, and the creation of narrative tools needs a good understanding of how those tools should be working within the individual gameworld. This will usually be predominately defined by the genre, platform, and gameplay. However, the vogue for genre blending is picking up the pace in the search for new gameplay experiences—for example, *Overlord* mixed together action-adventure, role-playing, and strategy elements.

Now more than ever, game writers need to be fully aware of the medium they're writing for. It's a tall order, especially if you didn't grow up playing games, but it can be an immensely rewarding one. The fact that you are interested in writing for games and have picked this book up suggests that you already have some interest in games and gaming. If not, then go away and do your homework.

When it comes to project lengths, then writers on a new IP will be looking at quite a meaty time commitment. Depending on the genre and importance of narrative within the game, this can be spread over anything from four to eight months for the bulk of the story work, with a couple of extra months for recording, pick-ups, and ambient-dialog writing (if you're lucky). If a writer is brought onboard quite early on, then they may be only required to roughly scope out a story and characters and then return to a project further on down the line when the story needs properly embedding into the game and production schedule.

Some writers do charge more for anything that falls into the IP creation/world creation workload, given that often they are helping create the building blocks of a franchise, rather than just a standalone game. It's certainly worth both writers and developers checking with the Writers Guild of America or Writers' Guild of Great Britain (both of which represent games writers) to see just what the current rates are for early-stage narrative work. However, it usually falls to the individual writer and their employer to define exactly where early-stage IP creation begins and ends.

14.2   Innovation or Familiarity?

New IPs fall into two rough categories: complete, standalone, original games such as *Psychonauts*, *Call of Juarez*, and *Bioshock* (*Overlord*, *Heavenly Sword*, and *Mirror's Edge* also fall into this category) and games related to an existing (or upcoming) IP such as a movie (*The Chronicles of Riddick*, *Spiderman 2*, *Hulk: Ultimate Destruction*),

TV series (*Little Britain: The Game*), comic (*The Darkness*, *Rogue Trooper*), or old game licence revamped (*World of Warcraft*, *Half-Life 2*, *Doom 3*).

Standalone IPs

A new, standalone IP isn't any cast-iron guarantee of gameplay innovation, although this is the place you're most likely to find it. From a writer's point of view, much of the project will be geared towards delivering on the gameplay experience, as should be the case. The story and narrative can sometimes take a back seat until the gameplay is considered a solid and enjoyable experience.

Whilst this can be frustrating for a writer at first, it's ultimately for the best. You're unlikely to be able to cram a great story into a title with poor gameplay and stop the game from the inevitable press pounding, but solid gameplay gives the writer a great basis from which to build an immersive narrative world and avoid the afore-mentioned narrative custard effect. For the most part, we are writing for games; games aren't gameplaying our stories. Needs of the gameplay do need to come first, especially if a new, standalone IP is to have longevity in the marketplace.

But it's certainly not doom and gloom here. Creating new worlds and compelling characters (covered in more depth later) are incredibly important with standalone IPs precisely because they do help bolster a single game into a burgeoning franchise. If you are given free, or at least freer, rein to create your own characters and world structure then pretty much every narrative and character creation technique is at your disposal, as long as it conforms with those old game-narrative bugbears of pacing, gameplay, and memory requirements. Whatever you create, keep one eye firmly on the extension of your world (the sequel, the downloadable content, the ports, the comics, the animation, even the movie) because you can be damn sure that your publisher will have. And being a few creative steps ahead always helps come contract renewal time.

Existing Franchise IPs

New game IPs attached to another franchise really aren't the kiss of death that they used to be. As the rest of the entertainment world becomes a little more savvy about games and game development, there's thankfully less pressure to turn out a fourth-rate game and hope the name alone will sell it.

From a writer's perspective, franchise IP can often come with its own restrictions piled on top of the existing game-related ones. This is especially true if the game is tied to an upcoming movie, which may well dictate not only the content but also the release date. It is also likely that any script or story work will have to be passed through the franchise holder for signing off (such as J. K. Rowling, in the case of the *Harry Potter* games).

There's also the added benefit (or curse, depending on your viewpoint) that as far as characters and world go, a lot of the work has already been done for you. Of course, that doesn't mean the end of creativity for the writer/story designer. Even realizing the same story in an interactive world is a whole different ball game. However, allowing a game to cover an element of the franchise world that isn't necessarily covered in, say, an upcoming movie is starting to become quite popular.

Just look at the success Starbreeze had with the *The Chronicles of Riddick: Escape from Butcher Bay*, which ran as a prequel to *Pitch Black*, which was released alongside the movie sequel entitled *The Chronicles of Riddick*. Arguably, the game was much better received than the movie. Starbreeze also went on to follow this up with another franchise tie-in, *The Darkness* (originally a comic), which also received the twin golden kisses of critical and sales success.

14.3 Building Narrative Worlds

The narrative elements of a game have their own pre-production phase, too. This is unlikely to run alongside the rest of the game's pre-production phase, unless the studio has a dedicated narrative team as part of their day-to-day staff.

In the case of *Heavenly Sword*, there was actually a first draft script in place when I came onboard, which had been written by Tameem Antoniades, the game's Creative Director. The story, or at least the spine of it, had been conceived before the gameplay and levels had been completely nailed down, which almost never happens in the game industry. My role was to help flesh out the world, the characters, their relationships, backstories, and character arcs through the game, as well as doing a full, page-one rewrite on the script.

Flesh on the Bones

The important thing to remember when faced with creating a narrative world is that there are usually a lot of team members who will also need to be involved in this process; predominately art and design, because narrative world design is rarely just about the words. *Bioshock* and *Half-Life 2* are great examples of where the story is told as much through what you see as what you hear, demonstrating one of the greatest rules of visual narrative: "show don't tell." Unfortunately, as desirable as that is, the game industry is in the rather unfortunate position that showing can often cost just as much as, if not a lot more than, telling!

I've always found it beneficial to flesh out the world as much as possible for my own benefit as a writer, even if it never gets further than a Word document. In all likelihood, like the proverbial iceberg, the players will only see the actual tip of it in the game. Nevertheless, that narrative support structure is vital for a writer. Not only does working out things like the politics, socioeconomic make-up, power-structure, industry structure, and world history actually help develop your characters and support level design and narrative, but it also provides great fodder for expanding the world further down the line. Story, character, and even gameplay can be far better supported in a world that feels real, or at the very least coherent, in its structure

If a game has a heavy story element then it may be part of your role to create a story bible for that world that is easily accessible by all members of the team but with its content controlled by you. This should contain information on the main story arc, character profiles, casting notes, and concept art. It should also contain information on the narrative side of the world. Conceivably, then they could include elements such as the political make-up, gang structure or culture, pre-history, slang used, relationship networks, companies, organizations, etc. It should be the go-to guide for anyone seeking information on the story and narrative world, which will frequently include you, the writer.

The Story Without and the Story Within

One aspect of game narrative that makes it unique among entertainment forms is that it has the ability to allow players to tell the story, or at least part of it, to themselves. This is done with clever use of design, environment, and narrative markers. It is also something that any writer or story designer needs to be especially aware of when they are shaping a new IP world, as any additions along these lines will greatly increase the game's narrative strength.

Again, this works on the "show don't tell" principle. But because a player is moving around inside and shaping this narrative world, what we're talking about really is self-narration. Sometimes this can be spun out of a certain feeling elicited in the players; for example, the feeling of isolation in *Shadow of the Colossus*, the feeling of loss in *Ico*, or the feeling of vulnerability in *Fatal Frame/Project Zero*. Sometimes it can be in the little details in the world: the burnt-out playgrounds and sad tic-tac-toe games on the walls in *Half-Life 2*, the macabre arrangement of corpses in the Fort Frolic level of *Bioshock*, or the *Deb of Night* radio show in *Vampire: Bloodlines*.

What is really demanded of writers on new IP is to help create the world not just with text and dialog but with vision and feel. It's a task far more akin to part director, part set builder, part writer, part actor. Any game writer who truly loves the medium should learn to be a skilled interactive story designer as well—bricks, mortar, and walls, the whole shebang!

As I'm sure you are aware, game writing is a young enough writing discipline that there are no hard-and-fast rules yet. There is merely good, solid advice born out of success, failure, frustration, and elation. Part of the reason for this is that every game is different, in demands, expectation, and time frame. So to invoke the "show don't tell" principle, I'm going to help convey how to deal with world creation and new character creation for a new IP by showing you how I tackled it in *Overlord*. Okay, so technically, I'm showing you in words, but the game is available at all good entertainment retailers should you wish to see it yourself. (End of blatant plug.)

14.4   Case Study: The World of *Overlord*

The Home of Evil Deeds

When I arrived aboard the good ship *Overlord* (published by Codemasters and developed by the Holland-based Triumph Studios), the game had already been in devel-

Figure 14.2. Ransacking cute villages and setting fire to halflings proved to be very popular in the *Overlord* world.

opment for a year. The basic story of this action-adventure title was that the player assumed the role of a newly appointed evil overlord tasked with bringing the smiting stick down hard upon the seven heroes who killed their predecessor and looted their dark tower. The gameplay premise, namely that the player would use an ever-expanding army of gremlin-like minions to do their evil (and not so evil) deeds, was already pretty solid and fun to play.

Many of the levels were already in development and had been designed around the fall of the seven heroes, who had fallen from grace in the manner of the seven deadly sins. So the halfling hero (who represented greed) had eaten himself into this disgusting blob, enslaving the inhabitants of his realm to perpetual food-farming in the process. Meanwhile, the holy Paladin's trips to the local brothel and weakness for succubi had caused a city-wide plague. He, unsurprisingly, represented lust. You get the idea.

Although the game itself never shouted about it, the use of deadly sins made a nice, easy-to-grasp framework for the heroes (handy when explaining things to the press) and also bled through to the environments and the quest and level design.

The environments themselves were deliberately quite typical fantasy fare: rolling green meadows, magical forests, war-torn cities, scorching deserts, and ruined castles. And since the mood of the game was very tongue-in-cheek, the level design and sheer exuberant joy of heading up a rampaging horde of angry minions gave the world more of a dark twist, as much in gameplay action as in looks. So the player could well find themselves setting fire to halflings, performing genocide on the elven race, battling drunken dwarves, and generally giving the good, bad, and ugly of fantasy land a good, solid thrashing.

Writer Onboard

I was very lucky that *Overlord* already had a wonderfully fun sense of humor instilled in its gameplay and level design. When I started on the project, my role was really to help enhance that through the creation of a coherent story that held all the levels and the player's journey together, plus help create a cast of suitably mad, bad, and dangerous-to-know characters. From a world-creation perspective, it was about giving each domain its own unique narrative feel, its own story-within-a-story, based around the particular hero who dwelled there.

Though hardcore RPGs are less common than they used to be, the benefits of creating story webs (mini stories that link back and forth to other stories, as well as helping describe the arc of an overall story) still reverberate across the genres and are particularly important in anything that has quite a definite level-by-level, linear structure. Although in the case of *Overlord*, you could go back (and were, in fact, encouraged to) and revisit previous levels. This was both through the needs of the gameplay (harvesting the various colors of life force to keep your Minion horde topped up) and built into the story, such as when the player has to pursue Kahn, the Barry White soundalike warrior hero, as he rampages through several domains.

I also had to make sure that the less linear aspects of the world—for example, when the player had a choice of domains to go to next—could be reflected in a flexible storyline. In that instance, the narrative had to be constructed so it could be experienced in various orders without confusing the player. Giving each level its own feel and individual story was probably the most useful tool in achieving this. That way, the game had an encapsulated mini-tale, along with nonlinear nuggets of narrative about the overall story. What makes this particularly important for new IPs is that it's all about creating a narrative world, rather than one single narrative path.

The desire to create a specific feel to the different areas was also echoed in our casting choices. The halfling domain was populated largely with both American and British rural voices, the elves became annoying American emos (a very deliberate move, since I felt that elves get far too much good press), and the more urban areas had tougher, American and British semi-city accents. Despite the fact that the *Overlord* world is a fantasy one, we really wanted it to feel as coherent to the players as any real-world franchise, yet still keep the fun and humor elements very much in the foreground.

Ambient and level dialog is also very important for capturing the essence of the world and, perhaps more importantly, giving the player narrative feedback on the results of their chosen path through it (just how evil they'd chosen to be). Some quests, such as the much sought-after "maiden collection" quests, were deliberately triggered as the result of the player marching around being very nasty to everyone they met.

Although it's often left until last, the role of ambient dialog as a feedback mechanism, and a world-coloring tool, should not be underestimated. There's always a certain percentage of players that may skip cutscenes (the brutes!), but almost every

Figure 14.3. *Overlord* allowed Minions to wear all sorts of items, like these natty pumpkin hats.

player will hear ambient narrative. For this very reason, it's often where dialog and story nuances have the most impact. So do not neglect your ambient dialogue—it can really be an interactive writer's best friend.

As mentioned earlier, we cast our NPCs very specifically for our different domains to help create this world idea and also to create a feel for the races within it. So now an *Overlord* player would go into a future *Overlord* game expecting the peasants to be affable but rather foolish, the elves to be sulky and deliberately overwrought, and the dwarves to be little more than angry beards on legs who'll do anything for a pint of beer and a pocket full of gold.

Expanding the World—*Overlord: Raising Hell*

When we came to creating the expansion content, *Overlord: Raising Hell*, we spun out the story by introducing a hell-themed sub-domain where the previously defeated heroes and their cronies were going through perpetual punishments. The elves were being forced to watch a play about their downfall, the halfling hero was forced to eat and eat until he exploded, and the gold-obsessed dwarf king had been encased inside a golden statue. Both the narrative themes and gameplay were created with the desire to kick up the dark humor and evilness a few notches. This was in part a reaction to some player feedback on the main game, namely that they didn't think you could be quite wicked enough.

The solid base we'd established in the first game made it much easier to spin off new mini-stories that felt coherent and linked to the original game, rather than just being tacked on. Gnarl, the Minion Master character in the game and the player's always on-hand guide, had proved very popular with players (thanks to the vocal talents of Marc Silk), so we decided to make him play a central narrative role in the expansion. My role as writer and co-story designer went very smoothly on *Raising Hell* precisely because I'd spent so long helping to flesh out the narrative parts of the world and characters in the original game. It meant I could worry less about coloring and building the narrative world and more about creating fun stories and dialog that complemented the gameplay.

14.5   Importance of Character

In the past, iconic game characters have been predominately defined by their looks: Lara Croft (certainly in the early years), Mario, Sonic, Samus Aran, Gordon Freeman, etc. They haven't had any real character traits or arcs either because it was deemed unnecessary or, in the case of Mr. Freeman, they weren't even given the luxury of speech.

When it comes to singling out one area not related to gameplay that will make a new IP stand out from the rest, then it's in addressing these areas of character and character development. In every other entertainment form, characters and their experiences are vital for bringing a story to life, and games should be no acceptation.

Obviously, strong visuals are still important. The marketing and coverage of *Heavenly Sword* was certainly helped by the strong artistic look of not only Nariko, the red-haired lead character, but also the rest of the (relatively small) cast. Small casts are often a lot more fun for a writer to work with because there's much more opportunity to shape and grow them as distinct personalities. Often games with a larger cast of characters suffer from the same character voice being split between multiple characters, even main-cast characters. If new IP characters are going to stand out and help bolster the IP and franchise then they need to have unique and individual voices that will require time and attention from you the writer to create and communicate to the audio/dramatic direction team.

As with any other entertainment medium, you need to love your characters, at least a little bit. Love all your characters, even the bad guys—in fact, those tend to be fairly easy to love. If you don't care about your characters, how do you expect players to?

14.6   Character Case Studies: *Overlord*—Mistress Rose and Mistress Velvet

Rose and Velvet were NPC characters that the player encountered at various points during the game. Initially Rose joins the player's little tower community after the completion of a mandatory quest to find a Mistress for your tower. Later on in the game, you meet Rose's younger sister Velvet and get the chance to swap sisters, each sister giving you different Minion upgrades as a possible incentive for choosing them.

While the Mistresses' main role was to provide ambient feedback on the way the player has been progressing through the game, Rose and Velvet also came to play quite a significant part in the overall story—more than was originally envisaged before I came onboard. The following extras from the characters' original bios detail a little bit of insider information about the creation of these two virtual ladies.

Mistress Rose

Figure 14.4. Left: Mistress Rose in concept-art form. Note the sensible neckline and hemline! Right: Rose in the game, ready for some organized and orderly evil action!

Gender/Age: Female, late twenties.

Keywords: Reserved, sharp, diplomatic, charming at times, bossy, classy, slightly soothing voice (girl next door rather than vamp), rather cold sometimes, kindly (towards Minions), twisted Mary Poppins.

Rose's Background

Rose is the older sister of Mistress Velvet. Rose and Velvet are both the daughters of the "Good" Wizard, born to him before he was taken over by the Old Overlord. Whilst they share the same father, Rose is not so immediately inclined towards evil deeds as her sister is. She is neither completely good nor completely bad.

Rose and Velvet were raised together, but their father the "Good" Wizard was somewhat of an absentee parent, always far more focused on going out adventuring, questing, and smiting evil than raising his own children. Rose ended up looking after her sister and trying to cover up Velvet's naughty childish ways until she got fed up and left home to make her own way in the world. Since then, Velvet has left home, too, and fallen in with a "dark crowd." Neither of them have had much contact with each other for years.

Rose During the Game

Rose is the first of the two Mistresses that the player will encounter. She is practical and sensible, she's a great planner and strategist, and she knows how to make things run properly no matter whether they are good or evil. She dislikes sloppiness and bad management wherever it might appear.

Rose could be a great asset to either side, should she actually make the choice between good and evil once and for all, but Rose prefers to go where she sees the work, regardless of alignment. Rose acknowledges killing as a necessity (just a necessity for other people), and if there's to be evil in the world (and Rose understands the need for balance) then it should at least be done properly.

Although Rose is attractive, she does not use that to get what she wants, as compared to the gushing and flirting of her sister Velvet. Rose does have a soft spot for the Overlord's Minions, though, and speaks about them in a much more kindly way than she ever does about the player.

Rose's Vocal Requirements

Rose has a pleasant but somewhat "teacherish" voice, like a slightly twisted Marry Poppins. She is quite well spoken (think English Rose) although not to the extent of sounding too posh, as that is likely to be off-putting. Her tone goes slightly cutesy when she's talking about/to the Minions.

Example lines to the player:

ROSE

"Sire, that girl that William the Paladin was going to marry. Well... she's my sister, Velvet.

We don't speak. Speaking usually means she's got herself into some kind of trouble... *again*.

Judging by this place, Velvet's in it up to her silly little neck."

Example lines to Velvet:

ROSE

"Sir William summoned an over-sexed demon, started a city-wide plague, and now he's dead. I can see why you might be *emotional*! But stay out of my business!"

Rose Postmortem

Rose's character was quite a hard one to voice, as we wanted to make sure that her character traits came off as amusing, rather than annoying, and that her voice was still pleasant to listen to. We had to go through a couple of voice actresses to get the right tone and performance.

Lots of players seemed to think that Rose was the "good" sister, rather than the "less evil" one. I think this is in part because players are used to thinking in quite black-and-white terms when it comes to the representation of evil in games. Rose would actually make one hell of a dictator, given half a chance. However, unless players kept Rose in their tower for the whole game, they wouldn't see her more Machiavellian side emerging. In retrospect, I probably should have made her even more openly evil.

Rose's character was very much an attempt on my part to get away from the typical "wench" character that's so often seen in fantasy games and to create a character who was strong but still had the fun, dark spirit of the game. She came together well in the end, thanks to the vocal talents of Fay Maillardet.

Mistress Velvet

Figure 14.5. Left: Mistress Velvet in concept-art form, working the sexy-evil look. Right: Velvet gets a bit of a wiggle on in the game.

Gender/Age: Female, mid twenties.

Keywords: Naughty/flirty, sexy, seductive, a little crazy, calculating, ruthless, charming, classy (or at least thinks she is!), decadent, selfish, spoilt, slightly snobbish.

Velvet's Background

Velvet is the younger sister of Rose. She craves attention, adulation, and wealth and doesn't care how she gets it.

She was always a naughty child but was used to being protected and covered for by her Rose, since her father wasn't around very much (constantly off thwarting evil, having adventures, etc.). But when Rose left home seeking her own life away from her demanding little sister and her absentee father, Velvet spiraled downwards, fell in with the wrong crowd, and became a "Mistress of evil."

Velvet in the Game

Velvet is very attractive and sexually alluring. This is 100% deliberate, and she knows how to manipulate men, especially the Paladin. Rather like an evil soccer player's wife.

Velvet is attracted to the monetary, aesthetic, and amoral trappings of evil. When we meet her, she is the spurned about-to-be-bride of the once heroic Paladin who has given himself over to his lustful side. Even worse, his relations with the succubi at the local brothel have caused an STD-like zombie plague throughout Heaven's Peak. The wedding has been canceled, and the Paladin has locked up his ex-would-be-bride in his private bedroom, while he and his followers have somewhat dodgy parties in the main Citadel.

Rose doesn't like her sister that much, but she's still worried that she may be in serious trouble. When the player and Rose rescue Velvet, Rose remembers exactly why she doesn't get along with Velvet!

Once the player kills the Paladin, Velvet will join up with the player if the player forsakes Rose. Velvet is very flirty (but with an undertone of making sure she gets what she wants) towards the player, although she doesn't like the Minions much and constantly refers to them as "pixies."

Velvet's Vocal Requirements

Velvet should sound very much like her name, namely the sultry seductress voice (think Liz Hurley in *Bedazzled*). This is partly for effect as much as anything else, because when she's angry, frustrated, or caught off guard (such as when she's arguing with Rose), the seductress voice drops a little, and she can sound more like a petulant, stubborn child. But she tries to maintain the act at all times because she's pretty convinced that this is what evil mistresses *should* sound like!

Example lines to the player:

VELVET

(Shouts from the bedroom) "I'm in heeerrre!

And tell that greedy dwarf King that he can't have his wedding presents back!

If I'm not going to have a wedding, I at least want *presents!*"

"Well hello... dark stranger. The rumors do not do you justice."

"You've brought me a gift... some little *pixies*? You *really* shouldn't have!

Next time make it something shiny... and expensive!

Now... let me thank you *properly*."

Velvet Postmortem

Velvet was deliberately meant to be the sexy, slightly goth, fantasy wench, but the difference is that she knows it. This was what I tried to build into her character, as well as her cleavage! She was an easier character to write than Rose but still a lot of fun, as I could offset her flirtatiousness with a more spoilt, childish side. This was expertly captured by the lovely Jonell Elliot—a former Lara Croft voice, no less!

Overall, the sisters made a nice pairing, and their scenes together were a lot of fun. Given more time, we would have definitely involved the Mistresses more in the general gameplay. However, in the creation of Rose and Velvet, I in-build a few narrative hooks that will ideally spin them into future incarnations. In fact, at the end of *Overlord: Raising Hell*, it's strongly suggested that your chosen Mistress will have a very literal role in spawning future evil!

Rose and Velvet Narrative Character Hooks

- They had distinct personalities, voices, and ways of looking at the world, as well as very different visual looks. There's certainly no mixing Velvet and Rose up!

- Both had conflict with each other, the player (depending on who the player spurned), and other characters in the game.

- The chosen Mistress has a *special* bond with the player, which remains unbroken at the end of the game.

- They are both alive at the end of the game. Death, especially in video games, isn't always the end, but it's not too easy to get back from!

- They both have a strong insight into and about the gameplay—namely being evil. And there's certainly the indication that if they managed to get along and team up, they'd be a formidable force.

14.7   Conclusion

I've been very lucky that the majority of my game writing and story design work have been for new IPs, and so far they've not been consigned to Mr. Allison's 93% failure graveyard. New IPs may be the greatest risks, but creatively they can be the biggest wins as well. This is really where the metal meets the meat, and it's a fertile area for writers to get involved and do some good. There are worlds out there for you to create and populate and stories to be spun. Go forth, good writers, and be narrative gods!

14.8   Exercises

1. Take a game you've enjoyed and create (in document form, unless you're feeling really creative) a new area of the gameworld that has a particular emphasis on narrative and storytelling. This could be to create more interest in a particular character or event, or even to cover what you see as a plot hole in the original game. Keep it small and think about narrative features such as cutscenes, interactive dialog, and combat dialog within that area.

2. Create your own backstory for an NPC character of your choice, either an existing NPC or one of your own making. Think about how the character's backstory could be folded into the gameworld.

15

Script Doctoring

Richard Dansky

In a perfect world, game writing follows a defined process that establishes room for creativity. The writer works with the team start to finish, provides the dialog, story, and other writing elements that the game requires, and is able to satisfy the needs of the project while still carving out a satisfying space for creative endeavor. The process flows smoothly, the schedule is reasonable, and the needed content is appropriate to both the needs of the game and the capability of the writer or writers producing it.

Unfortunately, this doesn't always happen. Things go wrong, or at least go differently from the initial plan. Scope changes. Deadlines shift. The need for five thousand extra lines of dialog suddenly materializes. People roll onto and off of projects, levels get redesigned, features get added or cut, and so forth.

In other words, stuff happens, and stuff happening is the main reason that game writers are sometimes called on to fill the role of script doctor.

Technically, the term isn't quite accurate. After all, a writer coming onto a project mid-development cycle may be asked to do anything from polishing up the dialog to getting involved in major reworking of the story (and, by extension, gameplay). The script is a large part of a game writer's focus under those circumstances, but it's not always all of it. Sometimes, it's not even the most important part.

15.1 What Is Script Doctoring?

Script doctoring for video games is a catch-all term for coming onto a project to assist with any and all writing-related tasks. It can be as light a task as polishing the dialog to make sure all the slang is appropriate, or as heavy as doing a complete story and character overhaul. It can be a couple of days of in-and-out, or it can be a task requiring months of work.

What it is not is an entirely original task. A script doctor's work is to get a game's writing where it needs to be, and that implies that there's already a game in place to be doctored. And if there's a game in place, odds are that there are characters, levels, and suchlike, elements that pin down what a writer has to work with. Even if your mandate as a script doctor is to tear the whole story down and start again, odds are you won't be allowed to toss the main character or the game's central concept. Depending on how far along the other assets are and how close ship date is, you may even be asked to try to make a narrative out of previously existing assets, putting them into some kind of logical order.

If that doesn't sound like a boundlessly creative task, that's because it isn't. It's task-oriented, not necessarily art-oriented, and the most important thing to focus on is making sure the game gets done.

15.2   The Basics

The most important thing any game script doctor can do is figure out what they're actually there to do. Going in with a mistaken idea about their mandate, authority, or permitted scope of change is a recipe for 180-proof disaster. After all, if a new writer is being brought in, there's a good chance that they're being brought in for a particular reason. Sometimes that reason is as broad as, "The last guy didn't work out"; sometimes it's as narrow as, "We need to you take a pass on this to add some humor to a couple of the characters." But nobody randomly says, "We need to bring another writer on now," without a very good reason, and without knowing what that reason is, the script doctor is setting himself up for immediate, spectacular failure.

Craft, Not Art

One of the things you have to deal with as a script doctor is recognizing that you're doing a very different job than the game writer who's on the project from the word go. You are often there to fix something, to do rewrites, or to plug holes, not to create art. And while you may perform Herculean feats of prose in the service of your project, nine times out of nine and a half, that's not going to be on a level playing field with a game that's had tight story and writing development since its very beginning. Just getting a game to "decent" from "unlistenable" might be the work of ages, but nobody outside the development team will know that, nor will they care. The players care about the end product, not what might have been, and there are no writing prizes for "best patch job."

So, instead of focusing on art, script doctors need to focus on craft—plugging plot holes, getting things done, and making sure all of the game's needs are met. This is an honorable approach to the work, and has done much to make many games playable, but it's not the sort of labor that's necessarily going to always be easy on the ego. That's not to say that script doctors shouldn't try to do the very best work they can, but the demands they're likely to face—lots of work, short turnaround, existing assets to be dealt with and incorporated—mean that there's a lot less wiggle room for creativity and art.

Scope

The first thing to find out is the scope of the work being asked for. This is both harder and more important than it sounds. It's harder, in that the people remaining on the team may not actually know what is wanted or needed. After all, many of them were probably on the team when the circumstances requiring a script doctor's attention were created. On the other hand, they may have just been brought on themselves, which means their grasp of the project may be imperfect.

Establishing scope. Without knowing how much there is to do, you can't get started. Without knowing how much work there is to do in the time available, you can't prioritize your time appropriately, and you risk spending either too much time or too little on the first deliverable you tackle. That means that the first thing you have to do is figure out what you have to do.

Find Out What the Actual Assignment Is

"Fix the writing" sounds great on paper, but in real life it's spectacularly unhelpful in providing direction. What any script doctor actually needs to know is the answer to one simple question: What am I expected to do? Without getting a definitive answer on that question, you're going to have tremendous difficulty in going forward with the actual work of writing. So it's vital to get your actual expected deliverables mapped out and agreed upon.

Find Out the Assignment Parameters

What anyone doing script doctoring needs to know can be measured with numbers: How many lines overall? How many variants on each line (if necessary)? How many cutscenes? What's the total word count allowed by disc footprint? Find out parameters before you start writing, or you may end up throwing out work when you overwrite a strict guideline. That, incidentally, is the one thing you absolutely cannot afford to do: waste time on work that can't or won't be used.

Time. Knowing how much time you have is key. Knowing exactly when each chunk of what you're doing needs to be delivered is vital prioritization. When you're on a tight deadline—and script doctoring deadlines can be as tight as, "We're in the studio now, can you think of a better way to say this?"—organizing the tasks at hand by priority is an absolute must. Having a firm schedule to order your workflow around will make your life easier; not having one will make your life impossible.

Number of lines/scenes/etc. The quantitative side of what you're doing is important, as well. Knowing how many lines/scenes/missions you have to write tells you how much time you can give to each one. Getting those numbers laid out for you by the person you'll be reporting to serves another purpose, as well; it's protection in case someone else suddenly decides to add an extra thousand lines when nobody's looking. If you have a list of deliverables, you can use it to ward off excessive, ill-thought-out, or impossible requests.

Existing assets. By definition, a script doctor is playing with someone else's toys. Something—levels, characters, mission designs, you name it—is already in place in the game and would cost too much time or money to replace. That means that you have to suck it up and work with it, for good or for ill. On one hand, it can be a situation where there are twenty levels built and you get to craft a storyline putting them in order; on the other, it may be, "Here's all our gameplay and mission design. You get to write the dialog to support it because the last guy couldn't stop bitching about the plot holes."

On the bright side, finding out what's already in place that you can or have to use helps you build a structure for your work. It also answers questions about what you have to work with and potentially gives you something to match your work against, providing a useful standard.

Other restrictions (rating, number of voices, etc.). There are a lot of hidden restrictions on writing that you may not know about. For example, the character pipeline may be tapped, or the voice-recording budget may be stretched thin, so you might not be allowed to add any new voices or characters. The game's motion set doesn't include, say, smoking a cigarette, so you can't write a cutscene where your dastardly villain lights up and blows smoke in the captured hero's face. The publisher may have mandated a certain rating, either US or European, and that places definite restrictions on the sort of language you can use. Finding out what all of these secondary parameters are before you start writing helps focus your efforts, and it keeps you from being frustrated later at having to chop stuff you thought was good to go. There's nothing quite like having to go back through a 20,000 line script taking out every instance of profanity worse than the word "darn" to make you appreciate the importance of getting the boundaries of what you're doing straight before you start.

Integrating with the Team

In video games, no one works in a vacuum, and a writer called on to script doctor is no exception. And because time is generally short for a script doctor, there's precious little room for the sort of extended getting-to-know-you period that might otherwise have taken place. A script doctor needs to integrate with the team seamlessly and immediately, or they're already behind.

On a basic level, that means being introduced to everyone you might be working with, getting shown the tool set you'll need to use, and otherwise finding your way around. Everything from security badges to knowing where the coffee machine is falls under this particular rubric. In a broader sense, it means getting yourself ready to work immediately. On the other hand, there are certain particulars that need to be addressed first that aid in the larger integration of the script doctor into the team.

Find a point of contact. Ideally, there should be one key point of contact for a script doctor. While it's fine to talk with other folks on the team for informational or social purposes, there really needs to be a dedicated point of contact: one person to report to, one person to give tasks, one person to funnel requests or concerns through. Otherwise, you run the risk of getting hit from all sides with requests, complaints, feedback, and ideas, none of which will help you do what you're actually there to do.

Set up a chain of communication. This goes hand in hand with finding a point of contact. You need to establish how your docs are getting out and whom they're going to, or else your work may just fly off into the ether. You also need to know who has approvals on your work, whom you should be talking to about particular characters or features or levels, and generally establish whom you'll need to talk with and why.

If there's a clear chain of communication in place, then the set-up cuts down on the number of potential surprises heading your way. It also lets you prioritize your email and other messages; the guy who sounds utterly urgent and desperate may not be in a position to actually ask you to do anything.

Set up a chain of command. It can't be said often enough: game writing doesn't happen in a vacuum. Multiple people are going to be clamoring for writing deliverables, or giving them out, or commenting on them, and that's just during the normal chaos of game development. Add in the caffeinating factor of script doctoring, and you have the potential for a snarl that looks like a wad of taffy in an industrial loom.

It is vital, then, to establish very clearly whom you report to and who gets to tell you what to do. It's equally important to lay out who needs to see your work and who doesn't. This isn't an attempt to hide your writing from the team, but if every single team member has final cut on the script, then the script's never getting done. Instead, it's best to solidify a relationship with a single point person. All deliverables go out through them; all requests come in the same way. And together with them, you can figure out who needs to see each deliverable so that proper workflow is maintained.

Ultimately, this comes down to two clear lists: who gets to make assignments, and who gets signoff. A subset of signoff is who gets the right to edit, but once your work is approved, the editing process should be over anyway. Keeping both lists short, clear, and public saves you from distraction and saves the project from the horrors of having a writer being pulled in multiple, possibly contradictory, directions.

Prioritization

Knowing what to do first is almost as important as knowing what to do, period. Sadly, script doctoring is generally done under serious time pressure, and that means you can't agonize over and polish each line. It also means that, more than ever, some stuff is more important than others. Going the extra mile to make the bark pools 25 lines deep instead of 15 is admirable, but if that means you don't get to two characters' main dialog before recording starts, you've made a bad time-management decision somewhere.

Instead, work out with your point of contact what your schedule should be. What gets done first, what gets cut first, and who needs what when—these are the things that you need to know.

What gets done first. What gets done first is, by necessity, most important. Odds are this is the stuff that the most other features/work schedules are hanging on, so it's that much more important to get it nailed down and handed off. This, too, is where knowing team schedules is vital. If the guy doing the cutscenes needs the scripts to block the sequences and feed the animators, object builders, etc., then you'd better get those scripts to him quickly. Conversely, if the guys following him in the pipeline aren't ready, you can re-prioritize.

What gets cut first. Because there are always unexpected delays, mishaps, and other catastrophes lurking in the shrubbery, you always need to figure out what can go first. This isn't a decision that you can make solo, but mapping your intentions and getting them approved means that there are fewer tears and faster reactions when the axe inevitably comes down.

Style. Almost without exception, shorter and cleaner is better when it comes to script doctoring. Clear and concise should be your watchwords. There isn't time for potentially confusing or ambiguous phrasings, no time for multiple loops of revision. Instead, you need to make things as clear as possible the first time to make sure there isn't a need for a second—or a third, or a fourth.

(Here's a quick litmus test. If you can't say a line of dialog you write in a single breath, mark it as suspect. Not every one needs to go, but it's a handy red flag for when time is short.)

This works from a logistical standpoint as well. Write shorter lines and fewer lines, and there's much less work in the recording studio, for the sound engineers, the localization team, and so forth. You're not only making your life easier you're making the lives of a lot of people down the line easier, as well—not to mention the player who has to listen to the dialog over and over again.

Script Doctoring in the Studio

Sometimes, the writer is asked to tag along on voice shoots. This can be for a variety of reasons, ranging from providing context and character motivation to, inevitably, rewriting lines on the fly. Simply put, not every line works as written. Sometimes the actor can't make it work, sometimes the rhythm's better for the written word than the spoken, and sometimes it's just plain off. When that happens, you may be called on to do a rewrite on the fly, and if that happens, there are some things you can do to make life easier for all concerned parties.

One, don't fight it. If the actor can't read the line, the actor can't read the line. Be willing to make changes for the sake of getting a better reading. If you've got a good enough relationship with the voice director and actor, you can even volunteer it when something's not working, and the admission that your stuff isn't deathless prose may win you some respect. On the other hand, don't do this too often. Save it for when the line, or the actor, is really floundering. Otherwise, it's easy to slip into artiste-ville, and you should have thought of that before you stepped into the very-expensive-per-minute studio.

Two, listen. There's usually one spot in the line where the actor is obviously having trouble. That's where you want to make your change. Your ears should tell you what your fingers should change.

Three, chopping is usually winning. The shorter a line is, the less chance there is for something to go wrong with it. When in doubt, throw words out.

And finally, remember that you're not in charge. It's the voice director's show, not the writer's, and your role is to support, assist, and inform. Keep to that, and establish a good working relationship with the voice director, and everything else is details.

Quick-and-Dirty Secrets

The basics aside, there are certain tips and tricks that you can use when script doctoring to make your life easier, your work come out better, and your inevitable panic attacks end more quickly. While nothing replaces the basics of being organized, efficient, and open, there are ways to shave time off the corners of what you're doing while strengthening the quality of the work.

Break assignments into manageable sizes. Trying to tackle everything at once is foolhardy, not to mention potentially very depressing when you constantly look up and see how much is left to do. Instead, you're better off taking some time at the start to chop the work into manageable chunks that you stand a good chance of finishing quickly. The sense of accomplishment that comes from wrapping up a discrete piece of work is often vital fuel in powering on to the next one, and the next, and the next.

Furthermore, it helps your coworkers. If you're completing stuff in chunks, you can hand it off in chunks, and the people down the deliverable chain can get working on it that much sooner. Sitting on the entire script until it's done means that other folks are potentially twiddling their thumbs waiting for you, something that no project can afford. Writing in easily handled units also helps with setting up feedback loops, and with helping to make sure that problems get tackled quickly and before they get out of hand. After all, if the team cuts a level, it's a lot easier to make the necessary adjustments a few hundred lines at a time, as opposed to a few thousand.

Set up quick feedback loops. Figure out who needs to sign off on what you're doing (as opposed to who just wants to get their fingers in the pie), and make sure you set up a clean and easy process for getting feedback from them. This is imperative for producing a fast workflow, otherwise one party or the other is going to be sitting around waiting, unable to move forward.

Building the loop means building the parameters—who gets it, how much time they have to turn it around, and what happens if they don't. The number of people involved should be pared back as far as possible; the more people involved in any given feedback process, the longer it takes, and the rate of increase is most decidedly not linear. Be merciless in chopping unnecessary names, and get the producer or the equivalent to back your play. Otherwise, you run the risk of getting bogged down in endless review meetings and revision cycles, as everyone needs to get their two cents in.

Instead, what setting things up like this means is that everyone who's appropriate is in the loop but that there's a mechanism built in to keep the system from bogging down. Getting feedback fast means making corrections fast, which hopefully everyone can get behind. It also shortens the time until final version and allows for fast, on-the-fly adjustments to what you're doing instead of waiting until the end and making one titanic change.

Have something to show fast. The sooner you get feedback from the appropriate team members, the sooner you know if you're doing things right. If you're not doing things right, the sooner you know, the less work you have to redo and the less time gets wasted. If you are doing things right, getting the confirmation early lets you charge ahead with more confidence, knowing you're on target.

So, setting up a quick deliverable—even just a few lines per character to make sure you have tone and voice right—for key team personnel to look at can save a lot of time and heartbreak on the back end. Getting a small chunk of work into the right hands quickly and setting a short deadline for turnaround on the feedback ensures that you're in sync with the team's needs and that you're not plunging ahead with an incorrect mental image of what you should be doing. In other words, it's a great safety feature for both you and the team.

Ask questions as needed. If you don't ask questions, you don't get answers. If you don't get answers, you can't do the job right unless you're very, very lucky at guessing. So, if you have a question—any question at all—ask it. Making bad guesses simply means lots of backtracking and repair later. Sitting there and hoping that someone magically answers your question by reading your mind generally doesn't cut it, and doesn't get you your answer, either. Don't be afraid of embarrassment; the other team members would generally prefer you ask rather than get something wrong.

If you have a lot of questions for one individual or workgroup, it might be best to schedule a sit-down meeting to make sure you work through everything. Otherwise, there's no reason not to throw your issue out there as soon as it makes itself known as a problem. Email it out, walk over to someone's desk, write it on a paper airplane and toss it over—it doesn't matter. What matters is asking the question quickly and cogently, so that you're not sitting there for months waiting on an answer.

What Not to Do

Oddly enough, sometimes the most important thing in a script doctoring situation is knowing what not to do. With so many potential pitfalls, having a good sense of at least the obvious ones that can be avoided goes a long way towards establishing smooth relationships with the team and getting into a good working dynamic as quickly as possible.

Don't come in and insult the work that's been done already. Odds are that some of the people you will be working with have contributed to the material that has been deemed unsatisfactory, and they may still have an emotional attachment to it. Remember that they've been asked to believe in that material for months, if not years. Or, they may still be friendly with a writer who is no longer on the project and feel the need to defend their work. In either case, trying to establish yourself by putting down what has already been done is a sure-fire way to make enemies, and to make your job harder.

Remember, your job is not to come in to pass judgment on the work that's in place. It is to figure out what's needed to move forward, and one of the best things you can do towards that end is examine what's been done for its good points. Being respectful toward the work that's been done shows respect for the people who did it.

Don't try to reinvent the game unless you're told to do so. A corollary of the need to discover the scope of work you're empowered to do, this axiom is about as straightforward as it gets. Everything you do—add characters, rewrite lines, add cutscenes—has the potential to cause other people to have to do more work or spend more money. Throwing your creativity around willy-nilly will create confusion about what assets are actually needed, not to mention who's doing them and whether there's room for it in the budget. More to the point, doing a complete overhaul of the game based on your vision is fraught with all sorts of peril. Odds are you don't understand the asset pipeline and schedule completely, so demanding new assets, motion sets, cutscenes, and the like isn't going to endear you to people you're going to be working with. It might not even be possible at all, and if you're relying on those new assets to make your stuff work, you'll be out of luck.

And the project will be, too.

Don't set yourself up as the final authority. As seductive as the fantasy of coming in at the last minute to save the day can be, it shouldn't be confused with the reality of the situation. The odds of a writer being handed complete control over a project to make sure everything else jibes with the story are somewhere between "low" and "nonexistent." Instead, make sure you set up working relationships with the point people on the team so that you're in the loop on decisions that relate to story. This can work just fine and makes sure that writing concerns are taken into account when changes are made. What won't happen is everyone else kowtowing to writing's needs, and if you expect it to go that way, you'll look foolish.

It's perfectly sensible to expect to be in the loop when changes affecting story get decided on. And yes, this can include everything from level design to seeing which motions are included in the animation set. But expecting story—and by extension, yourself—to be the final arbiter over what goes in the game is asking for trouble and a very short working relationship with the rest of the team.

Don't prioritize your agenda over the team's. There are a lot of people working on a game at any given time, and ideally, they all have the same agenda: to make the best game possible under the constraints of time, resources, and technology. The only way that goal is achievable is if everyone is pulling in at least roughly the same direction. That means that the game comes first, not the writing. The writing is an element in making a good game, one of many. It's an important element, but it's still just one piece of the puzzle. Trying to prioritize your tasks over the rest of the team's, when in many cases team members are waiting on your deliverables, has the potential to derail the development process significantly.

Don't be a jerk. This one should be self-explanatory. As in any professional situation, when you join an established team, you have a professional obligation to integrate yourself with that team so that everyone feels comfortable working with you. For one thing, it's the right thing to do. For another, it helps the project. A prima donna script doctor is going to make it that much harder for everyone else to get their work done. If you slow the rest of the team down, it doesn't matter how good your dialog is, you're hurting the project. That's precisely the opposite of why you're there, after all, and thus is a circumstance best avoided.

And if that weren't enough reason to leave the jerk juice at home, there's the simple matter of self-preservation. If you're disrespectful, rude, and no fun to work with, the team won't want to work with you—and there's a lot more of them than there are of you. So, it's in everyone's interests—the project's, the team's, and yours—for you to approach the team as well as the project with respect and good manners.

The Script Doctoring Secrets of the Hidden Masters

- Do *not* expect perfection. If you do, you will be disappointed.

    - Do the best job that you can, but recognize that you are working under constraints. Art is the enemy of deadlines. You will need to balance your creative skill and perfectionist intent with the need to get things done, or you won't get things done.

    - Some stuff, you just can't fix. Learn to live with this, or you'll drive yourself crazy.

- Chop your deliverables up into discrete chunks—and do them.

    - It's easier to get something smaller done.

    - It's tangible progress, so you'll feel better along the way.

    - You have something to hand off relatively quickly for feedback.

- Solicit feedback on one chunk while you're working on the next one.

    - This lets you know early if you're on the right track.

    - It gives the people watching you something to do.

- Schedule regular check-ins so you can. . .

    - see how you're doing so far;

    - see what's changed since the last check-in—and something *always* changes.

- Be consistent in the changes you make.

    - Keep character voice consistent—if you're pulling all of the contractions out of one character's speech, do it all the way through.

    - Consistent spelling and capitalization go a long way towards reducing confusion and making you look professional.

    - And of course, consistency in formatting is essential.

- What you are there for is the *difference*—the changes you make. Therefore, make it easy for people to find those changes and comment on them.

    - Highlight changes you make for easy identification.

    - Summarize what you've done so readers can look in the right place.

- Find reference points for what you're doing.

    - Actors, video clips, sequences in well-known books or movies—all of these make it much easier to communicate the changes that you're making.

    - It's much easier than making the folks you're working with hunt through line by line to get a sense of what you have done.

- Reference for yourself is important.

    - Pull together the "definitive" traits and lines of the characters you'll be writing for.

    - Refer to them to make sure the doctoring work you do blends seamlessly with the rest of the dialog.

- Don't give yourself closure until the box is on the shelf.

    - If you tell yourself that you're done, it will be that much harder to get into gear once the inevitable last-minute request comes up.

    - And if it's hard to get into gear, it's hard to do the work, which means it takes that much longer.

15.3   Conclusion

How you go about your work as a script doctor is as important as what you do, because in large part how you do it helps define what you're doing and how well you're
going to be able to do it. Assessing the task and setting up the systems and mechanisms to enable your success are essential steps to actually doing the work. Master
that, and you'll put yourself in the best place possible, giving you the maximum available time and attention for writing, which, after all, is why you're there in the first
place.

15.4   Exercises

1. (Rewrites)

   (a) Look at the following paragraph of dialog. Rewrite it so that it flows like
       actual conversation without losing any of the factual information.

       "Hello. My father is at war fighting Marchizia. He left me in
       charge. That makes me as good as a king while he's gone. So
       don't make me mad."

   (b) Look at the following paragraph of dialogue, which suffers from an excess
       of personality. Rewrite it so that it's half its current length without losing
       any of the factual information it contains.

       "Oh, hello Sir Reginald! So good of you to come! Do you
       want some wine? Something to eat, perhaps? I'll have a ser-
       vant prepare your quarters—we weren't expecting you so early!
       Now, I'm sure you're dying to know why I've summoned you,
       and make no mistake, it was a summons. With my father off
       on the Marchizian frontier, I am, for all intents and purposes,
       king. You would do well to remember that, don't you think,
       the next time you consider spreading sedition and lies about
       me. I'd hate to have to shorten you by a head, but I must
       do what is best for the kingdom, and the best thing for the
       kingdom is most certainly ridding it of traitors. Wouldn't you
       agree?"

2. (Writing barks) You have 20 minutes to write as many variations on "I've been
   shot" as you can. At the end of the 20 minutes, count how many you have
   and make sure each of the ones you've written is unique. Try this once a day
   for a week. See how many you can do at the end of the week as opposed to at
   the beginning.

3. (Adding characterization) Imagine that you've been asked to work on a fantasy
   RPG. The helper NPC character is a crotchety old wizard, but the dialog that's

been written for him so far has been painfully generic. In order to pump up his uniqueness and make him more interesting, do the following.

(a) Come up with a list of five words or phrases that he uses that define his speech patterns. Think about *why* he always uses these five.

(b) Come up with a list of five words or phrases that he'd never use—this also helps define his speech patterns and diction.

(c) Write a one-paragraph monologue for the character in which he discusses dragons. At the end, look at what you've got and determine if the character's diction, rhythm, and other speech patterns are consistent and distinct. If they aren't, try again until you're satisfied you have the character's distinct voice down.

(d) Once you have the character voice nailed, write a ten-exchange conversation between the character and a standard fantasy innkeeper wherein both characters are happy.

(e) Now try it if the wizard is angry.

(f) Now try it if the innkeeper is an old friend.

(g) Now try it if the innkeeper doesn't like wizards. Make sure you keep the wizard's voice consistent throughout.

4. (Story pitches) You're doing a game based on *Snow White and the Seven Dwarfs* when suddenly word comes down that there's only enough time in the schedule for four dwarves. How do you change the story? Write up three distinct one-paragraph pitches detailing new approaches that will make use of the assets you've got.

5. (Putting a story together) You're working on a science-fiction game, and all of the levels are designed and in production. One is a desert planet, one is a giant orbiting space station, one is a deserted spaceship, one is an urbanized technological utopia with a dark underside, and one is current-day Earth. Create three possible game stories that use all of these spaces at least once.

16

Game Writing and Narrative in the Future

Evan Skolnick

Previous chapters in this book have focused on practical, usable information on the process of writing for today's video games. For this final chapter, however, we will allow ourselves a flight of fancy, turning our attention from the actual to the theoretical; from what is to what might be. For even the most experienced traveler must occasionally look up from his carefully plotted map and allow himself to dream of distant, unknown places barely visible on the horizon. In our case, it is the self-indulgent act of imagining what video game narrative might look like in the future.

16.1 Growing Pains

As a mass-market entertainment medium, video games are still in the equivalent of early childhood, stumbling alongside—or sometimes trailing directly behind—older siblings such as motion pictures, radio, and television. This is not to say that in terms of sheer size or popularity video games are lesser or inferior to these older forms. Indeed, in terms of gross revenue, the video game industry is more than competitive with any of them. But as a creative art form, video games are still in what will surely be looked back upon (by future generations of gamers and game developers) as early formative stages.

This is particularly true of game narrative development, which has continued to be a relatively underappreciated, undervalued, and undeveloped component of modern video games—especially when compared with other, more obvious aspects such as graphics rendering power, realistic physics engines, and gameworld sizes. As the hardware has become more powerful, the main emphasis has been to concentrate on ways to make games look, sound, and feel more realistic and immersive. Storytelling, in general, has been left behind, and many games that are modern in all other respects still sport the same type of subpar story structure, painfully stereotypical characters, and cringe-inducing dialog that were common (and ridiculed) in video games of decades past.

There are, of course, compelling exceptions to this rule coming from certain developers renowned for putting high-quality game writing near the top of their priority list, and who sometimes reap substantial rewards for doing so. However, these exceptions aside, most developers still do not prioritize writing. One would probably have a very hard time getting the management team of any game development studio to admit to this, but look at their actual investment in this area and you'll see the reality. There are only a small handful of game development studios that bother to retain full-time fiction writers or editors. Instead, game designers with varying degrees of writing ability are usually tasked with producing narrative content.

16.2   Near Future: Pro Writers, Early Involvement

The days of this "good enough" philosophy toward video game writing—i.e., that game designers with rudimentary writing skills will be able to generate narrative content that is "good enough" for what the game needs—seem to be slowly, inexorably drawing to a close. The existence of this book and books like it, combined with the active nature of the IGDA's Game Writing Special Interest Group and the ever-increasing number of freelance game writers and game writing consultancy groups, can be seen as harbingers of a slowly changing landscape.

Perhaps even more importantly, game reviewers are beginning to pay increasing attention to game stories and narrative elements, adjusting their scores up or down in relation to perceived quality in this area. With some studies showing a positive correlation between review scores and game sales, even the stodgiest developers and publishers will eventually need to take game narrative development more seriously than ever before if they wish to remain competitive.

Staff Writers/Editors

The most forward-thinking of developers, especially those who specialize in narrative-focused games, are hiring on-staff fiction writers and editors to ensure consistently strong and well-integrated story content. This group is admittedly small but seems to be slowly growing.

Other studios, unwilling or unable to invest so heavily in narrative development, may ask one professional-level writer or editor to oversee all story content development, either on a full-time or part-time basis (while also shouldering other, non-narrative responsibilities). This role often has less to do with hands-on writing than with reviewing and improving the work of narrative content, generated by on-staff game designers, freelance writers, or a combination of the two.

For both of these cases—an entire staff of writers and editors, or just one—there is an increased probability of bringing the professional fiction writing skill set into the game narrative development process early enough to actually do some good. It's difficult to overstate the significance of this early involvement, since most missteps in fiction writing happen at the story outline stage, and these "baked in" errors can be the hardest to address later on.

Dipping their toes into the shallower end of the game narrative pool are the majority of developers, who see the value of quality writing in their games but choose not to invest in full-time (or even part-time) staff members devoted to it. These studios tend to either handle all writing by assigning in-house game designers or by hiring freelance writers on a short-term basis.

Freelance Writers

For many people in the game development business, writers are most associated with dialog writing. Perhaps it is because for the world's dominant forms of storytelling—movies and television—the writer's main deliverable tends to be a script (which consists largely of dialog). Other elements generated by the writer on the way to delivering that script—a high concept, a corkboard full of index cards, an outline, a treatment, a beat script—are rarely seen by people outside the business. And so the impression held by the average game developer is that what writers are for is generating dialog scripts. Not surprisingly, then, the solution for studios unwilling to invest in staff writers is often to develop the core narrative materials in-house and turn to a professional freelance writer or writers only when the time comes to generate dialog.

This is often a recipe for mediocrity. Unless the game designers happen to also be excellent fiction writers or editors, the aforementioned story structure or characterization problems are likely to be permanently embedded in the narrative. The frustrated freelance writers, brought on board far too late to address these core issues that they can so plainly see, find themselves in the all-too-familiar position of being asked to "polish the turd"—to use their dialog-writing skills to add flair and panache to a fatally flawed work.

Additionally, the choice of writers may be made based on "name" value rather than actual competency at the very specific skill of writing for games. Movie and television writers who are struggling to find regular work will sometimes see the video game business as an excellent place to pick up some extra income while waiting for their sure-to-be-a-blockbuster film script to emerge from Development Hell. The cosmetic similarities between video games and movies only help to convince these writers—as well as star-struck game producers looking at a Hollywood writer's résumé—that writing for games is the same as writing for movies or television. Anyone who has read this book up to this point should be able to appreciate the folly of such a notion.

Write Your Own Beginning

In the coming years, people with expertise in fiction writing for video games will more and more consistently be brought into the development cycle from the very earliest stages, especially for games that have a strong narrative focus. In some cases, these experts will be on-staff "narrative designers," editors, or writers, while others could be freelance writers. But the unifying factor will be that professional-level writers will be involved early on.

Additionally, game writing may eventually emerge as its own discipline, as opposed to being considered a mere subset of game design. Game audio—for many years also considered a design subset—has already begun to emerge in this fashion, much like game design itself broke off from game programming so long ago.

16.3   Far Future: The Emergence of Emergence

What about further down the road? What form might video game narrative take in 20, 30, 50 years? In order to even begin to guess where things are headed, it's useful to get some perspective on where they really are today.

When we look at modern video games, it's easy to stand in awe of their eye-popping graphics, motion-picture-quality digital audio, bone-crushingly realistic physics, and continually evolving gameplay mechanics. And even in the arena of story and character dialog, while the industry as a whole continues to lag in this area, there are still shining examples of excellence in game writing.

However, in terms of the size of the story possibility space, today's games remain shockingly limited with regard to what the player can actually *do* and how many different ways the fiction can react to him.

How many meaningful narrative choices can a player make in a video game? Choices that can propel the game story into entirely unexpected and original new directions? The fact is, while many modern games do give the player the illusion of choice or perhaps even provide a small set of meaningful choices that can result in a small set of variable game outcomes, no game has come close to providing a truly open possibility story space for the player.

Sandbox games tend to provide the player more of an opportunity to chart her own course, but often the resulting "story" is not really a story at all, just a series of events that may or may not be related to each other or form any kind of rising action. The outcome (assuming there is one) is either a narrative mishmash that has no perceived cohesion at all or a play space that regularly and inevitably corrals the player back through the narrative gates that lead to the next sandbox.

Size Doesn't Matter

Modern video games, especially in the RPG and action/adventure genres, have more and more voiceover lines, usually topping out in the tens of thousands. However, despite these impressive numbers, the main limiting factor continues to be the need for a human to write each line—meaning that someone has to anticipate every single thing in the game that can be said by any character, ever.

This is a brutally constricting limitation, and it's a big part of the reason that even games with hundreds of thousands of recorded words still have very limited narrative choices and possible outcomes.

For contrast, let's consider the granddaddy of all computer role-playing games, the original paper-and-dice RPG, *Dungeons & Dragons*. As any video gamer with a sense of history knows, *D&D* is played in person with a Dungeon Master (DM) guiding the players through a pre-planned adventure that unfolds as they explore it. In this way, it sounds very much like computer RPGs such as *Diablo*, the *Ultima* series, or the *Final Fantasy* games. However, in *D&D*, the pre-planning work is left largely incomplete and is flexible. Whether working from an adventure he created himself or utilizing one of the ready-made scenarios that can be purchased from TSR (now Wizards of the Coast), the DM starts the game session armed only with a rough framework for the adventure. He is expected to improvise, embellish, add to, and fill out that skeleton, largely in reaction to the players' unfettered and wonderfully unpredictable actions.

Imagine, if you will, the Dungeon Master who guided his players through one of the ready-made adventures and was completely unable to adapt to anything that was not covered within that slim guide. Players would tell him what they wanted to do, and if it did not jibe with what was anticipated by the author of the adventure, the DM would reply with, "Sorry, that action isn't supported. Please try something else." It's hard to believe that players would be satisfied with such a rigid, unimaginative Dungeon Master.

And yet when players enjoy even the most modern of computer/console RPGs and MMOs, that is *exactly* what they must be satisfied with, because it's all the rigid game structures are capable of delivering.

Of course, you may argue that players within those games do have limitless choices. They can move in any direction at any moment, decide when and where to fire their weapons, etc. But the choices the player can make that truly affect or change the *narrative direction* of the adventure are few and far between, if existent at all.

Tear away all the flashy graphics, room-shaking sound effects, and dazzling game-play mechanics, and you are left with this sad truth: today's story-based video games, in terms of the real narrative choices that are offered to the player, are the digital equivalent of having a *Choose Your Own Adventure* book read to you. Yes, occasionally you're asked which direction you want the story to go, but in between those decision points you're basically being read to.

What the human DM brings to a session of *Dungeons & Dragons* is the ability to speak original dialog for any monster or non-player character (NPC) in the game-world, to invent wholly new concepts and characters on the fly, and to work with the players to determine an entirely unique, fitting, and satisfying ending to the story that wasn't conceived until that very moment.

What if our games could do *that*?

The Game Story Generation System

In order to generate a fully-realized, emergent game space like a paper-and-dice RPG with almost limitless narrative possibilities, a game in the future would need to have the core abilities of a human DM. Described in terms of a feature set, this hypothetical game system—let's call it the Game Story Generation System, or GSGS for short—would incorporate the following abilities.

- Create and name new NPCs, and place them appropriately in the gameworld.

- Control the fully realized, dynamic behavior of game characters.

- Write realistic-sounding and appropriate character dialog, on the fly, in response to player actions or world conditions.

- Generate audio speech that sounds realistic and can appropriately express emotion and emphasize certain words for meaning.

- Recognize player speech and decode it for meaning, with back-ups in place for knowledge gaps.

- Story-checking that compares the current narrative flow against optimal narrative structures and can guide NPCs and world events to move the story in structurally sound directions.

Of course, the technology to pull off some of these requirements is pretty far down the road, while others exist in at least a crude form already.

Create and populate the world. Large teams of developers have proven again and again that they are capable of creating massive worlds for players. The best examples are in the MMOs, which need to be large enough to avoid feeling claustrophobic to thousands of players at a time.

A space this large should be big enough to contain potential for a seemingly infinite number of adventures. Additionally, dungeon-like spaces could be generated on the fly, much like the maps in the venerable *X-COM* turn-based strategy games.

Programmatically generating new NPCs with unique names, looks, and personalities would also be within today's existing technology.

NPC behavior. The artificial intelligence (AI) programming behind many of today's video game enemies and NPCs seems fairly rudimentary when compared with the capabilities of a human DM. AI motivations are usually quite simple (i.e., follow the player, aim at the player, attack the player) and lack the finesse that a live human is able to infuse into a character.

AI programming in general seems to have hit a brick wall in the past several decades, with the once seemingly attainable goal of creating machines that think like a human having settled, according to *Wired* magazine, into "a long AI winter of shrunken budgets and general indifference."[1]

It's difficult to predict how long it could take for AI programming to rise from this extended plateau and be applied to gaming at the level required to fully realize this feature. However, it seems safe to assume it is not just around the corner.

---

[1] *Wired* 15.10, Geekipedia insert, 9.

NPC dialog and speech. Making video game characters speak pre-written, pre-recorded dialog is no challenge at all for today's game developers. However, transitioning from this pre-canned system to one that can convincingly create and speak original dialog is a technological challenge that would rival anything achieved in the last decade in the area of, say, game physics.

To begin with, the text-to-speech improvements that would need to be made are significant. While it's true that computers are getting better and better at synthesizing basic human speech in a fairly convincing manner, storytelling requires so much more, such as emotion, emphasis, sarcasm, subtext, and so on. Anything less would feel robotic and potentially disturbing.

Even more daunting are the technological leaps that would be required for a game engine to write realistic-sounding human dialog on the fly. It would require no less than a system that could successfully pass the Turing test.

This test, conceived back in 1950 by mathematician Alan Turing, was a proposal on how it might be possible to determine if computers can think. In the test, a human judge sits at a computer terminal in one room and uses it to engage in a natural-language interaction with a human and with a computer, neither of which are in the room, and both of which try to convince the judge that he's conversing with a human. If the judge can't reliably tell which is which, then the computer is said to have passed the test, proving that computers can think.

Of course, no computer or computer program has ever passed this test.

The Turing test has been criticized for being a poor indicator of true artificial intelligence, and there are few scientists today who would claim that it would be, in and of itself, a reliable way to gauge whether machines can think. However, the goal of developing a computer program that can convincingly write natural-sounding, conversational dialog has direct application to game development.

There have been a number of computer programs that do a decent job of faking their way through a conversation with a human, dating back to the early days of the personal computer. ELIZA, a virtual psychologist "character," is perhaps the most famous of these programs, now collectively referred to as "chatterbots." Here is a conversation an actual user is reported to have had with this digital psychotherapist.

> Young woman: Men are all alike.
>
> ELIZA: In what way?
>
> Young woman: They're always bugging us about something specific or other.
>
> ELIZA: Can you think of a specific example?
>
> Young woman: Well, my boyfriend made me come here.
>
> ELIZA: Your boyfriend made you come here?
>
> Young woman: He says I'm depressed much of the time.
>
> ELIZA: I am sorry to hear you are depressed.

Young woman: It's true. I'm unhappy.

ELIZA: Do you think coming here will help you not to be unhappy?

Young woman: I need some help, that much seems certain.

ELIZA: What would it mean to you if you got some help?

Young woman: Perhaps I could learn to get along with my mother.

ELIZA: Tell me more about your family.

Young woman: My mother takes care of me.

ELIZA: Who else in your family takes care of you?

Young woman: My father.

ELIZA: Your father.

Young woman: You are like my father in some ways.

ELIZA: What resemblance do you see?

Young woman: You are not very aggressive but I think you don't want me to notice that.

ELIZA: What makes you think I am not very aggressive?

Young woman: You don't argue with me.

ELIZA: Why do you think I don't argue with you?

Young woman: You are afraid of me.

ELIZA: Does it please you to believe I am afraid of you?

Young woman: My father is afraid of everybody.

ELIZA: What else comes to mind when you think of your father?

Young woman: Bullies.

ELIZA: Does that have anything to do with the fact that your boyfriend made you come here?[2]

As you can probably tell, ELIZA is little more than a clever mimic, picking up on certain keywords and throwing your own answers or comments back at you in the form of new questions or pat psychological observations.

A chatterbot perhaps of more interest to game writers is PARRY, a program that instead of asking questions answers them, while simulating the personality of a paranoid. As you read this actual conversation a user reportedly had with PARRY, imagine it taking place in a game environment, with the player as interviewer and Parry as an NPC in the world.

---

[2]Joseph Weizenbaum, *Computer Power and Human Reason* (New York: Freeman, 1976) 3–4.

Interviewer: How are you today?

PARRY: OK.

Interviewer: What is your name?

PARRY: My name is Frank Smith.

Interviewer: How old are you?

PARRY: Twenty-eight.

Interviewer: Are you married?

PARRY: No.

Interviewer: What sort of work do you do?

PARRY: I work in the Post Office.

Interviewer: Why are you in the hospital?

PARRY: I shouldn't be here.

Interviewer: Who brought you here?

PARRY: The police.

Interviewer: What trouble did you have with the police?

PARRY: Cops don't do their jobs.

Interviewer: What do they do instead?

PARRY: Cops arrest the wrong people.

Interviewer: They arrest the right ones sometimes.

PARRY: The law should get those Italian crooks.

Interviewer: Are you Italian?

PARRY: My background is British, but I was born in this country.

Interviewer: Do you know any Italian crooks?

PARRY: I try to avoid the underworld.

Interviewer: Are you afraid of the underworld?

PARRY: The mafia are the worst gangsters.

Interviewer: Are you connected with the mafia?

PARRY: You know, they know me.

Interviewer: How do they know you?

PARRY: They spy on me.

Interviewer: Why do they?

PARRY: They want to get false evidence to frame me.

Interviewer: What do they have against you?

PARRY: They are out to get me.

Interviewer: What for?

PARRY: I have incriminating evidence against the mafia.

Interviewer: Are you sure of all this?

PARRY: You don't believe me?[3]

The above sample conversations were typed by the human user and answered with a computer-generated string of onscreen text. They would probably feel a lot more realistic if the user were able to speak his questions and hear human-sounding speech in response.

Beyond just generating dialog that sounds right, has the correct inflection and emotional emphasis, the GSGS would need to have a good understanding of character motivation and how those motivations might evolve and change over the course of a game based on what the player does and what happens in the world.

Comprehend player speech. Of all the required components, the ability to recognize human spoken language is probably the least formidable. Many off-the-shelf programs already do a fine job of this. In fact, it's surprising that more games don't already take advantage of this rapidly improving technology.

However, processing and interpreting the meaning of improvised player sentences is something else entirely. More than a clever mimic like ELIZA, the GSGS would need, on some level, to truly understand human language. This feature is as challenging as the earlier requirement to generate original dialogue, perhaps even more so. It requires a system that can consistently pass the Turing test, and it is something we may have to wait a very long time to have at our disposal.

Storytelling. Finally, the Game Story Generation System would need to have a sense of the dramatic, incorporating a good understanding of story structure and plot devices. This is perhaps one of the hardest things to imagine a computer program accomplishing, though even today there are software packages that claim to do just that. Dramatica, for example, is a combination fiction theory and software package that is billed by its creators as the "ultimate writing partner"—a computer program that fiction writers can use to analyze and improve their stories' structure.

When it comes to crafting a tale, certainly no game story system will ever be able to favorably compare to a talented human writer. However, the requisite story quality level will not be nearly as high for an interactive system, either. That is because whereas most storytellers are judged by observers, game story systems will be judged by participants only. And a story that you're in the middle of instantly becomes much more potentially interesting than a story about someone else.

This brings us back to *D&D*: have you ever noticed that when a *D&D* player tries to recount an adventure he experienced, no matter how excited and enthusiastic

---

[3] Bertram Raphael, *The Thinking Computer* (New York: Freeman, 1976) 201.

he is about what "happened," it doesn't translate well when being retold to someone who wasn't involved? As a direct participant in the adventure, he isn't noticing the poor story structure or the uneven pacing; he's enraptured by the experience he had because he was *in* it and *collaborated* on it. Whereas as a listener afterward, even though the story may have many of the elements of a fine tale—intriguing characters, imaginative locations, a devious villain, sharply defined conflict—you find that it's not holding up as a linear, nonparticipatory story.

The difference between these two experiences can be likened to that of a practiced, well-executed musical performance versus a jam session.

Performance	Jam session
tight	loose
practiced, polished, vetted	in-the-moment, fluid, improvised
entertaining	involving
memorable	most memorable
predictable and repeatable	unpredictable and unique
best for audience	best for participants

For a musician, the chance to see his idol play live is exciting. However, that excitement would pale in comparison to his reaction at the opportunity to actually jam with his idol. Conversely, an audience who paid good money to see a live performance by their favorite band might be more than a little disappointed to be witness to an improvised jam session.

In the future, the game player will be more and more of a participant and less and less of a mere audience member. Writers who can't or don't want to adapt to this shift may be left behind.

16.4 Embrace the Future

Today's video game writers struggle with the innate conflict between story structure and player agency. You as the writer want to tell a story with specific beats, rising action, a climax, and a resolution. But the player wants to grab control of your story and feel like she's in charge of where it goes. It is the irreconcilable dead end that confounds nearly every game writer, the unsolvable problem that is by now almost a cliché.

Let's be honest. We writers are never going to win the tug of war between player agency and author's intent. Gamers want to play, and increasingly they want control. And if that's what the audience wants, then the market will continue to try to cater to it. But if we're going to lose this contest, is there a way to do it that still serves both sides?

Ironically, the answer may lie in that most ancient and decidedly non-narrative game, chess.

There was a time when it was imagined that if a computer could learn to play chess at a grandmaster level, it would have developed enough intelligence to pass as a human. It was also considered unlikely to ever happen.

However, in 1997 the IBM supercomputer known as Deep Blue beat reigning world chess champion Garry Kasparov in a six-game exhibition match. Chess experts around the world were stunned. How could a piece of hardware have overcome Kasparov's decades of experience, brilliant strategies, and unpredictable, insightful human brain?

Deep Blue's programmers had taken a game that was considered a gentleman's contest requiring subtlety, intuition, and deviousness and reduced it to a programming problem. With the ability to analyze 200 million chess positions per second, Deep Blue solved the chess-playing problem not with finesse but with brute force. However, it was not all about computation. The programming team for the supercomputer included a human grandmaster chess player, whose intimate knowledge of the game helped improve Deep Blue's performance beyond just number-crunching.

Is the challenge of developing Deep Blue really that different from taking on and solving the problem of creating something like the Game Story Generation System?

It's the End of Game Writing As We Know It

BioWare, one of the few game development studios that employs a full staff of narrative writers and editors, regularly posts job postings for such positions, and in addition to a résumé, applicants are required to submit a dialog sample embedded in a module created using the *Neverwinter Nights* toolset. While not a hugely intimidating barrier to entry, it does require that a writer be familiar with at least one BioWare game (i.e., *Neverwinter Nights*) and gain an understanding of some of the underlying technology that drives its NPC dialog engine.

When completed, the writing sample will not resemble anything a movie, television, or book writer has probably ever seen before. This requirement may represent a small step in the direction that the entire industry could eventually move, with only the most game-savvy writers able to have any hope of garnering work.

In the future, the game writer role itself may bear little resemblance to its current incarnation. Instead of generating plot outlines, branching story diagrams, cutscene scripts, and reams of character dialog, the game writer of tomorrow may instead be more of a co-architect—much as the grandmaster chess player was for the Deep Blue project—working with AI programmers, speech/audio programmers, psychologists, and fiction analysis engineers to create a system that can interactively weave an infinite number of story possibilities at runtime based on player actions.

Today's video game writer may be appalled by this vision of the medium's narrative future. Where is the authorial intent, the writer's intuition and muse? These notions are borne of *non-interactive* storytelling—vestiges of prior forms that we are clinging to because they are familiar and comfortable, or because the technology is not yet here to free us from them.

Much as early movies initially mimicked the conventions of stage plays, today's video games continue to ape the conventions of this era's dominant storytelling forms: the movie and television show. But over time, this medium will evolve its own narrative conventions and forms, best suited to its unique abilities and strengths.

The most forward-thinking of game designers and writers are already preparing for this sea change. "I love to write game stories," admits 2K Boston founder and *Bioshock* Creative Director Ken Levine. "But, frankly, any game story I wrote won't be half as interesting as the emergent experience you [the player] create based on the variables we throw out and you set in motion."[4]

In keeping with this final chapter's theme of wistfully gazing to the horizon, the Game Story Generation System is only a fanciful imagining of what the narrative elements of a futuristic game might someday look like. We may never get there, but like a guiding star, it represents the general direction we should probably be headed. So, instead of concentrating so much effort on making even more realistic-looking CGI hair and fur simulations for games, perhaps some savvy technical folks could get started on this little project instead? It's hard to exaggerate the transformational impact that could result from the unleashed imagination of a game storyteller being married to the almost incomprehensible computing power of future home game consoles.

Traditionalists, fear not: the game writer of the far future will still need a deep understanding of classic story structure, characterization, and drama in order to generate starting story parameters and to evaluate and help improve the performance of real-time story generation systems.

And regardless of whether this system or something like it ever becomes a reality, it seems clear that the game writers of today and of the near future will need to know more and more about how games are really architected and created. Familiarity with many kinds of games, deep knowledge of game development processes, and fluency with various proprietary storytelling engines and tools will no longer just be what separate successful game writers from the "slumming" writers from other media— they will be required to get in the door at all.

The long-term result will be video games with superior narrative content, further differentiating them from non-interactive narrative media, evolving a new and unique kind of storytelling...and perhaps someday offering the most compelling stories ever to be experienced.

---

[4] *Electronic Gaming Monthly*, May 2006, 55.

A

Script Samples for Chapter 2

Wendy Despain

A.1 *Bratz: Forever Diamondz* Game Script Excerpt

SF3-5: Special Feature 3-5 - Fashion Show Gameplay

<u>Task Detail:</u>
Player will need to enter the fashion show from the now open backstage door. Player will then complete the fashion show gameplay mix of posing and photography.

<u>Dialog:</u>
(The task dialog for the fashion show will play over the actual gameplay, in the style of a show commentator. Byron Powell will not be visible for the duration of the task.)

Model 1 approaches pose point#1
BYRON POWELL
Alright, let's show these people the hottest fashion in Manhattan.

Model 1 approaches pose point#2
BYRON POWELL
They need to see all the angles - hit it.

Model 1 approaches pose point#3
BYRON POWELL
Own the stage, girl. You look great.

Model 2 approaches pose point#1
BYRON POWELL
Okay, time for you to show us what you've got.

Model 2 approaches pose point#2
BYRON POWELL
Spotlight's on you!

Model 2 approaches pose point#3
BYRON POWELL
This is it - make it a good one!

[Successful pose dialogue will be randomly selected from the following selection every time the player succeeds in performing a pose move from the current pose list]

Successful pose#1
BYRON POWELL
Nice!

Successful pose#2
BYRON POWELL
Woo!

Successful pose#3
BYRON POWELL
Gorgeous!

A.2 *Pests* Script Sample

Line ID	Story	Section	Character	Line	Voice Direction	Triggered	Context
101	Oni	Prolog	Shoki	Shoki here. Yes. I understand. Keep calm. We'll be there soon.	All business, answering phone.	Start of story	In Shoki's library at night, the towering bookshelves are lit with candles in sconces and a chandelier. (cont.)
102	Oni	Prolog	Lucy	Not such a quiet evening after all?	Distracted. Still reading her book.	Next	
103	Oni	Prolog	Shoki	Downtown. A maintenance chief just had a conversation with a worker who died on site fifteen years ago. He's a little upset.		Next	
104	Oni	Prolog	Lucy	I thought we didn't do hauntings.	Curious. Paying full attention now.	Next	
105	Oni	Prolog	Shoki	We don't. At the end of their conversation the "ghost" turned into a rat and ran away		Next	

Line ID	Story	Section	Character	Line	Voice Direction	Triggered	Context
106	Oni	Prolog	Lucy	Okay. that's weird. Can I drive?	Deadpan.	Next	
107	Oni	Prolog	Shoki	Only if you stay off the freeway.	Cautious.	Next	
108	Oni	Prolog	Lucy	It's a deal.	Excited.	Next	
109	Oni	Driving 1	Shoki	[Whistles a dog summons] Come on, Kyrie		Car door opens	Shoki lets Lucy drive the car. (cont.)
110	Oni	Driving 1	Lucy	Oh neat. Backup.	Deadpan.	Dire hound arrives.	
111	Oni	Driving 1	Shoki	She likes rats.		Next	
112	Oni	Driving 1	Lucy	Welcome to the Lucy express. Please keep hands, noses and tails inside the vehicle at all times and be prepared for sudden stops, sharp corners and the occasional collision		Engine starts	
113	Oni	Driving 1	Shoki	Erm		Sharp corner - random	
114	Oni	Driving 1	Shoki	Ung		Sharp corner - random	
115	Oni	Driving 1	Shoki	Careful!		Sharp corner - random	
116	Oni	Driving 1	Shoki	[Sharp intake of breath through teeth]		Sharp corner - random	
117	Oni	Driving 1	Shoki	No, left. Left. Your other left.	Steel calm.	Wrong turn - right - random	
121	Oni	Driving 1	Shoki	Right. Go right. The. . . right.	Slightly agitated.	Wrong turn - left - random	
122	Oni	Driving 1	Shoki	But. . . back that way.	Slightly confused.	Wrong turn - left - random	
123	Oni	Driving 1	Shoki	Okay, that's not right.	Calm.	Wrong turn - left - random	
128	Oni	Driving 1	Shoki	Annnnnd. . . forward		Car pauses too long	
129	Oni	Driving 1	Shoki	Go.		Car pauses too long	
130	Oni	Driving 1	Shoki	Foot on the gas, not the brake.		Car pauses too long	
131	Oni	Driving 1	Shoki	Any time now.		Car pauses too long	
132	Oni	Driving 1	Shoki	And we're here.		Car arrives at destination	
133	Oni	Driving 1	Lucy	Weee!		Car corners too tight	
134	Oni	Driving 1	Lucy	Um, I meant to do that.		Car collides with something	
137	Oni	Driving 1	Lucy	You have to admit it's more interesting my way.		Car arrives at destination	
138	Oni	Driving 1	Maintenance Chief	Oh good, you're here. It's this way.		Lucy and Shoki get out of car	

A.3   Actor-Friendly Format Sample

The IGDA Game Writing SIG actor-friendly format sample was originally written by Steve Ince.

Basic Format

Scene Name	Conditional	Line Number	Character	Dialog Line	Comments
Scene—Edwards talks to Wilks					
		[20201]	Edwards:	Hey, Wilks.	*// Greeting used every time*
	First Time				
		[20202]	Wilks:	What's up?	
		[20203]	Edwards:	I heard that you witnessed the shooting.	
		[20204]	Wilks:	That so?	*// Nervous, but puts on brave face*
		[20205]	Edwards:	Just tell me what happened!	
		[20206]	Wilks:	Get lost! I didn't see nothing!	
					// Edwards looks angry – he should have handled it better
	Other times (not talked to Wilks about Johnny)				
		[20207]	Wilks:	I got nothing to say.	
	IF Edwards has talked to Johnny				
		[20208]	Edwards:	Your friend Johnny saw you with the body.	
		[20209]	Wilks:	That junkie ain't fingering me!	
		[20210]	Edwards:	It's not looking good, man.	
					// Wilks thinks, weighing his options
		[20211]	Wilks:	Look, all I saw was a guy in a leather jacket running away. The woman was already dead.	
		[20212]	Edwards:	Thanks.	
	IF all information has been obtained (Repeated response line)				
		[20213]	Wilks:	Get lost, will you?	

Actor Format

<u>Scene – Edwards talks to Wilks</u>

[20201]	**Edwards:**	Hey, Wilks.	*// Greeting used every time*

First Time

[20202]	**Wilks:**	What's up?	
[20203]	**Edwards:**	I heard that you witnessed the shooting.	
[20204]	**Wilks:**	That so?	*// Nervous, but pouts on brave face*
[20205]	**Edwards:**	Just tell me what happened!	
[20206]	**Wilks:**	Get lost! I didn't see nothing!	
			// Edwards looks angry – he should have handled it better

Other times (not talked to Wilks about Johnny)

[20207]	**Wilks:**	I got nothing to say.	

IF Edwards has talked to Johnny

[20208]	**Edwards:**	Your friend Johnny saw you with the body.	
[20209]	**Wilks:**	That junkie ain't fingering me!	
[20210]	**Edwards:**	It's not looking good, man.	
			// Wilks thinks, weighing his options
[20211]	**Wilks:**	Look, all I saw was a guy in a leather jacket running away. The woman was already dead.	
[20212]	**Edwards:**	Thanks.	

IF all information has been obtained (Repeated response line)

[20213]	**Wilks:**	Get lost, will you?	

B

Script Samples for Chapter 3

Erin Hoffman

B.1 *Food Finder* Pitch Doc

FOOD FINDER AND THE QUEST FOR THE GOLDEN WALNUT
A Game Concept for the Nintendo DS

Erin Hoffman
Game Designer
1st Playable Productions

in partnership with

Dr. Ernie Medina, JR., DrPH
Preventive Care Specialist
Co-founder and Chief Executive Officer, XRtainment Zone
Assistant Clinical Professor of Health Promotion, Loma Linda University

with advisement by

Dr. Roy Vartabedian
Preventive Care Specialist
Bestselling Author, *Nutripoints: Healthy Eating Made Simple*

Overview

Food Finder and the Quest for the Golden Walnut is an action adventure for the Nintendo DS that directs kids to healthier eating habits by turning healthy foods into exciting game objective items in an action adventure side-scroller for the portable Nintendo DS system.

Players take the role of the Last Food Finder, a Nutrinaut who collects foods of various types to perform amazing feats of strength and dexterity in their quest for the Golden Walnut, a fabled nut with so much nutritional value it could feed an entire city for a month. They're set on this quest by Rufus Carrotwright, a retired Nutrinaut who bears a striking but entirely coincidental resemblance to Robert Preston, and who guides the player through each of their adventures.

The "geist" of the project, or the desired emotional response from the player, is for kids to associate healthy foods with excitement. By making especially healthy foods rare in the game and by giving the player exciting abilities associated with them, we aim for a "Look! A sweet potato!" excited reaction fueled by a kid's natural collector gameplay instinct (see Pokemon) and underscored by the symbolic value we give to the power-ups players receive.

Along the way, the player can meet other characters in the game and convince them to join the quest and become Nutrinauts themselves, creating more Food Finders. By connecting to DS wifi, kids can connect with other kids and share special food items across the network for use in the Food Lab, and compare their Food Finder scores against those of other players.

In the "Plaque Attack" minigame, players track foods fed to a character by watching as food dragged to the character's mouth passes through their digestive system and impacts the pulsing heart on the bottom screen. Caffeine speeds the heart up, while unhealthy foods such as donuts and greasy cheeseburgers create plaque buildup in the bloodstream that the player must scrub away using their stylus. In the "Food Lab" minigame workshop, players can take apart foods that they've gathered in the main game and combine them into new ones, creating unique power-ups while learning about the vitamin makeup of the foods they've collected. In a third lightweight, fast minigame, players choose between two food items displayed on a set of scales, attempting to identify the healthier food and attempting to get through as many rounds as they can in a short period of time. All of these minigames link in with the primary game story, providing the player with special power-ups and collectible items that make the primary game more fun while educating at the same time.

By placing fun first, *Food Finder* keeps a primary objective of keeping kids entertained and excited about rare food items and nutritional power-ups, educating through the natural game format of points collection and an action-and-consequence gameplay.

Objectives

Numerous health organizations including the US National Institute for Health and the World Health Organization have identified obesity as one of the fastest growing and serious health crises in North America and in the world. Childhood incidences of what once were exclusively adult-onset conditions,

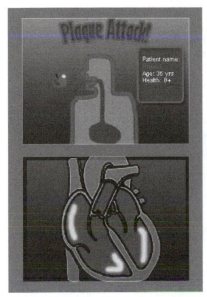

such as insulin resistance, type 2 diabetes mellitus, and hepatic disease, are rapidly on the rise. In June of 2006 US Surgeon General Richard Carmona addressed the American College of Sports Medicine Annual Conference in Denver saying that "The greatest threat to our national security is pediatric obesity."

At the 2006 Games for Health conference Connie Dresser from the National Institute for Health addressed attendees with the NIH's request for games that enhance self-awareness that leads to health awareness; games that educate users about the physical impact of healthy/unhealthy eating habits, good/poor exercise habits or using smoke/smokeless tobacco products. She commented that "Most people don't know about what happens from the time that you take a drink of juice or eat a piece of food – what it does in a positive way, or in the same case, unhealthy foods and how they adversely affect the human body," and noted that "If they can't see how something visually impacts the body, they are less likely to do something about it."

In addition to being one of the most serious threats to public health, nutrition is also a health concern most readily influenced by lifestyle change and patient motivation. Because strong early habits can lead to a lifetime of health, it is especially critical to target kids. As a subject with a strong kid-focus and a big opening for motivation (a game specialty), the subject of nutrition is one of the highest potential impact areas for positive game development.

To this end, *Food Finder* aims to:
- educate kids about healthy eating habits through an interactive and stealth-education game format;
- use minigames to allow kids to build their own nutritious foods in a Food Lab workshop;
- use minigames to allow kids to trace the effects of eating various food types through a simple visual interactive bloodstream simulator;
- get kids excited about healthy foods by presenting them as action game objectives;
- deliver an easily transportable pick-up-and-play game suitable for kid-style rough play and short play sessions;
- deliver a portable game with wifi capabilities particularly helpful for keeping kids socialized and interacting with others even when hospitalized, and learning at the same time.

Audience

Food Finder is aimed at children aged 8 to 14, squarely within the Nintendo DS majority demographic and also targeting the age where kids begin to take initiative with their own eating habits, and therefore are at a prime age to establish healthy patterns. While the game will have a quirking and engaging storyline with gameplay appeal for all ages, testing will focus on kids in this age demographic.

Platform

The Nintendo DS is uniquely suited to fit the objectives of *Food Finder* and other lifestyle behavior enhancing games because of its many innovative attributes:

- a **touchscreen** promotes workshop style gameplay and gets players involved in creative activities that enhance action-and-consequence learning;

- the **rugged shell** and strong design of the machine make it a sure choice for kids, who can be hard on electronics and less careful or coordinated than older players; this is particularly in contrast to the other primary handheld device, the PlayStation Portable, whose construction is considerably more delicate;

- its **portability** and **small size** make it a perfect fit for kids who are constantly on the move, and the compactness of the system provides a less intimidating physical interface for small hands, and especially girls;

- the **self contained** nature of the system – with no requirement for cords or an exterior monitor – makes the system a natural choice for a hospital or any group environment environment that has to keep track of a large amount of equipment, and share equipment between numerous patients;

- **wifi capability** enables the system to contact other DS systems and the Internet, allowing for updatable content and social play between systems, a must for replayability and social engagement for enhanced retention and enthusiasm as the game is shared with friends.

Game Mechanics

In the action segment of the game, players pursue clues that will eventually lead them to the Golden Walnut, with a special leading clue and power-up item at the end of each level.

Action takes place on the upper screen, with the lower screen devoted to the player's interface. A beating heart shows the character's exertion rate, with certain foods (such as caffeinated beverages) causing it to require energy faster and burn it more rapidly.

Other status bars measure key attributes that the player will use to execute special moves:

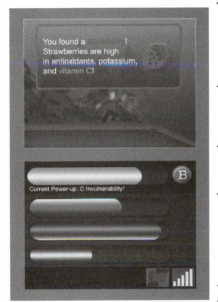

- a **calcium** meter is impacted by the foods the player collects on their way, with high-calcium foods such as milk and broccoli raising the bar – which, when full, allows the player to create a magical calcium bridge that will gain them access to higher levels, highlighting the strengthening effect of calcium;
- a **vitamin C** meter, charged by strong citrus foods, when maxed out allows the player to become temporarily invincible, highlighting the importance of vitamin C for the immune system;
- a **protein** meter, charged by healthy proteins found in nuts and legumes, when maxed out and accessed provides the player a boost in energy and strength;
- a **heart healthy** bar, charged by foods high in fiber and heart-healthy elements such as flaxseed oil, is the hardest to fill, but triggers a special bonus mode where the player can run through a level with all enemies frozen and collect as many special heart tokens as they can, for a high score at the end of the game.

These bars sit on the bottom screen and can be queued up with touches from a fingertip or the stylus. The top queued bar represents the special ability (ex Calcium Bridge, C Invulnerability) that will be triggered when the player presses the 'B' action button during regular gameplay.

Whenever the player encounters a new food type, a popup dialogue reveals the new food in a shower of sparks, and gives the player a fun fact about its value. These items then fill out an electronic "smartbook" that the player uses to record all of the foods they've encountered, such as pomegranates, sweet potatoes, salmon, and over a hundred others. Though the game's storyline can be completed without filling the smartbook, players must find every food type in the game in order to reach 100% completion.

All of the collected foods the player may also use in the FoodLab minigame and Plaque Attack. In the FoodLab they can combine basic foods into superfoods and retain these in their inventory for special use later, to rapidly charge up their power bars for facing Bacteria Bosses that guard the clues leading them to the Golden Walnut.

Nutripoints Partnership

An option explored by the *Food Finder* project team is a partnership with Vartabedian & Associates, founders of the bestselling Nutripoints program. A partnership with Nutripoints would provide an instant "hierarchy" database of target foods presented by the game, and leverage Dr. Vartabedian's over

25 years of experience as a nutritionist and 6 years of experience with the world-renowned Cooper Clinic. The Nutripoints method evaluates over 3,600 individual foods, and as a supplement to the *Food Finder* game, if a license were pursued to utilize Nutripoints, a simple "Nutripoints Calculator" would be included with the game for quick typed-in lookup of individual foods, delivered on the portable DS system. This calculator would be entertaining for children as they accompany adults on grocery shopping excursions, but would also expand the game's audience and utility to the many participants and proponents of Nutripoints.

Budget and Schedule

The advantage to a handheld game title is that because of its interlocking reliance on minigames in addition to the primary storyline, it is a highly modular game style that can be expanded or specifically tailored to a variety of budgets.

For the features described above in full, a team of 6 total developers with a ten month projected project life cycle from pre-production to Nintendo lot check would total $650,000. The breakdown of the team would be as follows:

- 1 Programmer (Gameplay)
- 1 Programmer (Engine)
- 1 Programmer (Networking)
- 1 3D Animator
- 1 3D Modeler
- 1 2D Artist (User Interface)
- 1 Designer

Due to *Food Finder*'s unique focus on nutrition, from a marketing standpoint the project would best be served by a tailored strategy that reaches outside both game- and health-based standard advertising channels. Placement in grocery stores, hospitals, and department stores, established with precedent by other games such as Yourself!Fitness would work well for *Food Finder*, as would partnerships with schools in addition to gym and exertainment centers such as Dr. Medina's XRtainment Zone, which would serve as the first testing ground and launch point for *Food Finder*.

Team Experience

- **Erin Hoffman** is a game designer with eight years of experience working on a variety of game styles from Massively Multiplayer online environments to action adventures to handheld titles for kids. *Cabbage Patch Kids: Patch Puppy Rescue,* which she worked on with 1st Playable Productions, received a Parents Choice award in 2006, and an iParenting Media Award.
- **Dr. Ernie Medina** is a preventive care specialist who has spent the last 12 years working at Beaver Medical Group helping patients of all ages overcome lifestyle-related diseases such as obesity, diabetes, high blood pressure, and high cholesterol. He is the CEO and co-founder of the XRtainment Zone, a specialized gym targeted at young adults that utilizes a variety of video game consoles and custom exercise machinery to get kids motivated about exercise.
- **1st Playable Productions** is an award-winning handheld development studio located in upstate New York, founded by CEO Tobi Saulnier. Details can be found at www.1stplayable.com. This project is not directly affiliated with 1st Playable, but initial discussions with Ms. Saulnier indicate that should funding be available for the project 1st Playable would be first in line to make it a reality.

C

Script Samples for Chapter 9

Wendy Despain

C.1 Minigame Barks from *Bratz: Forever Diamondz*

MGD: Mini-game dialog

MGDP: Pairs

Successful pair matching - Cloe#1
CLOE
Great!

Successful pair matching - Cloe#2
CLOE
Yes!

Successful pair matching - Cloe#3
CLOE
Sweet!

Successful pair matching - Cloe#4
CLOE
Oh yeah!

Successful pair matching - Jade#1
JADE
Woo!

Successful pair matching - Jade#2
JADE
Hey, yeah!

Successful pair matching - Jade#3
JADE
I can do this.

Successful pair matching - Jade#4
JADE
Yay!

Successful pair matching - Sasha#1
SASHA
Right on.

Successful pair matching - Sasha#2
SASHA
I knew it!

Successful pair matching - Sasha#3
SASHA
Phew!

Successful pair matching - Sasha#4
SASHA
Hey, nice!

Successful pair matching - Yasmin#1
YASMIN
Perfect!

Successful pair matching - Yasmin#2
YASMIN
Sweet!

Successful pair matching - Yasmin#3
YASMIN
Alright!

Successful pair matching - Yasmin#4
YASMIN
Woo!

Unsuccessful pair matching - Cloe#1
CLOE
That's so lame

Unsuccessful pair matching - Cloe#2
CLOE
Oh no!

Unsuccessful pair matching - Cloe#3
CLOE
Oh man!

Unsuccessful pair matching - Cloe#4
CLOE
Bummer!

Unsuccessful pair matching - Jade#1
JADE
Oh, come on.

Unsuccessful pair matching - Jade#2
JADE
Hey, wait!

Unsuccessful pair matching - Jade#3
JADE
No way!

Unsuccessful pair matching - Jade#4
JADE
Awww.

Unsuccessful pair matching - Sasha#1
SASHA
Wait?

Unsuccessful pair matching - Sasha#2
SASHA
But I?

Unsuccessful pair matching - Sasha#3
SASHA
Argh!

Unsuccessful pair matching - Sasha#4
SASHA
Hey!

Unsuccessful pair matching - Yasmin#1
YASMIN
I say?

Unsuccessful pair matching - Yasmin#2
YASMIN
No!

Unsuccessful pair matching - Yasmin#3
YASMIN
Come on.

Unsuccessful pair matching - Yasmin#4
YASMIN
Ouch!

Unsuccessful pair matching with only four cards remaining - Cloe#1
CLOE
Noooo!

Unsuccessful pair matching with only four cards remaining - Cloe#2
CLOE
I'm so gonna lose!

Unsuccessful pair matching with only four cards remaining - Cloe#3
CLOE
That's so uncool!

Unsuccessful pair matching with only four cards remaining - Cloe#4
CLOE
Whatever!

Unsuccessful pair matching with only four cards remaining - Jade#1
JADE
Wait a minute!

Unsuccessful pair matching with only four cards remaining - Jade#2
JADE
Hey!

Unsuccessful pair matching with only four cards remaining - Jade#3
JADE
But I thought?

Unsuccessful pair matching with only four cards remaining - Jade#4
JADE
Oh no!

Unsuccessful pair matching with only four cards remaining - Sasha#1
SASHA
Gasp Can't be!

Unsuccessful pair matching with only four cards remaining - Sasha#2
SASHA
No way!

Unsuccessful pair matching with only four cards remaining - Sasha#3
SASHA
Hrm. I can still do this.

Unsuccessful pair matching with only four cards remaining - Sasha#4
SASHA
Uh oh!

Unsuccessful pair matching with only four cards remaining - Yasmin#1
YASMIN
Oh dear!

Unsuccessful pair matching with only four cards remaining - Yasmin#2
YASMIN
(worried) Oooohhh!

Unsuccessful pair matching with only four cards remaining - Yasmin#3
YASMIN
(sanguine) Bad karma!

Unsuccessful pair matching with only four cards remaining - Yasmin#4
YASMIN
No way!

Cloe wins#1
CLOE
I can't be beat!

Cloe wins#2
CLOE
I'm too good!

Cloe wins#3
CLOE
I'm so sweeeeet!

Cloe wins#4
CLOE
I'm unstoppable!

Jade wins#1
JADE
I rock!

Jade wins#2
JADE
Whoohoo!

Jade wins#3
JADE
Winner!

Jade wins#4
JADE
Oh yeah, I'm good.

Sasha wins#1
SASHA
You know it.

Sasha wins#2
SASHA
Take that!

Sasha wins#3
SASHA
That's what I'm talking about.

Sasha wins#4
SASHA
Exceptional!

Yasmin wins#1
YASMIN
Perfection!

Yasmin wins#2
YASMIN
Alright!

Yasmin wins#3
YASMIN
squeals with glee

Yasmin wins#4
YASMIN
Watch me win again!

Cloe wins perfect#1
CLOE
That's embarrassing

Cloe wins perfect#2
CLOE
Perfection is my middle name

Cloe wins perfect#3
CLOE
I'm just too good

Cloe wins perfect#4
CLOE
Perfect!

Jade wins perfect#1
JADE
Way cool!

Jade wins perfect#2
JADE
Perfect!

Jade wins perfect#3
JADE
I'm the best!

Jade wins perfect#4
JADE
All the way.

Sasha wins perfect#1
SASHA
Exactly!

Sasha wins perfect#2
SASHA
I knew I could do that.

Sasha wins perfect#3
SASHA
Way to go me!

Sasha wins perfect#4
SASHA
(hushed voice) Stylin'

Yasmin wins perfect#1
YASMIN
Wow, I'm good.

Yasmin wins perfect#2
YASMIN
Look at me go!

Yasmin wins perfect#3
YASMIN
Oh, wow!

Yasmin wins perfect#4
YASMIN
Woohoo!

C.2   Sample Task Spreadsheet

Task Description	Time Estimates	Milestone Deadline	Approval #1	Approval #2	Contacts
6 episode summaries	12 hours	15-Dec	JD - 12/6	AS - 12/10	jd@somwhere.com
6 episode summaries	12 hours	10-Jan	JD - 1/3	AS - 1/9	as@somwhere.com
2 episode scripts	20 hours	29-Feb			
2 episode scripts	20 hours	15-Mar			
2 episode scripts	20 hours	15-Apr			
2 episode scripts	20 hours	15-May			
2 episode scripts	20 hours	15-Jun			
2 episode scripts	20 hours	15-Jul			
Revisions	20 hours	1-Aug			
Pick-Ups	20 hours	15-Aug			

D

Script Samples for Chapter 11

Haris Orkin

D.1 Casting Sides for *Call of Juarez*

REVEREND RAY

For twenty years I followed the light and denounced the darkness. Day in and day out, I labored to save lost souls. All for you, Lord! So why have you forsaken me? How could you let this happen? Help me, Lord! Please! Tell me! What do you want from me?

BILLY CANDLE

I'm Billy. Ma would never say who my father was, so... I don't got no last name. She gave me this medallion before I could talk. It's engraved with a candle stick, so that's what kid's called me. Candle. Beats spic or pepper gut. Yeah, my Ma's from Mexico. The town I grew up in is just over the border and the folks there are mostly white. Like my step-father. Thomas. A big, mean son of a bitch who would just as soon backhand me as look at me.

JUAREZ

Don't you see the resemblance, muchacho? I'm your padre. 17 years ago, your mama ran off with another man. You were still in her womb. My only son, my pride and joy. I've been searching for you ever since.

JONES

Hey! You wouldn't shoot 'ol Jones, would you? I got nothing against you... We don't need no trouble now!

SHERIFF TIM

My, my... Billy Candle! Been a long time, boy. I don't think Thomas'll be too pleased to see you. You come back to set things right with him? Fine... (sarcastic) Welcome back. Just don't do anything stupid, son.

UNDERTAKER

Billy Candle! Is that you? Boy, you're growing like a weed! Stand still... Let me take a measure... Hm... Just in case... Well now. Looks like you're as tall as Reverend Ray. If it comes down to it, what do you prefer? Pine...or Oak?

SUZY

Well, Billy Candle! Ain't you a sight for sore eyes! Here in town and you don't come see your old friend, Suzy? Get your skinny butt up here 'fore I change my mind.

D.2   Character List and Casting Specs for *Call of Juarez*

<u>56 Characters</u>

<u>1,027 lines of dialog</u>

Reverend Ray – Age 45-55. Intense, gruff, dangerous. Texas accent. A reformed gun-fighter who now preaches the word of God. Think Tommy Lee Jones or Sam Elliot. A fire and brimstone, holier than thou son of a bitch who believes he's the Lord's instrument of justice. Underlying all his self-righteousness is a prodigious amount of guilt and pain. (131 lines)

Billy – Age 17. His mother's Mexican, his step-father's white. He grew up in Texas, so he has a Texas accent with a touch of his mother's Mexican influence. He's angry, he's afraid, he's full of bluster, he's insecure. He's a rebel without a cause and he's right on the cusp of becoming a man. (182 lines)

Juarez – Age 45-55. Hispanic. A Mexican warlord. He can be charming when he needs to be, yet he's clearly an evil son of a bitch who can explode into a rage at any provocation. (81 lines)

Jones – Age 35-55. Farmer. Texas/rural accent. (19 lines)

Sheriff Tim – Age 35-45. A small town Sheriff. Earnest and reasonable, but can lay down the law when he needs to. (16 lines)

Undertaker – 35-55. Unctuous and a little too cheerful, which makes him kind of creepy. (5 lines)

Suzie – 18-25. A dance hall girl/prostitute. Older than her years. Bitter and cynical, but can turn on the charm to make a buck. (13 lines)

Buck/ Clyde Forrester – 40-50. Dangerous, mean, uncouth, but not stupid. A bully. Runs the local saloon. Texas accent. (21 lines)

Crazy Frank – 55-65. A Civil War veteran who hasn't been the same since Gettysburg. Talks to his rifle. Calls it Lucy. (11 lines)

Marisa/Intro – 25-30. Billy's mother. Mexican accent. Warm and nurturing. (2 lines)

Mrs. Powell – 25-35. Sheriff's wife. Proper. (5 lines)

Ned the Plague – 30-45. A hired gun. A psychopath. A perfect Jack Palance role. (18 lines)

Lieutenant Parker(Officer) – 35. By the book military guy. (5 lines)

Train Driver/Engineer – 30-50. Overly talkative. Nervous. Afraid. (6 lines)

Train Boss – 35-45. Blustery A fast-talker. A horse trader. Not up for a fight unless he doesn't have a choice. (3 lines)

Farmer – 55-65. Kind of a geezer. Gruff. Like Walter Brennen. (16 lines)

Chat – 35-40. Ranch Foreman. Pushes a little too hard. A quick temper. Doesn't take any guff. (8 lines)

Ferguson – 50-60. Ranch Owner. Molly's father. Rigid. Protective. (7 lines)

Molly Ferguson – 18. Young and a little spoiled. Idealistic and blunt in the way teenagers can be. (10 lines)

Ty Stewart/Butch – 40. A hired gun. Veteran of the civil war. A hard case and pragmatist who doesn't believe in anything but gold. (11 lines)

Tom Manson – 40-50. A Civil war era officer from Virgina who lost all sense of honor. A gentleman with the soul of a killer. (23 lines)

McClyde 1 – 33. Just as mean, but slightly smarter than his brother. Hails from Nebraska. (5 lines)

McClyde 2 – 34. Mean and stupid (2 lines)

Calm Water (Hermit) 45-65. An American Indian. Wise and kind in a zen master/Yoda sort of way. (32 lines)

Outgrowth (Boy), 10. Mexican. Outgoing and smart and full of anger and hurt. (20 lines)

Narrator (for introduction). Grounded and real, Texas accent. (1 line)

Bandit 1 – 25-45. Gravel voiced, American. (88 lines)

Bandit 2 – 25-45. Mexican accent. (84 lines)

Bandit 3/4 – 25-45. Blustery, Southern Accent. (43 lines)

Citizen of Hope 1 – 30-50. An Easterner who came west. (5 lines)

Citizen of Hope 2 – 50-60. Small town guy, Texas accent. (3 lines)

Citizen of Hope 3 – 25-35. (2 lines)

Cowboy 1 – 45-60. Grizzled saddle tramp. (1 line)

Cowboy 2 – 25-30. On the stupid side. (1 line)

Hyena 1 – 25-35. A low-life drifter. (3 lines)

Hyena 2 – 35-45. Whiny, high-strung. (4 lines)

Hyena 3 – 35-45. Aggressive, pushy. (3 lines)

Woman – 30-40. Farmer's wife. (3 lines)

Drunk 1 – 30-50. Hayseed. (2 lines)

Drunk 2 – 30-50. Mexican. (1 line)

Dying Soldier – 25-35. (2 lines)

Passenger 1 – 30-50. (4 lines)

Passenger 2 – 30-50. (2 lines)

Passenger 3 – 30-50. (2 lines)

Woman Passenger – 25-35. (4 lines)

Soldier 1 – 21-25. (5 lines)

Soldier 2 – 25-35. (6 lines)

Soldier 3 – 21-25. (3 lines)

Female Hostage – 21-35. (1 line)

Dying Officer – 35-45. (3 lines)

Rustic 1 – 25-30. (23 lines)

Rustic 2 – 35. (21 lines)

Rustic 3 – 20-25. (21 lines)

Thug 1 – 35. Mexican. (4 lines)

Thug 2 – 25. Mexican. (4 lines)

Whore (terrified scream) – 25-35. Excellent screamer.

Bandit shouts – in voices tab. (27 lines) (Give to Bandit 3 or divide up)

D.3 *Call of Juarez* Script Sample

EXT. NORTHERN MEXICO - DAY

The camera slowly moves forward over a desert landscape. An old Mexican
Church can be seen in the distance, obscured by waves of heat rising off
the desert floor.

                          NARRATOR (V.O.)
        The legend of the Lost Gold of Juarez has been passed from
        one generation to the next since the time of Hernando Cortez.
        It was said to be the ransom for Montezuma, held hostage by
        the Spanish in the great Aztec capital of Tenochtitlan. The
        treasure disappeared soon after the sacking of the city and
        some believe it's buried near the border town of Juarez. The
        legend relates that the Aztec Sun God put a curse on the treasure
        and that all who seek it will find only madness and their own
        perdition. This avaricious madness has come to be known as...
        The Call of Juarez.

The camera comes to rest on a headstone over an old grave.

EPISODE ONE

LOADING SCREEN SHOWING AN ARTISTS RENDITION OF BILLY.

He's nineteen, tall, wiry, with dark eyes and hair. He looks part Native American, part Hispanic. His voice has a Texas twang.

BILLY (V.O.)

I'm Billy. Ma would never say who my father was, so I don't got no last name. She gave me this medallion before I could talk. It's engraved with a candle stick, so that's what kid's called me. Candle. Beats spic or pepper gut. Yeah, my Ma's from Mexico. The town I grew up in is just over the border and the folks there are mostly white. Like my stepfather. Thomas. A big, mean son of a bitch who would just as soon backhand me as look at me.

EXT. MOUNTAIN SPRING - DAY

Billy is hiking home, crossing over a stream, and down a trail. The player controls Billy from a first person perspective. As the player navigates his way down the rugged trail, we continue to hear Billy's voice.

BILLY (V.O.)

I grew up in a town called Hope. Pretty much the most hopeless place I've ever seen. It's full of drunks and drifters, thieves and liars. And those are the leading citizens. Like my 'dear' stepfather who knocked the tar out of me at least once a day, rain or shine. Said he was teaching me how to be a man. But all he taught me is how to take a beatin'. The last time he laid a hand on me was over two years ago.

Billy (the player) continues to work his way down a steep mountain trail.

BILLY

I took off and didn't look back. I left to find my fortune. The legendary Gold of Juarez. Wanted to prove to that S.O.B. that I could be more than he ever was. But the world's a hard place and I didn't find squat. So now I'm back. Hungry. Broke. I don't have nothing. Not even a last name.

When Billy (the player) sees the town of Hope in the distance.

BILLY

Well, there it is...Hope. A haven for outlaws, assholes, and hypocrites.

When Billy (the player) sees Jones' Cabin just down the hill.

                                    BILLY
        Jones' cabin!   Good place to practice some shootin'...

When Billy gets caught walking onto Jones' property, old JONES, a crusty
old farmer chases him off.

                                    JONES
        What the heck are you doin'!?   This is private property!

Author Bios

Sande Chen

A Grammy-nominated music video director, Sande Chen is the co-founder, along with Anne Toole, of Writers Cabal (http://writerscabal.com). Her past game credits include 1999 Independent Games Festival winner *Terminus*. For her most recent game, *The Witcher*, she was nominated for a 2007 Writers Guild Award in the category of Outstanding Achievement in Videogame Writing. In 2006, she was profiled on *Next Generation*'s list of the Game Industry's 100 Most Influential Women. In addition to contributing articles to *Gamasutra* and other game development sites, Sande is the co-author of the book *Serious Games: Games That Educate, Train, and Inform* and was a contributor to *Secrets of the Game Business*. Sande graduated with a degree in writing and humanistic studies from the Massachusetts Institute of Technology. Afterwards, she specialized in screenwriting, earning an M.F.A. in cinema-television from the University of Southern California. She is a steering committee member of the Women in Games International Steering Committee and the IGDA Writers SIG. She has been a speaker at the Game Developers Conference, Women's Game Conference, South by Southwest Interactive Festival, and the Serious Games Summit.

Richard Dansky

Richard Dansky is the Manager of Design at Red Storm Entertainment and the Central Clancy Writer for Ubisoft. He has written for numerous games, including ones in the *Ghost Recon*, *Rainbow Six*, *Splinter Cell*, and *Might & Magic* franchises. Richard is also a novelist, and his most recent book is *Firefly Rain*. He lives in North Carolina with his wife and their feline masters. You can find him online at http://www.snowbirdgothic.com.

Wendy Despain

Wendy Despain writes dialog and does narrative design for video games through International Hobo. Her credits include writing for the console game *Bratz: Forever Diamondz*, the MMOG *ArchLord*, and ARGs for two Gene Roddenberry properties. She moonlights in science and video game journalism, writing for *Gamasutra* and *The Escapist*. She is chair of the IGDA's Game Writing Special Interest Group and a contributing editor to the book *Game Writing: Narrative Skills for Videogames*. Online, she's found at http://www.quantumcontent.com.

Beth A. Dillon

Beth A. Dillon is an Irish, Anishinaabe, and Metis writer specializing in the video game industry. She's currently based out of Vancouver, British Columbia, while she pursues a Doctorate in Interactive Arts & Technology at Simon Fraser University. She was previously the editor for *Gamasutra's Game Career Guide*. Her overarching efforts address indigenous representations in commercial games and development of games with indigenous content.

John Feil

John Feil is a game industry veteran whose duties have spanned from Quality Assurance, to Technical Writing, and finally to Level Designer and Designer. He's worked on such titles as *Star Wars: Jedi Starfighter*, *Star Wars: Battle for Naboo*, *Microsoft Flight Simulator*, *Forza Motorsports*, and *Justice League: Heroes*. John has written a book called *Beginning Game Level Design*, is a member of the board of directors for the International Game Developers Association, the Chairperson for the IGDA Credits Committee, and has a website at http://www.gamefeil.com.

Alice Henderson

Alice Henderson began her video game career at LucasArts Entertainment. She has written several Prima strategy guides and hint books, including *Star Wars: Obi Wan*, *Star Wars Galactic Battlegrounds: The Clone Campaigns, and Summoner II*. Now a full-time freelance writer, she also writes novels. Her *Buffy the Vampire Slayer* novel *Portal Through Time* recently won a Scribe Award for Best Novel. Please visit her at her website, http://www.alicehenderson.com.

Erin Hoffman

Erin Hoffman has been designing games since 1999 in a variety of genres including console action RPGs, massively multiplayer online games, sandbox social games, and handheld titles for kids. She also writes for *The Escapist*, the leading magazine covering commentary on gaming culture, which pulls in over 150,000 hits every month. In 2006, she was named one of the top 100 most influential women in games by *Next Generation*. In 2004, she wrote an essay on quality of life in the games industry that received international attention (including coverage by the *Los Angeles Times*, *New York Times*, *Wall Street Journal*, *CNet*, and others) and sparked widespread analysis and change in working development practices; the essay appeared in Joel Spolsky's bestselling *Best Software Writing I* in 2005.

Chris Klug

Chris Klug (some might know him as Gerry Klug), currently Creative Director for Cheyenne Mountain Entertainment's *Stargate Worlds* MMO, has had an interesting and varied career in the entertainment industry. While just prior to coming to CME Chris was a Visiting Professor of Game Design at Carnegie Mellon's Entertainment Technology Center, he has spent over 30 years as a professional in the entertainment business. In the beginning, originally trained as a theatrical lighting designer, Chris worked on Broadway, in regional theater and opera, and toured with various 70's rock n' roll bands. He won two Critic's Circle Awards for his designs. Through the intervention of a photographer friend, Chris began writing role-playing adventures for Simulations Publications Incorporated. This began a seven-year stint designing and writing traditional role-playing games. Chris won Best RPG of the Year for the *James Bond 007* role-playing game and oversaw the entire Bond product line. At Victory Games,

Chris designed a half-dozen more titles and was, for a time, Design Director. After leaving Victory Games, Chris became a freelance computer game designer and worked for SegaSoft, TSR, Hasbro Interactive, 3W, THQ, Simon and Schuster Interactive, Target Games, h2o Interactive, Gizmo Games, Westwood Studios, and GT Interactive. Some of his computer game credits include *Star Trek DS9: Dominion Wars*, *Europa Universalis*, *Duke Nukem: Time to Kill*, *Diamond Dreams Baseball*, and *Aidyn Chronicles: First Mage*. From 2001 through 2004 he was Creative Director for EA's MMORPG *Earth & Beyond*. A member of WGA, West, Chris is also a playwright.

Jay Posey

Jay Posey is a Designer/Narrative Designer at Red Storm Entertainment, where he has been employed for three years. Prior to joining Red Storm, his experience ranged from tech support to applications programming to screenwriting. His credits include work on Tom Clancy's *Ghost Recon: Advanced Warfighter* and *Blazing Angels: Squadrons of WWII*, and he is currently working as Narrative Designer on an as-yet-unannounced AAA title.

Rhianna Pratchett

Rhianna Pratchett has worked in the game industry since 1998, initially as a game reviewer for the likes of *PC Zone* and *The Guardian* and then moving into script writing and story design. She has worked as the main writer and co-story designer on original IPs such as the fantasy, martial-arts epic *Heavenly Sword* (Sony/Ninja Theory), which was nominated for a story/character BAFTA in 2007, the twisted and dark-humored *Overlord* (Codemasters/Triumph Studios), and most recently, *Mirror's Edge* for EA/DICE. She can be found at http://www.rhiannapratchett.com.

Haris Orkin

Haris Orkin has written for television, stage, film, and video games. Recently, he wrote *Fraidy Cat* for Walt Disney Feature Animation as well as the script for *Dragonshard*, a PC game from Atari and Liquid Entertainment. *Call of Juarez*, a game he wrote for Techland and Ubisoft, was released last June. *Kane's Wrath*, the expansion to the best-selling *Command & Conquer 3: Tiberium Wars*, is slated to be released in Spring 2008. Haris is currently writing new games for EALA and Techland, and his feature script, *Other People's Wishes*, is in development with Warner Brothers and Village Roadshow Productions.

Evan Skolnick

A former journalist and Marvel Comics editor, Evan has written for properties such as *Spider-Man*, *The Incredible Hulk*, *X-Men*, *Dr. Strange*, *New Warriors*, *RoboCop*, and many others. As editorial director for Vicarious Visions, he has written (or rewritten) for bestselling games such as *Spider-Man 3* for PS2, Xbox, Wii, PSP, and DS, *X-Men Legends 2* for PSP, *Spider-Man 2* for PSP and DS, *Ultimate Spider-Man* for DS and GBA, *Shrek 2: Beg for Mercy* for GBA, *Over the Hedge* for DS, *Crash Bandicoot Purple* for GBA, and *Spyro Orange* for GBA, among others.

Anne Toole

Anne Toole graduated from Harvard with a degree in Archaeology and studied abroad in Egypt. She co-founded, along with Sande Chen, the writing and game design partnership known as Writers Cabal (http://writerscabal.com). For her work on *The Witcher*, she was nominated for a 2007 Writers Guild Award in the category of Outstanding Achievement in Videogame Writing. Anne has worked in cable, syndication, broadcast primetime and daytime, comics, and video games. After writing dialog for children's games such as *Pet Pals*, she was hired as head writer for the MMO *Stargate Worlds*. In addition, she has written for daytime serial *Days of Our Lives* and for the original television pilot *Weho*. Anne has studied under the best writers in entertainment, including Dawn Prestwich and Nicole Yorkin (*The Education of Max Bickford*), Jan Oxenberg (*Cold Case*), Scott Lobdell (*X-Men*, *Chasing Alice*), and Mike Gold (comics editor).

Maurice Suckling

As a director of The Mustard Corporation, Maurice Suckling regularly writes as part of a writing team, having team-written ten titles over the last three years. Maurice has worked in computer games since writing the screenplay for GT Interactive's seminal *Driver* in 1998, which won a Moving Image Interactive BAFTA (1999). He went on to write the screenplays for *Driver 2* (2000), *Stuntman* (2002), and *Driver 3* (2004), all with the same development team. Simultaneously, Maurice worked as a script editor on Empire Interactive's light-gun game *Endgame* (2002) and on Atari's free-roaming RPG *Boiling Point* (2005). Aside from his work within The Mustard Corporation since 2005, Maurice has also written the script for and script edited *Little Britain: The Video Game* (2007).

Andrew S. Walsh

With 25 computer game credits and counting, Andrew Walsh is a dedicated game player as well as writer, game designer, voiceover director, and story consultant. He's worked for companies such as Electronic Arts, Sony, Creative Assembly, SEGA, Side, THQ Wireless, Koch, Egosoft, Nokia, Jadestone, Razorback, BAM, Vis Interactive, and G5. His most recent published game is *Harry Potter and the Order of the Phoenix*. Andrew has spoken about writing for games at both BAFTA and E.I.E.F. and to organizations such as the BBC. He has written on the subject for The Writers' Guild of Great Britain and *The Writers' Handbook 2005*.

With 35 games notched up on his CV, Andrew Walsh is a dedicated videogame addict, writer, voiceover director, game designer, and story consultant. His work has taken him to Electronic Arts, Ubisoft, Sony, SEGA, Koch, and Nokia with writing credits on titles such as *Harry Potter and the Order of the Phoenix*, *Heavenly Sword*, and the upcoming *Dirk Dagger and the Fallen Idol*. His directing credits include *Medieval Total War 2* and *Shinobido*. Currently working on AAA titles for Ubisoft and EA ,he occasionally researches tea, coffee, beer, and motorbikes (though not at the same time) and can be found lurking at http://www.andrewwalsh.com.

Index

The International Game Developers Association is the largest non-profit membership organization serving individuals that create video games. The IGDA is committed to advancing the careers and enhancing the lives of game developers.

The IGDA connects members with their peers, promotes professional development, and advocates on issues that affect developers.

Advance your career. Advance the game industry. Advance the art form of games.

Our community is over 14,000 strong. Become a member today!

http://www.igda.org/join

Together, we will play an active role in shaping the future of digital games.